The Glory of the Medieval World

THE GLORY OF THE
Medieval World

By
RÉGINE PERNOUD

Translated by
JOYCE EMERSON

London
DENNIS DOBSON LTD

First published in Great Britain in MCML by DENNIS DOBSON LTD, 12 Park Place, St. James's, London, SW1. Translated from the French *Lumière du Moyen Age* (BERNARD GRASSET, Paris, MCMXLIV) by JOYCE EMERSON. Printed in Great Britain by PAGE BROS (Norwich) LTD, THE PHOENIX PRESS, Norwich

32/R

ALTHOUGH in the study of the Middle Ages much distinguished work has been accomplished, understanding of the period has remained imperfect. It is curious to note that the researches of scholars, thanks to which it is now possible to form a fairly exact idea of the age, have not yet reached the general public. Possibly for lack of formal tabulation, knowledge of the medieval era is still the preserve of the specialist whose learning has not benefited even our school text-books, which are based more or less entirely on the rather over-simplified, and, in any case, inadequate, data of last-century historians.

This work is an attempt to present a picture of the Middle Ages slightly more in keeping with the most recent historical researches. Based on the study of domestic usages and the examination of manuscripts of the period, it corrects some of the most widely prevalent errors and rectifies as far as possible the false notions which have hitherto been accepted in the absence of sufficiently extensive documentation.

In this conspectus of French medieval society and civilisation, considered at their zenith in the twelfth and especially the thirteenth century, emphasis has been laid more particularly on points concerning which the layman knows little or nothing. The 'picturesque' aspects and 'local colour' of the period have been intentionally neglected so that the work may concentrate on demonstrating the topical interest of this age which presents, probably, more affinities with our own than is generally recognised.

All things considered, it is perhaps not an exaggeration to see in the medieval era the true *Grands Siècles* of French history.

Contents

List of Illustrations

.. *those ages which are called dark.*
MIGUEL DE UNAMUNO

IT has long been deemed sufficient, in order to explain
the medieval social system, to have recourse to the
time-honoured division into three classes: the clergy, the
nobility and the third estate. This is the impression still
conveyed by the history books: three clearly defined
categories of individuals, each with its own functions, each
sharply distinguished one from the other. Nothing is
farther from the historical reality. The division into three
classes is applicable to the *Ancien Régime*, to the seventeenth
and eighteenth centuries, when the various strata of
society did, in fact, form distinct classes, whose privileges
and relationships made up the structure of everyday life.
As far as the Middle Ages are concerned, however, such
a division is superficial; it explains the groupings, organisation and distribution of the various forces, but reveals
nothing of their origins, the motivating power behind them
or the depth of the social structure. Judging from legal
documents and literary and other writings, this was indeed
a hierarchy entailing a definite class system; but one which
differed vastly from the hitherto accepted conception of it,

being, primarily, very much more heterogeneous. One frequently finds, in deeds drawn up at that time, that the county squire or the parish priest appeared as witness in settlements between villeins, and that the *mesnie* of a baron —that is to say, his *entourage*, his household—included serfs and monks as well as persons of high rank. The functions of these classes were equally closely linked: the majority of the bishops were also nobles; many of these came of humble parentage; in certain regions a member of the middle classes who bought property belonging to the nobility became, himself, a noble. Thus, immediately one abandons history books to delve into documents, this conception of the 'three classes of society' appears both artificial and perfunctory.

Though approximating more nearly to the facts, a division into the privileged and unprivileged classes is not entirely satisfactory, for in the Middle Ages there were privileges on every rung of the social ladder, from the highest to the lowest. The meanest apprentice was, in some respects, a privileged person, for he shared in the privileges of his trade as a whole; the privileges attaching to the University benefited the students and even their valets as well as the doctors and professors. Certain groups of country serfs enjoyed clearly defined privileges which their lords were bound to respect. Thus, if one takes into account the advantages of only the nobility and the clergy, one gains a wholly false impression of the social system of the period.

In order to reach a proper understanding of medieval society it is necessary to study its domestic organisation, for therein lies the key to the whole age, and there too its salient characteristic is to be seen. Each relationship conformed to the pattern of family life, that of the lord and his vassal no less than that of the master and his apprentice. The explanation of rural life and the story of the soil in

France is to be found in the study of the manners and customs of the families who dwelt there. If it was desired to assess the importance of a village, it was the number of 'hearths' and not the number of individuals which was counted. In legislation, as in general practices, everything was designed to further the interests of the family and its descendants or—extending this conception of family life to a wider circle—those of the group, the members of a trade (itself no more than a great family, formed on the same lines as the family unit properly speaking). The great barons were, above all, fathers of families who grouped about them all the individuals who, by birth, constituted part of their patrimony; the battles of the nobility were family quarrels in which a share was taken by the whole of the *mesnie* for whose defence and administration they were responsible. The history of the feudal system is that of the principal families and, in effect, the history of the monarchy from the tenth to the fourteenth century is that of a family which had established itself thanks to its reputation for courage and the valour of which its ancestors had given proof; it was a family, far more than a man, which the barons placed at their head: in the person of Hugues Capet they saw the descendant of Robert le Fort, who had defended his land against the Norman invaders, and of Hugues le Grand, who had already worn the crown. This fact is apparent in the famous speech of Adalbéron of Rheims: 'Choose as your chief the Duke of the Franks, glorious by virtue of his deeds, *his family and his men*—the duke in whom you will find a protector, not only in public affairs, but also in your *private* concerns.' This family maintained its position on the throne by right of inheritance from father to son, and saw its domains increase less as the result of conquests than of inheritances and marriages. This is the history which has repeated itself thousands of times in

France at varying levels, and which has determined the country's fate once and for all by settling on the land families of peasants and artisans whose endurance through good and evil days has, in truth, created the French nation. It is in the family, as it was known and understood in medieval France, that '*l'éne françargieise*' has its roots.

There is no more effective method of grasping the importance of family life as the basis of the social system than that of contrasting, for example, medieval society, composed of families, with the society of ancient times which was made up of individuals. In the second case, *vir*, the man, took precedence in all things: in public life he was the *civis*, the citizen, who voted, who made the laws and took a share in State affairs; in private life he was the *paterfamilias*, the owner of a property which belonged to him personally, for which he was solely responsible and concerning which his powers were practically unlimited. Nowhere does one see his family or his heirs taking any share in his activities. His wife and children were completely subject to him and their status in relation to his remained one of perpetual minority; he had the *jus utendi et abutendi*, the right to use and abuse them, as in the case of his slaves or his landed property. The family appears to have existed only behind the scenes, living as a mere reflection of the personality of the father who was both military leader and high priest; legal infanticide must be set among the moral consequences of these conditions. In ancient times, moreover, the child was always the principal victim, a creature whose life depended on the paternal judgment or caprice; he was subjected to all the hazards of exchange or adoption, and even when the right to live was conceded to him, he remained dependent on, and under the authority of, the *paterfamilias* until the latter's death; even then he did not inherit his father's property by right, since the latter could dispose of his possessions as he chose, by will. When the State concerned itself with the child, it was in no way with a view to protecting a helpless being, but simply to educate the future citizen.

In medieval France nothing of this conception of life remained. At that time it was no longer the man, but the line, which was of importance. Ancient history could be—and is, in fact—studied by individual biographies: the story of Rome is that of Sulla, Pompey and Augustus; the conquest of Gaul is the story of Julius Caesar. But when one approaches the Middle Ages a change of method is essential: the history of French unity is that of the Capets; the conquest of Sicily is the history of the scions of a Norman family, grown too large for its patrimony. Fully to understand the Middle Ages one must see the period as a continuous whole. That, perhaps, is why it is less well known and much more difficult to study than ancient history, because it is necessary to unravel its complexities and follow the unbroken chain of events in their relationship to the *mesnies* which constituted the web of its history. It is not only those whose names have lived on account of the brilliance of their exploits or the importance of their estates, but also the very humble households, those of townspeople and peasants, whose private lives one must consider if one wishes to form an idea of medieval society.

There is, moreover, an explanation for this fact: during the period of unrest and disintegration which made up the early Middle Ages, the only source of cohesion, the only efficacious strength, lay precisely in the family unit, which was the embryo out of which French unity gradually developed. The family and its property tradition were therefore the starting point of the French nation.

The value set on family life in the Middle Ages produced a very marked preponderance in the significance of private

as opposed to public life. In Rome a man was of
consequence in so far as he exercised his rights as a citizen
by voting and by debating and participating in State affairs;
the struggles of the people to obtain representation by a
tribune were very significant in this respect. In the Middle
Ages public affairs rarely counted for much, or, rather, they
immediately assumed the guise of a family régime under
which estate accounts and settlements between tenants and
landlords were administered; even when the middle classes
demanded political rights at the time of the formation of the
communes, it was in order to be able to pursue their callings
freely without being inconvenienced by toll charges and
customs duties; political activities, as such, held no interest
for them. Rural life, moreover, was at that time infinitely
more active than urban life, though in both, the family and
not the individual took precedence as a social unit.

The essential motif of society, such as we see it from the
tenth century onwards, was this family solidarity which
emanated from barbarian Germanic or Nordic traditions.
The family was considered as a body in all of whose members
the same blood flowed—or as a microcosm wherein each
individual played his role, conscious the while of existing
as part of a whole. Thus, unity no longer depended, as in
Ancient Rome, on a nationalist conception of the authority
vested in the head of the State, but on this biological and,
at the same time, moral fact that all the members of a family
are united by flesh and blood, that their interests are identical
and that nothing is more to be respected than the affection
which they feel naturally one for the other. There was a
very lively realisation of this interdependence among the
members of one family:

> *Les gentils fils des gentils pères*
> *Des gentils et des bonnes mères*
> *Ils ne font pas de pesants heires*, (heirs)

wrote an author of the period. Those who lived beneath the same roof, who cultivated the same field and warmed themselves at the same fire—or, to use the language of the times, those who shared the same '*pain et pot*', who '*taillent au même chanteau*'—know that they could rely on one another and that, if the occasion arose, the support of the *mesnie* would not fail them. *Esprit de corps* was a more potent force in France at that time than in any other community, because it was founded on the irrefutable ties of blood-relationship and on equally obvious and self-evident common interests. Etienne de Fougères, the author quoted above, protested in his book *Livre des Manières* against nepotism among bishops; nevertheless, he recognised that they would be acting for the best in surrounding themselves with their relations, '*s'ils sont de bonne affaire*', for, he says, you can never be sure of the loyalty of strangers, but your own kin at least will not fail you.

Both joys and sorrows were thus shared: orphans or children of needy parents were welcomed into other homes and a whole household would fling itself into action to avenge a wrong done to one of its members. The right to wage private wars, which was recognised during a good part of the Middle Ages, was nothing more than the expression of family solidarity. At first this supplied a need: when the central authority was weak, the private individual could count on no assistance other than that of the *mesnie* to protect him, and, during the whole period of the invasions, he would have been delivered up to every kind of peril and disaster, had he been alone. In order to live, it was necessary to form a group and face the enemy—and what group could ever equal a resolutely united family?

Family solidarity, expressing itself, if need be, by armed aid, thus solved the problem of personal security and the defence of the estate. In certain provinces, notably in the

North of France, this sense of solidarity found expression in the home itself: the chief room in the house was the *salle*, the room which saw family conferences, where meals were taken and where marriages and birthdays were celebrated, and where watch was kept over the dead. This corresponded to the Anglo-Saxon *hall*, used for similar purposes—for medieval England had many customs in common with France, numbers of which still persist.

It was necessary for some person to be in charge of these common possessions and mutual affections, and it was naturally the father who took this role. But his authority was more that of a manager than the absolute and personal power of a leader, as wielded under Roman law: he was a manager, responsible for, and directly interested in, the prosperity of the household; but he discharged a duty, rather than exercised a right. His duty was to protect the weaker members, women, children and servants, who lived under his roof, and to ensure the efficient administration of the patrimony; but he was not considered as the master of the household for all time, nor as the owner of the estate. Though he enjoyed the patrimonial possessions, he had only a life interest in them and he was obliged to transmit them, as he had received them from his ancestors, to those who succeeded him by right of birth. The true owner was the family and not the individual.

In the same way, though he possessed all the authority necessary for his functions, he was far from having the unlimited power conceded by Roman law, over his wife and children. His wife collaborated with him in the *mainbournie*, that is, in the family administration and the education of the children; he managed the property which she owned because he was considered more capable than she of making it prosper—an achievement not attained without toil and trouble; but when for any reason he was obliged to absent himself, his wife resumed this management without any difficulty and without previous authorisation being necessary. The origin of her fortune was always clearly remembered so that in the event of a woman dying without children her own property reverted in its entirety to her family; no agreement could prevent this—such matters were automatically settled in this fashion.

With regard to the children, the father was the guardian, the protector and the master, but his paternal authority ceased when they attained their majority—at a very early age, nearly always at fourteen among commoners, though among the nobility this was advanced from fourteen to twenty years, since a nobleman had to render more active service in the defence of the fief and this demanded both strength and experience. The kings of France were considered to have attained their majority at their fourteenth or fifteenth year and it is well known that at this age Philippe-Auguste rode at the head of his troops. From the time of his majority the young man continued to enjoy the protection of his relatives and of the family solidarity, but, in contrast with what occurred in Rome and afterwards in countries having statute law, he acquired full freedom of enterprise and could leave home, found a family and administer his own property as he saw fit. As soon as he was capable of acting for himself, nothing hindered his actions; he became his own master while retaining the support of his family. It was a classic scene in the tales of chivalry for the sons of the house to leave the paternal dwelling as soon as they were of an age to bear arms and be knighted, and for them to roam over the world or enter the service of their suzerain.

This conception of the family rested on a material basis: the family property, generally landed property, for land constituted the sole source of wealth at the beginning of the Middle Ages and continued to remain the principal stable asset.

> *Héritage ne peut mouvoir*
> *Mais meubles est chose volage*

the saying went. This family estate, whether it were land held in fief or a nobleman's estate, remained for all time the property of the line. It was neither alienable nor distrainable; fortuitous family misfortunes could not affect it; no man could take it from the family's possession and the family was not entitled to sell or barter it.

When the father died the family estate passed to his direct heirs. In the case of a nobleman's fief the eldest son received almost everything, for one man, and an experienced man, was needed to be responsible for the upkeep and defence of an estate; that is the reason for the law of primogeniture, sanctioned by the great majority of usages. In the case of commoners' holdings, the custom varied according to the province: sometimes the property was divided, but generally the eldest son inherited the whole. It must be noted that it is only a question here of the principal patrimony, the family estate; in the event of there being other legacies, they were divided among the younger children, but the *chef manoir* was handed on to the eldest son with sufficient land to enable him and his family to live. This, moreover, was only just, since the eldest son had almost always assisted his father and, next to the latter, was the person who had had most to do with the upkeep and protection of the patrimony. In some provinces, such as Hainault, Artois, Picardy and certain parts of Brittany, it was the youngest, not the eldest son who succeeded to the principal heritage, and this too was compatible with natural law, for, in a family, the elder sons marry the first and establish themselves on their own account, while the last-born remains longest with his parents and cares for them in their old age. This *droit de juvégnerie* bears witness to the flexibility and diversity of customs which adapted themselves to family practices according to conditions of life.

At all events, what is chiefly to be noted in the system of the transmission of property is that it passed to one single heir, and that this heir was designated by right of birth. '*Pas d'héritier par testament*', it is said in common law. In the transmission of the patrimony the will of the testator was of no account: on the death of the father his natural successor took possession of it by right. '*Le mort saisit le vif*', it was also said in the language of the Middle Ages, which knew the secret of telling phrases. It was the death of the parent which conferred on his successor his title to the estate and put him *en saisine*, in possession of the land. For this no lawyer was needed then, as in our own times. If custom varied according to districts, considering as the natural heir now the eldest, now the youngest son, and if the manner in which nieces and nephews could claim the succession, if there were no direct heir, varied from province to province, one rule at least was constant: inheritance was dependent on natural ties linking the heir to the deceased man. That rule applied in the case of real estate, and testamentary bequests were concerned only with chattels and lands acquired during the testator's lifetime and not included in the family estate. When the natural heir was notoriously unworthy of his charge, or when he was, for example, simple-minded, modifications were permitted; but, in general, human will did not affect the natural order of things. '*Institution d'héritier n'a point lieu*', that is the adage of the jurists in common law. It is in this sense that it is still said, in speaking of royal successions: 'the king is dead, long live the king!' There is no interruption or abeyance possible when heredity alone determines the successor.

Thus the administration of the family estate was always ensured. All customs were designed to prevent the patrimony from being impaired, and for that reason there was never more than one heir, at all events in the case of a nobleman's estate. The parcelling out of property was feared, for this impoverished the land by dividing it *ad infinitum* and the division of lands has always been a source of disputes and lawsuits; it causes inconvenience to the husbandman and puts obstacles in the path of material progress—for in order to benefit from the improvements which science or labour bring within the reach of the peasant, a fairly large-scale undertaking is essential, one which can weather partial set-backs if the need arises and which can in any case provide a variety of resources. A large estate of the kind which existed under the feudal system, permitted the wise cultivation of the land, a part of which could be allowed to lie fallow from time to time and recover; in addition, crops could be varied while a harmonious proportion of each was maintained. In this way country life showed extraordinary activity during the Middle Ages and many crops were introduced into France during this period.

This was due in large part to the opportunities which the rural system of the time offered to the enterprising spirit present in the French people, for the peasant of those times was neither unprogressive nor lacking in initiative. The unity and stability of the estate were a guarantee, both for the future and for the present, in that they encouraged an uninterrupted family effort. Nowadays, when there are several heirs it is necessary to break up the estate and go through all kinds of negotiation and repurchases in order that one of them can carry on his father's work.[1] Cultivation

---

[1] Recently, clauses have fortunately been added to modify the law of succession.

ceases on the death of the individual. But when the individual dies the home remains, and in the Middle Ages there was a tendency to *remain*. If there is one significant word in medieval French terminology it is *manoir*, the place where one remains (*manere*). It formed the connecting link in the family whose members, past and present, were sheltered by its roof, and it enabled each generation to succeed the other in peace and security.

Also very characteristic was the agrarian unit known as the *manse*: the area of land sufficient to allow a family to settle and live. This varied, naturally, according to the region: a small plot in the rich province of Normandy or in the fertile Gascon land brought a better return to the cultivator than large expanses in Brittany or the Forez region; the *manse*, then, varied in size according to the climate, the quality of the soil and the conditions of life. Its area was determined by rule-of-thumb methods and, characteristically, from the point of view not of the individual but of the family. In itself alone it epitomised the most striking feature of medieval society.

In the Middle Ages the principal objective was to ensure an established base for the family, to rivet it, as it were, to the soil, so that it should take root there and bear fruit and endure. It was permissible to trade property in the form of chattels and dispose of them by will, since these were essentially impermanent and unstable; for the opposite reasons, real estate, the family property, was neither alienable nor distrainable. The man was merely the temporary guardian, the usufructuary; the true owner was the line.

A host of customs derived from this concern to safe-guard the family estate. For instance, in the event of there being no direct heir, the property from the paternal side reverted to the father's family and that from the maternal side to the mother—whereas under Roman law relationships on the male side alone were recognised. This custom of sharing out according to their origin the possessions of a family which had died out was known as the *fente*. Likewise, the *retrait lignager* gave to even distant relatives the right of pre-emption when, for one reason or another, an estate was sold. The method whereby the custody of an orphaned child was settled also exemplified a type of family legislation. The child was left in the care of the whole family, and whoever was entitled by his degree of kinship to administer the estate became, automatically, the child's guardian. Our family conference is merely a relic of the medieval custom by which the leases of fiefs and the tutelage of children were settled.

Furthermore, respect for the natural order of things and the avoidance of any hitch in the transmission of the family estate was deemed so essential in the Middle Ages that, in the event of the owners of a property dying without issue, their estate was not permitted to revert to their parents, but descendants, no matter how remote, cousins or distant cousins, were sought in order to prevent the property from reverting to its previous owners. '*Biens propres ne remontent*'—this expresses the desire to adhere to the natural course of life which is transmitted to members of the younger generation by their elders and does not retrace its steps; rivers never flow upstream and, likewise, the substance of life should nourish the future, represented by youth. It was, moreover, an extra insurance for the family estate that it should fall of necessity to the youngest and therefore the most active members, those most capable of turning it to good account for the longest time.

The transmission of property was sometimes effected in a form which spoke eloquently of the family feeling which constituted the principal strength of the medieval era. The family (those who lived from the same '*pain et pot*') formed a veritable personality, possessing in common the estate which the father administered. On his death the community was re-formed under the direction of one of the *parsonniers*, designated by kinship, without any interruption of tenure or any sort of transfer. Every member of the household, unless he had been expressly relegated '*hors de pain et pot*', belonged to this *communauté taisible*, as it was called, and the custom persisted until the end of the *Ancien Régime*. It was possible to cite cases of French families who had never paid any death duties and, in this connection, Dupin, the jurist, pointed out in 1840 that none had been paid by the Jault family since the fourteenth century.

Apart from the *communauté taisible*, the family, stretching across generations, remained in every case the true owner of the patrimonial estate. The father of the family, who received the property from his ancestors, was responsible for it to his descendants; whether he were serf or noble-man, he was never the absolute master: his right to use was recognised, but not his right to abuse, and he had, further-more, the duty of defending, protecting and improving the lot of all the persons and things of whom he had been appointed the natural guardian.

✱

Thus it was that France was created, the work of these thousands of families, resolutely settled on the land, in time and space. From the tenth century onwards, Franks, Burgundians, Normans and Visigoths, all the floating population whose unstable mass had produced so discon-certing a chaos in the early Middle Ages, constituted a nation, firmly rooted in the land, united by ties which were more solid than all the federations whose existence has ever been proclaimed. The ever-renewed exertions of these microscopic families had given birth to one great family, a macrocosm whose high standards were excellently symbolised by the Capet line which, from father to son, directed the fortunes of France so gloriously during three centuries. Certainly, one of the finest spectacles which History can offer is that of this family which remained continuously at the head of the French nation in direct and unbroken succession during more than three hundred years—a period of time equivalent to that which elapsed between the accession of Henri IV and the Second World War.

But the first essential is to understand that the history of the Capets themselves is no more than the story of one French family among millions of others. All French families possessed this same vitality, this same dogged perseverance on the land, to a more or less equal degree, save for the inevitable freaks and accidents of existence. The Middle Ages, born of uncertainty and confusion, of war and invasion, became an era of stability, of permanence in the etymological sense of the word.

This was due largely to family institutions, such as they are manifested in customary law. In these a maximum of individual independence was, in effect, combined with a maximum of security. Each individual found material assistance in the home and the moral protection he needed in the family solidarity; at the same time, as soon as he was able to support himself he was free, free to use his own initiative and to make his own life; nothing hindered the development of his personality. Even the ties which bound him to the paternal home, to his past and its traditions, did not in any sense fetter him; life in its entirety began afresh for him exactly as, biologically speaking, it begins whole and new for each being who comes into the world—or like personal experience, an incommunicable treasure which each man must store up for himself and which is of value only in so far as it is his own.

It is obvious that such a conception of the family sufficed to furnish a nation with all the vitality and all the strength it needed. The exploits of Robert Guiscard, who, with his brothers, the younger sons of an impoverished and over-numerous Norman family, emigrated and became King of Sicily, founding a powerful dynasty there, is typical of the medieval age, its daring, its family feeling and its fecundity. Customary law, which has been the source of France's strength, was here directly opposed to Roman law, by which family unity was dependent on the authority of the head, all the members owing him rigorously disciplined obedience their whole life long—a military and national-istic conception resting on an ideology of jurists and officials and not on natural law. The Nordic family has been compared to a hive which swarms periodically and multiplies and restocks—and the Roman family to a hive which never swarms. It has also been said of the family living under customary law that it bred pioneers and businessmen, while the Roman family gave birth to soldiers, administrators and officials.[2]

It is interesting to follow across the centuries the history of peoples moulded under these different systems of discipline, and to note their ultimate development. Roman expansion was political and military, not ethnical: the Romans conquered an empire by force of arms and their officials enabled them to keep their hold on it; this empire was united only while soldiers and officials were able to super-vise it with ease; as its frontiers were extended, so the dis-proportion increased with the centralisation which was the ideal aim and inevitable consequence of Roman law. When the thrust of invasions came to administer the *coup de grâce*, it collapsed of its own accord and through its own institutions.

[2] We owe these observations to M Roger Grand, *professeur à l'Ecole des Chartes.*

In contrast, the example of the Anglo-Saxon races can be cited, whose family institutions were identical with those of the French throughout the Middle Ages, and who, unlike the French, have continued to preserve them. Here, doubtless, lies the explanation of the prodigious Anglo-Saxon expansion throughout the world, for it is in fact in this way that an empire is founded, as a result of waves of explorers, pioneers, merchants, adventurers and dare-devils leaving their homes to seek a fortune, but without forgetting their native land and the tradition of their forefathers.

The Germanic countries, from which medieval France adopted a vast number of her customs, were to come very early under Roman law. Their emperors began to follow the traditions of the Western Empire and deemed Roman law an excellent instrument of centralisation for the uniting of the vast territories they had subjugated. Roman law was therefore instituted at an early date and from the end of the fourteenth century was firmly established as the universal law of the Holy Roman Empire, while in France, for instance, the first chair of Roman law at the University of Paris was not established until 1679. German expansion has, moreover, been more military than ethnical.

France herself was moulded principally by common law; undoubtedly one is accustomed to designate the Southern Loire and the Rhone valley as '*pays de droit écrit*', that is, under Roman law; but this signifies that the customs of these regions were inspired by Roman law, not that the Justinian Code was in force there. During the entire period of the Middle Ages, France preserved her family traditions and her domestic customs intact. It was only from the sixteenth century onwards that her institutions, under the influence of the jurists, became more and more latinised. It was a gradual transformation which was noticeable first in small modifications: the age of attaining majority was taken to twenty-five years as in Ancient Rome where, since the child was in perpetual minority in relation to his father, there was no objection to his majority being declared fairly late. Marriages, hitherto considered as a sacrament, as the joining together of two free souls for the fulfilment of their purposes, became associated with the idea of a contract, a purely human agreement, based on material stipulations.

The French family took as prototype a nationalist form of *régime* which had been previously unknown, and, just as the father began to concentrate all authority over the family in his own hands, so the State tended towards absolute monarchy.[3] In spite of appearances, the Revolution was not a starting-point but a goal, the result of an evolution which had been in progress for two or three centuries; it represented the final recognition of Roman law amid French usages at the expense of customary law. Napoleon merely completed the work by establishing the *Code Civil* and by organising the army, education and the entire nation according to the bureaucratic ideal of Ancient Rome.

It is, in any case, questionable whether Roman law, whatever its merits, was suited to the French genius or to the character of the French soil. Was it possible to substitute with impunity this body of laws, drawn up entirely by soldiers and jurists, this doctrinal, theoretical and rigid creation, for customs which had been founded on the experience of generations and fashioned gradually in accordance with the needs of the people—customs which were never more than habits noted and formulated in legal terms, the usages of each individual or, better, those of the group to which he belonged. Roman law had been conceived

[3] In this connection, the evolution of the law of property, which became more and more absolute and individual, is very characteristic. The last vestiges of collective property disappeared in the nineteenth century with the abolition of rights of user and rights of common.

with an urban State, not rural areas, in mind. To speak of
Antiquity is to evoke Rome or Byzantium; to conjure up
medieval France one must evoke not Paris but the Ile-de-
France, not Bordeaux but Guienne, not Rouen but Normandy; it is impossible to conceive of France other than as
she is represented in her provinces, with their soil rich in
good wheat and fine wine. It is a small but significant fact
that the man who was called the *manant* (he who remains),
became at the time of the Revolution the *'citoyen'*: in
'citoyen' there is *'cité'*; that is easily understandable, for the
town was soon to hold the political, and thus the greatest
power, since, as custom was no longer recognised, everything henceforward depended upon the law. France's new
administrative divisions, her *départements*, which were
centred on a town without consideration for the quality of
the soil in the surrounding country, clearly demonstrated
this mental evolution. Family ties were by this time
sufficiently weakened to permit the establishment of such
institutions as divorce, the alienability of the patrimony or
the modern laws of succession. The liberty of the individual
hitherto so jealously esteemed, vanished before the idea of
a centralised State run on Roman lines. Perhaps it is here
that we should seek the origin of the problems which later
presented themselves so forcibly: problems relating to
children, education, family life and the birthrate, none of
which had existed in the Middle Ages because the family
was a reality at that time and possessed the material and
moral basis, and the freedom, essential to its existence.

Chapter Two
The Feudal Bond

I T may be said that present-day society is based on a wage-earning system. At the economic level, a man's relations with his fellows are dependent on the relation of capital and labour. To perform a set job, receiving in exchange a set sum, that is the schema of social relations. Money is the vital nerve since, save for a few exceptions, a specific activity is first transformed into cash before being transformed again into one or other of the necessities of life.

In order to understand the Middle Ages one must picture to oneself a society based on a totally different system, in which the idea of paid labour or even, to some extent, of money, was absent or of secondary importance. Men's mutual relationships were founded on the double conception of fidelity on the one side and protection on the other. Security was expected in return for allegiance. A man did not undertake to complete a specific job for a fixed remuneration, but pledged his person or, rather, his loyalty, and claimed in return a livelihood and protection in all senses of the word. Such was the essence of the feudal bond.

This characteristic of medieval society is easily explained if one considers the circumstances of its formation. It originated in the chaotic Europe of the period from the fifth to the eighth centuries. The Roman Empire was crumbling beneath the double impact of internal disintegration and the onslaughts of invaders. Everything in Rome depended on the strength of the central authority; from the moment this authority was outflanked, ruin was unavoidable; neither the division into two empires nor any efforts at temporary recovery could check it. Nothing stable remained in this world where all living sources of strength had been virtually choked by a stifling bureaucracy; where the treasury squeezed the smallholders who had soon no course left open to them other than to cede their land to the State to pay their taxes; where the people were leaving the rural districts, content to call in for work in the fields those very barbarians who, on the frontiers, were being held in check only with difficulty; thus it was that the Burgundians settled in the Savoie-Franche-Comté region of Eastern Gaul and became the *métayers* there of the Gallo-Roman owners whose homes they shared. One after the other, either peacefully or by the sword, the Germanic and Nordic tribes spread over the Western world; Rome was sacked and sacked again by the barbarians; emperors were appointed and dismissed to suit the whims of the soldiery; Europe was no more than a huge battlefield where armies, races and religions confronted one another.

What means of self-preservation was there at a time when unrest and insecurity held absolute sway? The State was distant and powerless if not non-existent; it was, therefore, quite natural to turn to the only power still relatively strong and near at hand: the great landowners, who could ensure the defence of their domains and of their tenants; the small and the weak sought their aid, entrusting them with their

land and their persons on condition that they were protected from over-taxation and foreign incursions. From the
time of the Byzantine Empire, on an ever-mounting tide
of events during the seventh and eighth centuries, the
power of the great landowners increased as an outcome of
the weakness of the central power. The protection of the
senior was sought more and more as the sole active and
effective defence, an insurance against not only war and
famine but also against interference from the Emperor's
officials. Thus, deeds of privilege multiplied, by which the
humble folk attached themselves to a *senior* to ensure their
personal safety. The Merovingian kings, moreover, were
in the habit of surrounding themselves with an escort of
fideles, men devoted to them personally, warriors or others,
and this was later to lead the powerful men of the time to
gather about themselves, in imitation, the *vassi* who had
decided to swear allegiance to them. Finally, the kings
themselves often reinforced feudal power by rewarding, by
the grant of lands, the services of their own officials (whose
authority over the landowners had grown consistently less).

When the Carolingians succeeded to the throne, the
evolution was virtually complete: over all the land, nobles
enjoying varying degrees of authority and surrounded by
their men, their vassals, administered their fiefs, large and
small. Under the pressure of events, the central power had
given place to local authority which had, peaceably, absorbed
the smallholdings and was left, ultimately, as the sole
organised force. The medival heierarchy, the result of
economic and social factors, had grown up naturally and its
usages, fashioned by force of circumstances, were to be
maintained by tradition.

The Carolingians did not attempt to struggle against the
established order; Pepin's dynasty, moreover, had come to
power only because its representatives were among the

C

most influential landowners of the period. They were content to direct the forces in whose presence they found themselves, and to accept the feudal hierarchy and turn it to the best possible account. Such are the origins of medieval society, which differed vastly from any social system previously known: authority, instead of being concentrated at one single point, in an individual or an organisation, was dispersed over the land as a whole. The great wisdom of the Carolingians lay in not attempting to control the whole administrative machine themselves and in retaining as they found it the organisation which had grown up. Their direct authority extended to only a small number of people who themselves exercised authority over others, and so on, down to the humblest strata of society; but the central power could transmit an order by degrees in this way to the entire country, and could influence indirectly affairs over which it exercised no direct control. Thus, instead of combating the hierarchy which was to have so profound an influence on French customs, Charlemagne was content to discipline it; in recognising the legitimacy of the double oath of allegiance which every free man owed to his emperor and his lord, Charlemagne sanctioned the existence of the feudal bond. Such, then, are the origins of medieval society, and also of the nobility—a landed, not a military class as it has been too often believed.

An extreme diversity of conditions among both people and property resulted from this natural development which was shaped by events and by social and economic necessities,[4] for the nature of the commitments which bound the landowner and his tenant to one another varied according to circumstances, to the character of the soil and the mode

---

[4] The following excellent observation was made by Henri Pourrat: 'The feudal system was the living organisation imposed by the land on the men of the land.' (*L'homme à la bêche. Histoire du paysan*, p. 83.)

of life of the inhabitants; all kinds of factors combined to distinguish the relationship and hierarchy of one province from another, and even of one estate and another; what remained constant, however, was the reciprocal obligation: fidelity on the one side, protection on the other; or, in other words, the feudal bond.

During the greater part of the Middle Ages this bond was characterised chiefly by its personal nature: a precisely specified and particular vassal commended himself to an equally precisely specified and particular nobleman; he chose to attach himself to this lord and swore him allegiance, expecting from him material subsistence and moral protection. When Roland lay dying he referred to 'Charles, his lord, who nourished him', and this simple phrase suffices to indicate the nature of the bond which united them. It was only from the fourteenth century onwards that this link became more material than personal: it grew to be associated with the holding of a property and derived from the agreement between the nobleman and his vassal concerning the land; their relationship from that time onwards was more that of landowner and tenant, and it was the condition of the land which determined the condition of the individual. But, during all the medieval period properly speaking, bonds were made between individual and individual. *Nihil est preter individuum*, it was said, 'nothing exists apart from the individual.' A taste for all that was personal and particular and a horror of abstractions and anonymity are, moreover, characteristic of the period.

This personal link binding the vassal to his suzerain was affirmed during a ceremony which exemplified that symbolism so dear to the Middle Ages; for every obligation, every transaction and every agreement had at that time to be translated into a symbolic action, the essential visible form of inward acquiescence. When, for instance, land was sold, the act of sale was deemed to be the handing over by the seller to the new owner of a straw or a clod of earth from his field: if a written agreement was afterwards drawn up (which was not always the case) it served only as a memorandum; the essential act was the *traditio*, corresponding to the handshake in certain markets in our own time. 'I will give him a straw', says the *Ménagier de Paris*, 'or an old nail or a pebble, which were given to me as tokens of any important transaction.' The medieval period was one in which ritual was predominant, where everything which took place in the mind must necessarily be expressed in terms of actions; this satisfied a profoundly human need, that of a corporeal sign without which the reality remained imperfect, incomplete and evanescent.

The vassal took an oath of '*foi et hommage*' to his lord: he would kneel before him, his sword-belt unfastened, and place his hand in that of his *seigneur*—gestures signifying unreserved confidence, trust and fidelity; he would then declare himself his liegeman and give an assurance of personal devotion. In response, and to seal the pact which was henceforth to bind them to each other, the suzerain would kiss his vassal on the mouth. This gesture implied something greater than, and superior to, protection in the ordinary sense; it was a bond of personal affection which was to govern the relationship between the two men.

Afterwards there followed the ceremony of the '*serment*', of which the importance cannot be too greatly emphasised. '*Serment*' must be understood in its etymological sense: '*sacramentum*', a sacred thing. The oath was taken on the Gospel, and by this sacred act not only one's honour but one's troth and one's whole person was plighted. Such importance was attached to an oath that the word of honour of one or two witnesses was accepted even in extremely serious matters, for instance, as evidence of the last wishes of a dying man. To go back on one's oath was, to the medieval way of thinking, the worst possible disgrace. A passage from Joinville demonstrates very significantly that it was an extreme to which a knight could not go, even were his life at stake: at the time of his captivity, the dragomans of the Sultan of Egypt came to offer him his release and that of his companions:' "Would you," they asked, "surrender one of the castles belonging to the barons across the sea?" The count replied that he had no power to do so, since these were held from the German Emperor who was still living. Then they asked if he would surrender one of the *châteaux* of the Knights Templars or the Knights Hospitallers in exchange for our release. And the count replied that that could not be; that when the governor was installed he was required to swear by all the saints that he would never hand over the castles for the release of any man. And they answered that it seemed to them that we had no desire to be released, and that they would leave us and would send those who would practise their sword-play on us, as they had done upon the others.'[5]

The ceremony was completed by the solemn livery of seizin made to the vassal by his *seigneur*, who confirmed the man's ownership of the fief by an act of *traditio*, generally by giving him a rod or stick, symbols of the power which he could exercise over the property he had received. This was described as livery *cum baculo vel virga*, to employ the legal terms in use at that time.

The lofty conception of personal dignity which grew up during the Middle Ages is apparent from this ceremonial and from the traditions implicit in it. No other age has been so eager to set aside abstractions and theories and to rely exclusively on covenants between man and man; nor has

[5] That is to say, that they would massacre them as they had the others.

any other age appealed to higher sentiments as the basis for such covenants. It was a magnificent tribute to the human individual. The conception of a society founded on mutual loyalty was certainly a bold one; as was to be expected, there were abuses and shortcomings—the struggles of the kings with recalcitrant vassals offer proof of this. But, nevertheless, the fact remains that during more than five centuries faith and honour persisted as the essential foundation and the framework of social relations. When the principle of authority was substituted in the sixteenth and, particularly, the seventeenth century, it cannot be said that society gained by it; at all events, the nobility, already undermined for other reasons, lost their essential moral impetus.

During the entire medieval period the nobility, although its origins in the land and its estates were never forgotten, was a predominantly military one. Indeed, its duty of protection imposed upon it a primarily martial role: the defence of the estate against possible encroachments. Moreover, although efforts were being made to curtail it, the right to wage private war still existed, and family solidarity might entail the obligation of avenging by force of arms wrongs done to a kinsman. There was, in addition, a purely material aspect: as the nobility did, in fact, possess the chief, if not the only source of wealth—the land—they alone were in a position to maintain war-horses and to arm squires and men-at-arms. Military service was, therefore, to become inseparable from the service of a fief, and the allegiance sworn by a vassal presupposed his armed aid every time that '*mestier en sera*' (that there was need of it).

This obligation to defend the domain and its inhabitants was the foremost duty of the nobility and one of the most onerous:

L'épée dit: C'est ma justice[6]
Garder les clercs de Sainte-Eglise
Et ceux par qui viandes est quise.[7]

The most ancient strongholds, built during periods of unrest and invasion, bear the visible mark of this obligation: the village, the abodes of the serfs and peasants, clung to the slopes of the fortress where the whole population would take refuge in time of danger and seek help and provisions in time of siege.

The majority of customs among the nobility derived from its military obligations: the right of primogeniture originated in part from the need for entrusting the family heritage to the strongest individual, whose duty it was to guard it, often with his sword. Here, also, is to be found the explanation of the law of masculine succession: only a man could ensure the defence of a castle keep. Thus, when a fief fell to the distaff and a woman was the only surviving heir, the suzerain, whose responsibility this fief was, now that it had fallen into a position of inferiority, set about arranging a marriage for her. For the same reason a woman did not succeed to a property until after her younger brothers, and the latter did not succeed until after the eldest son, but received only apanages; moreover, the disasters which occurred towards the end of the Middle Ages were largely due to the over-large apanages left by Jean le Ben to his children, whose power was a perpetual source of temptation to them, and a source of disturbance for everyone during the minority of Charles VI.

The nobles had also the duty of dispensing justice to their vassals in all circumstances and of administering the fief. It was, in effect, the performing of a duty, and not the exercising

[6] Office, function.
[7] Those who were responsible for provisions and material necessities (peasants). *Carité*, poem by the Reclus de Molliens.

of a right, and very heavy responsibilities were entailed, since each lord was answerable for his estate to not only his family but also his suzerain. Etienne de Fougères depicts the life of the lord of a large domain as being full of cares and hard work:

> *Cà et là va, souvent se tourne,*
> *Ne repose ni ne séjourne:*
> *Château abord, château aourne,*
> *Souvent haitié,*[8] *plus souvent mourne.*
> *Cà et là va, pas ne repose*
> *Que sa marche ne soit déclose.*

Far from being unlimited, as has been generally believed, his power was much less than that of a captain of industry or of any landowner in our own time, since he never enjoyed full ownership of his lands, being always subject to a suzerain and, moreover, the most powerful suzerains being subject, ultimately, to the king. In our own days, in accordance with the Roman conception, payment for land gives the purchaser full rights in it. In the Middle Ages this was not so: maladministration exposed the nobleman to penalties which might amount to the confiscation of his property. Thus, no one governed with absolute authority and no one could escape from the direct surveillance of the person from whom he held his fief. This division of property and authority is one of the most characteristic features of medieval society.

The obligation binding the vassal to his lord also implied reciprocal obligations: 'The lord owes as much faith and loyalty to his man as the man to his lord,' says Beaumanoir. This conception of reciprocal obligations, of mutual service, is often to be met in both legal and literary contexts:

[8] Gay

Graigneur fait a sire à son homme
Que l'homme à son seigneur et dome,[9]

observes Etienne de Fougères, quoted above, in his *Livre des Manières;* and Philippe de Novare remarks, in support of this comment: 'He who accepts services and never repays them drinks the sweat of his servitors, which is a mortal poison to body and soul.' There is also the maxim: 'Good service merits fair return.'

As was only just, a higher standard of behaviour and moral rectitude was demanded from the nobility than from the other members of society. The fine imposed on a nobleman was much heavier than that imposed for the same offence on a commoner. Beaumanoir cites a crime for which 'a peasant pays a fine of sixty *sous* and a gentleman one of sixty *livres*'—a very considerable difference amounting to a proportion of one to twenty. According to the *Etablisse-ments de Saint Louis*, an offence for which an *homme coutumier*, that is, a commoner, paid a fine of fifty *sous*, resulted, in the case of a nobleman, in the confiscation of all his chattels. The same practice is also met with in the bye-laws of various towns: those of Pamiers fixed the scale of fines for stealing thus: twenty *livres* for a baron, ten for a knight, one hundred *sous* for a *bourgeois* and twenty *sous* for a villain.

Nobility was hereditary, but could also be acquired either as a reward for services rendered or else quite simply by the acquisition of a noble fief. That is what did in fact happen on a large scale towards the end of the thirteenth century; many noblemen had been killed or ruined on the great expeditions to the East and *bourgeois* families, who had enriched themselves, acceded *en masse* to the nobility, thus producing a reactionary tendency among the latter class. Knighthood also raised the man on whom it was conferred

[9] The lord owes more gratitude to his vassal than does the latter to his lord.

to noble rank. Lastly, there were, later on, letters patent of nobility, distributed, it must be admitted, very sparingly.[10]

Nobility could be acquired and it could also be lost, through disgrace resulting from a dishonourable sentence.

> *La honte d'une heure du jour,*
> *Tolt*[11] *bien de quarante ans l'honnour,*

it was said. Noble rank could be lost also by derogation in the event of a noble being convicted of following a commoner's calling or of engaging in any form of trading. He was, in fact, forbidden to make any departure from the role for which he had been cast and he must not seek to enrich himself by assuming duties which might cause him to neglect those to which his life should be dedicated. Trades were, however, excluded from those considered as commoners' callings when they demanded considerable resources and could hardly have been embarked upon by anyone other than a nobleman—for example, glass-making and iron-manufacture; in the same way, sea-borne trade was considered permissible because it necessitated, in addition to capital, a spirit of adventure which no one would have wished to curb. Colbert enlarged the field of economic enterprise among the nobility in the seventeenth century in order further to stimulate trade and industry.

The nobility was a privileged class, its privileges being, primarily honorary rights of precedence, *et cetera*. Some of these derived from the burdens borne by the class: thus, a noble alone had the right to spurs, sword-belt and banner; which reminds one that, originally, only the nobility

---

[10] The *Ancien Régime* tended more and more to forbid promotion to the nobility, and this constituted a contributory factor in the creation of an exclusive caste, isolating the king from his subjects. In England, on the other hand, the many ennoblements gave excellent results, in that they revived the aristocracy by the incorporation of new elements, making of it an open and a vigorous class.

[11] Effaces.

had the means to equip a war-horse. In addition, noblemen enjoyed certain immunities—those enjoyed in primitive times by all free men, such as exemption from tolls and certain indirect taxes whose importance, non-existent in the Middle Ages, increased continuously in the sixteenth and, particularly, the seventeenth century.

Finally, the nobility had certain well-defined rights which were of considerable importance: those which depended on the right of ownership, that is, for example, the right to collect rents and the right of sporting. The rents and quit-rents paid by the peasants were simply payment for the land on which they had received permission to settle, or which their ancestors had seen fit to convey to a more powerful owner than themselves. The nobles, in collecting these rents, were in precisely the same position as the owner of house-property. The distant origins of the right of ownership became gradually obscured, however, and at the time of the Revolution the peasant had come to consider himself the rightful owner of land where he had been the tenant for centuries. The circumstances were much the same with regard to the notorious right of sporting which has been represented as one of the most flagrant abuses in an era of terror and tyranny; but what could, in fact, be more reasonable than that a man should reserve his right to hunt on land which he rents to another?[12] At all events, both owner and tenant understood the nature of their mutual obligations when they made an agreement, and that was the essential. When the *seigneur* was hunting near the home of a peasant he was still on his own estate. It is possible—though not verifiable—that some of the nobles may have abused their rights and 'trampled the

[12] A distinction must again be drawn between periods: the right of sporting was reserved comparatively late, *circa* the fourteenth century—and then only for big game. Formal prohibitions were not made until the sixteenth century. Fishing rights remained free.

peasant's golden harvest beneath their horses' hooves'—as they say in the elementary school history books—but one can hardly believe that this could have been a systematic practice since a large part of their rent consisted in a quota of the harvest; it was, therefore, to their direct interest that the harvest should be abundant. The same applies in the case of the bannal mills: the seigniorial oven and wine-press were originally commodities offered to the peasants in exchange for which it was normal to exact a payment in kind—just as nowadays in certain districts the peasant hires a threshing-machine or other agricultural implements.

There is no doubt, however, that towards the end of the Middle Ages the burdens borne by the nobles gradually decreased without any corresponding reduction in their privileges, and that in the seventeenth century, for example, the rights—even the legitimate rights—which they enjoyed were flagrantly out of proportion to the trifling duties which devolved upon them. The great evil lay in the fact that when their connection with the land had been severed it was not found possible to adapt their privileges to suit their new conditions of life. From the time when the obligations of a fief and, notably, its defence, ceased to constitute an onerous duty, the nobility's privileges became purposeless. Here lay the origins of the decadence of the French aristocracy—a moral decadence which was to be followed by a well-deserved material decadence. The nobility was directly responsible for the ever-increasing misunderstanding between the people and the king; the aristocracy became useless and often harmful to the crown (it was among the nobles and thanks to them that the doctrines of the Encyclopædists, the irreligion of Voltaire and the ramblings of Jean-Jacques Rousseau were disseminated) and contributed largely in leading Louis XVI to the scaffold and Charles X into exile. It was only just that members of the nobility should follow each of them, though this must be counted as a heavy loss for France—a land without an aristocracy is a land without bones, without traditions, as it were, susceptible to every vacillation and every error.

I N the slightly superficial impression which is too often
formed of medieval society, there is room for only
seigneurs and serfs: on one side tyranny, despotism and
abuses of power, and on the other the poor people,
talliable and liable to forced labour at pleasure. Such is the
picture conjured up by the words '*Noblesse*' and '*Tiers état*'
—(and this is the case not only in primary school history
books). Common sense is enough, however, to make it hard
for one to concede that the descendants of fierce Gauls, of
Roman soldiers, of Germanic warriors and bold Scandinav-
ians, could have been reduced to leading, for centuries,
the lives of hunted animals. But it is a legend which dies
hard; contempt for the '*siècles grossiers*', moreover, dates
from before the time of Boileau.

In reality the *Tiers état* comprised a host of intermediary
conditions between the extremes of absolute liberty and
bondservice. There is nothing more varied or more con-
fusing than medieval society and the rural tenures of the
period. Their entirely empirical origins account for this
amazing divergence in both personal status and conditions

of tenure. As an example, during the Middle Ages, when the sub-division of a domain represented the general conception of the law of property, a tenure existed which is unknown in France to-day: land held absolutely, that is, by freehold, and exempt from every kind of charge or tax. This persisted until the Revolution when, all land being declared free, freehold property ceased, in fact, to exist, since everything was subjected to State control and taxation. It is to be noted, furthermore, that when a peasant settled on a piece of land and exercised his skill there, without being disturbed, for the prescribed time—a year and a day, that is, sufficient time to complete the cycle of work in the fields from ploughing to harvesting—then he was considered to be the sole owner of that land.

Thus one gains some idea of the unlimited number of varying agreements that were to be encountered. '*Hôtes*', '*colons*', '*lites*', '*colliberts*'—each of these terms designated a different personal status. And the variety of tenures was even greater: '*cens*', '*rente*', '*champart*', '*métairie*', '*tenure en bordelage*', '*en marché*', '*en quevaise*', '*à complan*', '*en collonge*'— one finds endless forms of agreement recognised concerning the holding of land, with one single point in common, namely that, except for the special case of the *franc-alleu* (freehold estate), there were always several owners, or at least several persons with rights in the same property. Everything depended on custom and custom adapted itself to every kind of land, climate and tradition—which was logical, moreover, since one could not impose the same obligations on those who lived on poor soil as on, for example, the country-people of Touraine or the Beauce region. In effect, scholars and historians are still struggling to disentangle one of the most complex subjects which have ever been presented to their wisdom: there is the abundance and the diversity of customs; and in each of these there is the multitude of different tenures ranging from that of the settler on virgin soil, from whom only a small part of his crops was exacted, to the established cultivator on land in full being, who must pay yearly rent and quit-rent. Errors are always possible as a result of the confusion of terms, for these sometimes embrace quite different realities, according to regions and periods. There is, finally, the fact that medieval society was in a state of perpetual evolution and that what was true in the twelfth century was no longer true in the fourteenth.

What is certain, however, is that during the Middle Ages there were a number of free men outside the nobility —and a no smaller number of individuals of rather indefinite status varying between freedom and bondservice—who swore an oath of allegiance to their *seigneurs* which was approximately the same as that sworn by noble vassals. Beaumanoir, the jurist, speaks of these sharply divided classes: 'All free men are not gentlemen. For they are called gentlemen who are descended from free lines, such as kings, dukes, counts or knights; and this nobility is always inherited from the father. But the freedom of the *homme de poosté*[13] is different, for his freedom is inherited from his mother, and whoever is born of a free mother, he also is free and has the right to do as he pleases. Those of the Third Estate are bondsmen. But all members of this class are not equal in status, for there are several ranks among bondsmen.' It is evident that there are plenty of distinctions to be made.

All town-dwellers were free men: towns, of course, multiplied from the beginning of the twelfth century and the large number of those who, to-day, bear the name '*Villefranche*', '*Villeneuve*', '*Bastide*', *et cetera*, are a reminder to us of the charters of settlement by which all men who came

[13] *Homme de poosté* signifies the villain in the general sense.

THE BANKS OF THE SEINE
(*early Fourteenth Century*)

to take up their abode in these newly established towns were declared free, as were the *bourgeois* and artisans in the *communes* and, in general, in all the cities of the realm. Furthermore, a large number of peasants were free: notably those who were called *roturiers* or villains, these terms not, of course, having the pejorative sense that they have since acquired: a *roturier* was a peasant, a ploughman, for *rutura*, *roture*, signified the action of breaking up the earth with the ploughshare; the villain, generally speaking, was a man who lived on a domain, a *villa*.

Then there were the serfs. The word has often been misunderstood because of a confusion between bondservice, which was peculiar to the Middle Ages and the slavery which was the basis of the social hierarchy in ancient times, and of which *no trace* remained in medieval society. As Loisel explains: 'All people are free in this realm, and as soon as a slave reaches its borders and is baptised, he is freed.' As the Middle Ages, owing to force of circumstances, borrowed its vocabulary from the Latin tongue, it was tempting to assume from the similarity of terms a similarity of meaning. But the status of the serf was totally different from that of the slave in ancient times: the slave was a thing, not a person; he was under the absolute domination of his master who held the power of life or death over him; all personal activity was denied him and he knew neither family, nor marriage nor property.

The serf, on the contrary, was a person, not a thing, and was treated as such. He possessed a family, a home and a field, and owed nothing to his *seigneur* after he had paid his rent. He was not subject to a master, but was attached to an estate; he was not in personal bondage but rendered actual bondservice. The only restriction imposed on his liberty was that he could not leave the land he was cultivating. But it must be observed that this restriction was

D

not without its advantages for if he could not leave his holding, *neither could it be taken from him;* this fact was considered in the Middle Ages almost as a privilege and, in effect, the term is to be found in a collection of customs, the *Brakton,* which says explicitly, in speaking of the serfs: '*tali gaudent privilegio, quod a gleba amoveri non poterunt*' (they enjoyed this *privilege,* that they could not be removed from their land)—this being more or less equivalent to a guarantee against unemployment in our own times. The free tenant-farmer was burdened with all sorts of civic responsibilities which made his destiny rather precarious: if he ran into debt his land could be seized; in time of war he could be obliged to take his part, or his home could be ravaged without the possibility of compensation. The serf, however, was protected from the vicissitudes of fortune; the land he cultivated could not be taken from him, just as he could not leave it. This attachment to the soil was extremely revealing of the medieval mentality, and, let it be observed in this connection, the nobleman was subjected to the same obligation as the serf, for he could not under any circumstances part with his estate or separate himself from it in any way whatever; at the two extremities of the hierarchy, the same need is found for stability and permanence, which was inherent in the medieval soul and which was to shape France and Western Europe generally. It is not a paradox to say that the peasant to-day owes his prosperity to the bondservice of his ancestors; no institution has contributed more to the fortune of the French peasantry. Continuing his labours during centuries on the same land without civic responsibilities and *without being liable for military service,* the peasant became the true master of the land; only bondservice could bind a man so intimately to the soil and make of the former serf the owner of the land. If peasant conditions in the East of Europe, in Poland and elsewhere, have remained very wretched, it is because the protection of bondservice was lacking; in times of upheaval the smallholder, left to his own resources and responsible for his land, experienced the most appalling difficulties which paved the way to the creation of immense estates, thus giving rise to a flagrantly unbalanced society, the exaggerated wealth of the big landowners contrasting with the deplorable conditions of their *métayers*. The fact that the French peasant has been able until recent times to enjoy a life of ease compared with that of the Eastern European peasant, has been due not only to the richness of the soil but also, and most particularly, to the wisdom of our ancient institutions which assured his future at the moment when he had most need of security, and preserved him from the military obligations which afterwards constituted the heaviest burden upon peasant families.

The restrictions placed on the liberty of the serf all derived from this attachment to the soil. A *seigneur* had the right of pursuit of a serf, that is to say, he could bring him back to his estate by force in the event of his running away, for, by nature of his status, a serf was not allowed to leave his land; the only exception made was for those who went on a pilgrimage. The right of *formariage* involved the prohibition of marriage outside the seigniorial domain, which would have been weakened or, as it was said, '*abrégé*', as a result; but the Church protested continually against a right which interfered with family liberties, and which was, in fact, modified from the tenth century onwards; the custom was then instituted of claiming only a pecuniary indemnity from the serf who left a fief to marry into another; there lies the origin of the famous '*droit du seigneur*', concerning which so many foolish remarks have been made. This implied merely the right of the *seigneur* to authorise the marriage of his serfs; but as in the Middle Ages everything was expressed in terms of symbols, the *droit du seigneur* gave rise to symbolic gestures, the significance of which has been exaggerated: for instance, the placing of his hand or his leg on the conjugal bed (whence the terms sometimes employed: '*droit de jambage*' or '*de cuissage*', which have occasioned unfortunate, and, moreover, entirely erroneous, interpretations).

The most irksome liability for the serf was, doubtless, that all property acquired by him during his lifetime was held in mortmain and had, after his death, to return to the *seigneur;* but this obligation also was soon modified and the serf had the right to dispose of his chattels by will (his holding passed in any case to his children). Moreover, the system of *communautés taisibles,* allowed him to evade this law in accordance with the custom of the district, for the serf, like the *roturier,* could form a sort of society with his family, grouping together all those who shared one '*pain et pot*', under a temporary head whose death did not interrupt the life of the community, which continued to enjoy the goods in its possession.

Finally, the serf could be emancipated: emancipations did, in fact, increase from the end of the thirteenth century because the serf had to buy his liberty, either with money or by undertaking to pay an annual quit-rent in the same way as the free tenant-farmer. There is an example of this in the emancipation of the serfs of Villeneuve-Saint-Georges, a dependency of Saint-Germain-des-Prés, for a lump sum of one thousand four hundred *livres*. This obligation of buying their freedom explains, doubtless, why those who benefited from the emancipation often accepted it with a very bad grace: the decree by which Louis X le Hutin in 1315 emancipated all the serfs of the royal domain met with the ill-will of 'recalcitrant serfs' in many places. When customary law was recorded in writing in the fourteenth century, bondservice was not mentioned except among the customs of Burgundy, Auvergne, La Marche, Le Bourbonnais and the Nivernais district, and among the local customs of Chaumont, Troyes and Vitry; everywhere else it had disappeared. A few islands of a very mild form of bondservice persisted here and there, but Louis XVI abolished these definitively in the royal domain in 1779 (ten years before the dramatic action of the too-famous night of August 4th) and invited the *seigneurs* to follow his example; for it was regarded then as a matter of individual right over which the central authority did not claim the power of legislation. Records show, moreover, that the serfs had nothing of the attitude of whipped curs before their *seigneurs*, as has been too often supposed. One finds that they argued, asserted their rights, exacted respect for ancient conventions, and claimed their due without hesitation.

★

Is it permissible to accept without verification the legend of the wretched, uncultivated (this is quite a different story), and despised peasant, which a well-established tradition still imposes upon a great many of our history books? His general mode of life and nourishment gave no grounds for pity, as we shall see. The peasant in the Middle Ages did not suffer any more than mankind in general at all periods of humanity's history. He underwent the after-effects of wars; but have his descendants in the nineteenth and twentieth centuries been spared such misfortunes? Also the medieval serf was exempted from all military service, as were most *roturiers;* the baronial hall was a refuge for him in time of distress, and the Peace of God a guarantee against the brutalities of armed men. He suffered from hunger when the harvest was bad—as the whole world suffered until transport facilities enabled assistance to be brought to threatened areas—and even since that time. But he had the expedient of resorting to the granary of his *seigneur*.

There was only one really hard period for the peasant in the Middle Ages, but it was so for all classes of society without discrimination. That was the time of the disasters produced by the wars marking the decline of the era— a period deplorable for unrest and disorders engendered by a fratricidal struggle, during which France experienced distress comparable only to that of the Wars of Religion, the Revolution and our own times: bands of soldiers ravaged the country, famine provoked rebellions and peasant risings, and as a final blow there came the horrifying epidemic of the Black Death which depopulated Europe. But that constituted a part of the cycle of ills endemic among humanity, from which no people has been exempt; our own experiences should satisfy us on that point.

Was the peasant more despised? Never, perhaps, has he been less so than in the Middle Ages. Certain literature in which the villain was often ridiculed should not be allowed to create an illusion—it bore witness only to the rancour, old as the hills, felt by the *jongleur* and the vagabond for the peasant, the '*manant*', whose home was permanent, whose wits were sometimes slow and whose purse-strings were often tight; and it expressed also the typically medieval aptitude for poking fun at everything, including what seemed most to be respected. In reality, relations between the so-called ruling classes—in this case the nobility—and the people, had never been closer; relations facilitated by the conception of the personal link which was an essential feature of medieval society, and strengthened by local ceremonies and religious and other feasts, during which the *seigneur* met his tenant, learned to know him and shared his existence much more intimately than, in our own time, the middle classes share the lives of their servants. The administration of the fief obliged him to bear in mind all the details of the peasant's life: births, marriages and deaths in serf families had to be taken into account by the nobleman, as directly affecting his estate; the *seigneur* had judicial duties which obliged him to assist the peasants, to settle their law-suits and to arbitrate their differences; he had thus a moral obligation towards them, just as he was materially responsible for his fief to his suzerain. In our own time the owner of a factory is free from all material and moral obligations towards his workers as soon as they have received their pay-packets; one seldom sees him throwing open his home to entertain them to a banquet on the occasion of, for instance, the marriage of one of his sons. All things considered, a radically different conception from that prevailing in the Middle Ages when, as M. Jean Guiraud, has said, roughly speaking, the peasant occupied the foot of the table, but it was the table of his *seigneur*.

One can easily realise this by glancing at the artistic heritage bequeathed by this period and by noting the place occupied in it by the peasant. In the Middle Ages he was everywhere: in pictures, tapestries, cathedral sculpture, illuminated manuscripts, everywhere one finds work in the fields the most general theme of inspiration. What hymn to the glory of the peasant will ever equal the miniatures of the *Très riches heures du Duc de Berry*, or the *Livre des prouffictz champestres*, illuminated for the Bastard Antoine de Bourgogne? Or, again, the little scenes of the months on the portal of Notre-Dame and so many other buildings? And, let it be observed, in all these works, executed for the public or for the noble patron of the arts, the peasant appears in his genuine everyday life: turning the soil, wielding the hoe, pruning the vines, killing a pig. Is there any other period which can show so many exact realistic and lively pictures of rural life?

It is possible and even certain that individually some noblemen and some *bourgeois* showed contempt for the peasants; but has that not been so at all times? However, considering the tendency to mock which was prevalent in those days, the general attitude was one of great awareness of the fundamental equality of men across the inequalities of their condition.

> *Fils de vilain preux et courtois*
> *Vaut quinze mauvais fils de rois*

says Robert de Blois, and the Reclus de Molliens, in his poem *Miserere* protests vigorously against those who believe themselves superior to others:

> *Garde qui tu as en dédain,*
> *Franc hom, qui m'appelles vilain.*
> *Jà de ce mot ne me plaindrais*
> *Si plus franc que moi te savais.*
> *Qui fut ta mère, et qui la moie?* (mine)
> *Andoi* (both) *furent filles Evain.*
> *Or mais ne dis que vilain sois*
> *Plus que toi, car je te dirois*
> *Tel mot où a trop de levain.*

It was a jurist, Philippe de Novare, who differentiated between three types of human being: the 'free people', that is, 'all those who have a free heart—and he who has a free heart, no matter whence he comes, he must be called free and noble; for if he is from a bad place and he is good, then should there be all the more honour to him'; tradespeople, and villains, that is, those who render service only because they must, 'all those who do so are villains, just as if they had been serfs or *gaeigneurs* . . . Nobility or worthy ancestors only deepen the disgrace of bad heirs'.

It would be possible to quote many of these proclamations of equality, as, for instance, in the Roman de Fauvel:

> *Noblesse, si com dit le sage*
> *Vient tant seulement de courage*
> *Qui est de bons moeurs aorné:*
> *Du ventre, sachez, pas ne vient.*

From the more general point of view, is it possible that a human being holding a position in the forefront of the artistic and literary achievements of a nation could have been despised by that nation?

On this point, as on so many others, periods have been confused. What is true of the Middle Ages is not so of all the period known as the *Ancien Régime*. After the end of the fifteenth century a split occurred between the nobility, the educated classes—and the people. From that time onwards, these two classes lived parallel lives, but grew to sympathise with, and understand, each other less and less. As was natural, high society drew intellectual and artistic life to itself and the peasant was struck from the culture of the country as he was from its political activity. He disappeared from painting, save for a few exceptions—from fashionable painting, at all events—and from literature, these having come to be regarded as the concern of the great. The eighteenth century knew only a quite artificial imitation of rural life. There is not any doubt that the peasant has been, if not actually despised, at least scorned and misunderstood from the sixteenth century[14] to the present day, but neither is there any doubt that in the Middle Ages he occupied a position in the first rank of French life.

---

[14] It must be noted that in the sixteenth century the same contempt for manual crafts was evinced, which had been characteristic of antiquity. The Middle Ages traditionally placed the 'sciences, arts and crafts' on an equal footing.

A S soon as the invasions were ended, life spread beyond the boundaries of the seigniorial domain. The manor ceased to be self-sufficient; men took the roads to the cities, trade was organised and soon, overlapping the ramparts, suburbs sprang up. The period from the eleventh century onwards was one of great urban activity. Two factors of economic life, which had remained secondary until then, became of prime importance: trade and commerce. With them a class grew up which was to exert a major influence over the future of France—although it did not come into power effectively until the time of the French Revolution, from which it alone derived real benefits: the *bourgeoisie*.

Its strength, however, dated from much earlier and from the outset it held a predominant position in urban government, while the kings, from Philip the Fair, in particular, were glad to call upon members of the *bourgeoisie* to act as counsellors, administrators and agents of the central authority. It owed its greatness to the growth of the communal movement, of which it was, moreover, the chief motive power. There was nothing more alive or more dynamic than this irresistible force which, from the eleventh century to the beginning of the thirteenth century, drove the towns to free themselves from the authority of the *seigneurs*. And once they had been acquired, nothing was more jealously guarded than these communal liberties. The fact was that the taxes levied by the barons became intolerable from the moment when there was no more need of their protection. In times of unrest, dues and tolls were justified, for they represented the cost of policing the roads; a merchant who was robbed on the land of a *seigneur* could claim compensation from him; but a re-adjustment had to be made to suit new and better days, and this was accomplished by the communal movement. Thus, the Middle Ages succeeded in shaking off the past, a necessary achievement, but difficult to effect in the evolution of society in general. It is very probable that if the same re-adjustment had been made at the proper time in the rights and privileges of the nobility, many disorders would have been avoided.

The monarchy offered an example of the general trend by the conferring of liberties on rural *communes*. The 'Charte Lorris' granted by Louis VI did away with forced labour and bondservice, reduced taxes, simplified judicial procedure and, further, stipulated the protection of markets and fairs:

'No man of the parish of Lorris shall pay customs duty nor any other dues on that which is necessary to his subsistence, nor dues on crops produced by his labour or that of his animals, nor any tax on the wine from his vines.

'Of no man shall it be required that he ride or journey to any place from which he cannot return the same day to his dwelling, if he so desire.

'No man shall pay toll as far as Etampes, nor as far as Orléans, nor as far as Milly en Gâtinais, nor as far as Melun.

'And he who has his property in the parish of Lorris shall not be subject to the confiscation of this property in the event of his committing some offence, unless it be an offence against Ourselves or our people.

'No man coming to the fairs or market of Lorris or returning therefrom shall suffer arrest or interference, unless he have committed some offence that day.

'No man, neither Ourselves nor any other, may levy taxes from the men of Lorris.

. . . . .

'No man among them shall perform forced labour for Us, except once in the year, to bring our wine to Orléans, and to no other place.

. . . . .

'And whosoever shall have lived for a year and a day in the parish of Lorris, without complaint from any man, and provided that this has not been forbidden him by Ourselves or our provost, shall henceforward be free there and obligated to no man.'

The little town of Beaumont was granted the same privileges shortly afterwards and soon the evolution was taking place throughout the realm.

The evolution of a city in the Middle Ages was one of the most fascinating spectacles which history can show. Mediterranean towns such as Marseilles, Arles, Avignon and Montpellier, rivalling the great Italian cities by their daring in Mediterranean trade; centres such as Laon, Provins, Troyes and Le Mans; centres of textile industries such as Cambrai, Noyon and Valenciennes; all gave proof of unparalleled zeal and vitality. They were, moreover, looked upon with favour by the monarchy, for, in their desire for emancipation, did they not bring about the double advantage of both weakening the power of the great noblemen and of bringing unhoped-for additions to the royal domain—since towns which gained their freedom became automatically dependencies of the crown. Sometimes violence was necessary and there were popular risings, as in Laon and Le Mans; but usually towns freed themselves by means of barter, by repeated bargainings, or, quite simply, by the payment of money. Here again, as in all the details of medieval society, there is a striking diversity, for it was possible for independence to be incomplete: one specified part of a town or one particular right was retained by the feudal lord, while the rest reverted to the *commune*. A typical example was furnished by Marseilles; the port and the lower town, which had been shared by the viscounts, were acquired by the people, district by district, and became independent, while the upper town remained under the rule of the bishop and chapter, and a part of the roadstead opposite the port continued to be the property of the Abbey of St Victor.

What was, in any case, common to all the towns, was their eagerness to have these precious liberties they had won, confirmed, and their haste to organise themselves, to record their customs in writing, and to adjust their institutions to suit their own peculiar needs. Their customs varied according to their particular speciality: weaving, commerce, iron-manufacture, tanneries, maritime and other industries. During the whole of the *Ancien Régime*, France had a very special character resulting from these customs peculiar to each town. They were the fruit of experience, of lessons learned in the past, and, what is more, being established independently by the local authorities, they were therefore those best suited to the needs of each town. This variety between one town and another gave a charming and attractive aspect to the country. The absolute monarchy had the wisdom not to interfere with local usages and not to impose a uniform system of administration; this was a source of strength— and one of the charms of the France of those times. Each town possessed, to a degree which is to-day almost unimaginable, its own personality, not only externally, but internally in all the details of its administration and in all its conditions of existence. In general—at all events in the Midi—the towns were governed by consuls, varying in number: two, six, sometimes a dozen; or, again, one single governor combined all duties, assisted by a magistrate representing the *seigneur* when the city had not acquired full political rights. Often, too, in the Mediterranean cities a *podestà* was appointed—a rather curious institution, the *podestà* being always a foreigner (those of Marseilles were all Italian) to whom the government of the city was entrusted for a period of one or two years; in every town where this régime was adopted, it gave complete satisfaction.

In any case, the administration of the city included a council elected by the inhabitants, generally by some form of limited suffrage, and a plenary assembly of the population whose role was, on the whole, consultative. Trade representation always held an important place and the part played by the merchants' provost in Paris during the popular risings of the fourteenth century is well-known. The great difficulty which the *communes* came up against was financial embarrassment. Almost all of them showed themselves incapable of ensuring the efficient care of their resources. Moreover, the power was soon seized by a *bourgeois* oligarchy who proved to be harder on the lower classes than the *seigneurs* had been previously. Out of this state of affairs there rapidly developed the decadence of the *communes*. They were frequently disturbed by popular unrest, and began to totter in the fourteenth century. This development was assisted, it must be added, by the wars of the period and by the general unsoundness of the realm.

★

In the twelfth and thirteenth centuries trade expanded enormously, having received fresh impetus from an external cause: the Crusades. Relations with the Orient, which had never been broken off entirely, during the preceding periods, were strengthened anew; overseas expeditions encouraged French merchants to settle in Syria, in Palestine, in North

Africa and as far as the shores of the Black Sea. There was keen competition between Italians, Provençals and men from Languedoc, and a vast flow of trade was established. With the Mediterranean as its centre, it spread up the ancient road through the valleys of the Rhône, the Saône and the Seine, to the north of France, the Flemish countries and England. (This route had already been taken by the caravans which, before the founding of Marseilles in the sixth century B.C., carried tin from the Scilly Isles to the ports frequented by the Phoenician merchants.) It was the period of the great fairs in Champagne, Brie and the Ile-de-France: Provins, Lagny, Saint-Denis, Bar, Troyes, all received from Central Asia silks, velvets and brocades, alum, cinnamon and cloves, perfumes and spices, which had been bartered in Damascus or Jaffa for cloth from Douai or Cambrai, English wools and Scandinavian furs. The trading firms of Genoa and Florence had permanent branches at the French fairs; bankers from Lombardy or Cahors negotiated with the representatives of the Northern Hanse towns and issued bills of exchange valid as far as the remotest ports of the Black Sea. And the highways of France hummed with an extraordinary volume of traffic. The Oriental contribution was of cardinal importance in medieval civilisation; the early Middle Ages had already known the Orient through Byzantium: a part of the service in the churches of Paris was read in Greek; it was probably Byzantine ivories which taught the West the forgotten art of sculpture in wood and stone; and the illumination of Irish manuscripts drew its inspiration from Persian miniatures. But later the Arabs pursued their conquests with their accustomed brutality and cut communications for a while between the two civilisations. Then came the Crusades and this Oriental contribution (corresponding to a Frankish contribution in Asia Minor, brought to light by recent researches) spread over the whole of Europe, which came to know the excitement of trade, the dazzling display of exotic fruits, rich cloths, heady perfumes and sumptuous costumes—and bathed this era, already enamoured of colour and brightness, in its radiance. Above all, it encouraged the love of risk and the thirst for adventure which, in the Middle Ages, co-existed strikingly with an attachment to the soil. Never, perhaps, has the word 'epic' been better employed than in describing the Crusades; never did the spell of the East hold more fascination or lead, despite seeming set-backs, to more astounding results. One need recall only the settlements of Franks in the Holy Land, from the merchants' *fondoucs* (organised trading-posts which formed veritable little towns, with their own chapel, their public baths, their warehouses, the dwellings of their merchants, their law-courts and meeting-hall)—to the fortresses whose great mass still defies the sun: Krak des Chevaliers, the Château de Saône, the fortifications of Tyre—and the extraordinary feats of arms of men such as Raimond de Poitiers or Renaud de Châtillon, which make one feel that the Crusades, quite apart from their religious objective, were a fortunate safety-valve for the hot-headed zeal of the barons.

Europe was to lose much when, in the fourteenth century, its attention was distracted from the Orient. Saint Louis had glimpsed the opportunity of an alliance with the Mongols which, if it had been seized, would probably have changed entirely the destiny of the two worlds, the Eastern and the Western. His premature death, and the narrow views of his successors, left in embryo a project whose full importance has been demonstrated by the researches of René Grousset. The Mongols alone could offer an efficacious barrier to Islam; they were anxious for an alliance with the Franks and favoured the Nestorian Christians on their own territory. The relations established

LOVE AND THE CHASE
(*early Fourteenth Century*)

by Jean du Plan-Carpin, and, later, by Guillaume de
Rubruquis who, in 1254, visited Karakorum, capital of the
Great Khan, had made both sides aware of the advantages
which could spring from such a union. Did the Mongols not
offer to reconquer Jerusalem from the Mameluke Turks?
But their offer was not considered. The historian of the
Crusades, quoted above, has pointed out the coincidence
of the two dates: 1287, the fruitless mission of the Nestorian
Mongol Rabban Cauma to Paris to the court of Philip the
Fair—and 1291, the loss of Acre.

The Orient, crushed by Islam, became closed to European
trade and influence, and this marked the beginning of an
irremediable decadence for the Mediterranean towns and
for their shipowners, harried by pirates; only the Knights
of St. John Hospitaller continued the fight, foot by foot,
and from Rhodes to Malta struggled dauntlessly to keep the
road open to the East—an unequal but admirable struggle
which ended only with the capture of Malta by Bonaparte.

The organisation of the great Oriental trade was everywhere approximately the same. The trader entrusted to a
shipowner either a cargo or a sum of money to be utilised
to the best advantage; the destination of the voyage was
generally precisely specified, but sometimes the navigator
was left to his own initiative, *ad fortunam maris*. On his
return, he received a quarter of the profits or, if he had
shared the expenses, a proportionate share of the returns,
agreed upon in advance. This was the manner in which
commission or partnership contracts were understood
between merchants. One of the specific differences between
the Middle Ages and our own period was that at that time
it was the trader and not the shipowner who determined
the route; shipping companies had no fixed course—this
was a matter to be agreed upon with those who wished to
travel.

E

In connection with sea-borne trade, the Church tolerated usury, because the risks which were run justified the price of the money. The greatest of these risks, apart from ship-wreck, was the practice of jettison: a ship in peril or pursued by pirates, would unload part of her cargo to lighten. Collections of maritime customs, the *Constitutum Usus* of Pisa, and the Statutes of Marseilles, the Consulate of the Seas, gave careful rulings on the practice of jettison, the merchandise affected by it and the apportionment of the losses among the merchants on board at the time. Another risk arose from the right of reprisals which could be granted by a city to its citizens over the ships of an enemy city, or, more particularly, to a merchant who had been maltreated or whose cargo had been pillaged. It was, in fact, a form of the right of private vengeance.

In order to protect themselves the better, and in accord-ance with a custom dear to the age, merchants used to enter into partnership. There was, firstly, the custom of ships sailing in convoy: two or more ships would decide to make their voyage together, this decision being the subject of a contract which one could not break without exposing oneself to sanctions or a fine. Then again, the merchants of one city, wherever they happened to be, would form an association and select one of their number to act as administrator, and, if need be, to assume responsibility for the protection of their interests. The most important trading posts had a resident consul who at all times, or at least during the great commercial 'season', from the twenty-fourth of June to the thirtieth of November, governed the *fondouc*. Marseilles offers an example of this institution, which was very common in Mediterranean towns. The judgments of the consuls could not be quashed except by the governor of the *commune*, and assumed meanwhile the force of law. Marseilles had a consul in the majority of towns in Syria and North Africa, at Acre, Ceuta, Bougie, Tunis and in the Balearic Islands.

★

Together with commerce, the essential element of urban life was a man's trade. The way in which this was understood in the Middle Ages and in which its exercise and conditions were regulated, merits the particular attention of our own era, which sees in the corporate system a possible solution to the labour problem. But the only really interesting corporation[15] is the medieval one, understood in the broad sense of a confraternity or trade association, which was, however, soon debased by pressure from

[15] We use this term reluctantly, for it has been misused many times and led to much confusion on the subject of former French institutions. It must be noted that this is a modern noun, which did not make its appearance until the eighteenth century. Until then it had been a question only of *maîtrises* or *jurandes* (guild-masterships), which were chiefly characterised by a monopoly of manufacture in a town for a given trade. They were not very numerous during the hey-day of the Middle Ages; they existed in Paris, but not throughout the country as a whole, where they began to become the rule—still with many exceptions—only at the end of the fifteenth century. The golden age for the corporations was not during the Middle Ages, but in the sixteenth century, and from that time they began, at the instance of the *bourgeoisie*, to be monopolised by the masters, who turned the *maîtrise* into a sort of hereditary privilege. This tendency became so marked that in the following centuries the masters formed a veritable caste to which access was difficult if not impossible, for workers of slender means. The latter had no alternative but to form in their turn for their own protection autonomous and more or less secret societies, the trade guilds.

After being, to the minds of some historians, synonymous with tyranny, the corporation has been less severely judged and become sometimes the object of exaggerated panegyrics. Hauser was concerned chiefly with counteracting the latter tendency, and with demonstrating that one must avoid seeing a Utopia in the corporate system. It is quite certain that no system of labour organisation can be qualified as Utopian, the corporate no more than any other—unless, perhaps, in comparison with the situation created among the industrial proletariat in the nineteenth century, or with modern innovations, such as the Bedaux system.

the *bourgeoisie;* the following centuries knew only distortions and caricatures of the same thing.

One cannot define the medieval corporation better than by regarding it as family organisation applied to trades. It was the grouping into a single organism of all the elements of a specified trade: masters, workers and apprentices were gathered together, under no authority, but by virtue of the solidarity which grew naturally from occupation in the same industry. It was, like the family, a natural association, emanating from neither the State nor the king. When Saint Louis instructed Etienne Boileau to compile the *Livre des Métiers*, it was only to have a written record of customs already in existence, in which his authority did not intervene. The only role played by the king in connection with the corporations, as with all matters of private rights, was that of making sure of the loyal application of customs already current. Like the family or the University, the medieval corporation was a free body knowing no laws other than those which it framed freely for itself: that was its essential characteristic, which it was to conserve until almost the end of the fifteenth century.

All the members of the same trade belonged automatically to the corporation, but all did not, of course, play the same part in it: the hierarchy ranged from the apprentice to the *maîtres-jurés*, who formed the upper council of the trade. A distinction is usually made between three ranks—the apprentice, the journeyman and the master; but this was not applicable to the medieval period, during which, until about the middle of the fourteenth century it was possible in the majority of trades to become a master immediately upon termination of apprenticeship. There were not many journeymen until the seventeenth century when an oligarchy of rich artisans sought more and more to confine admission to the mastership to themselves, which promoted the

formation of an industrial proletariat. But during the whole
of the Middle Ages chances were the same for all, and
every apprentice, if he were not too clumsy or too lazy,
ended by becoming a master.

The apprentice was bound to his master by a contract
of apprenticeship (always one finds this personal link so
dear to the Middle Ages) which called for obligations on
either side; in the case of the master, that of training his
apprentice in the trade, of guaranteeing to provide him
with board and lodging in return for payment by his parents
of the expenses of his apprenticeship; in the case of the
apprentice, obedience to his master and diligence in his
work. One sees again, transposed into trade organisation,
the same double notion of fidelity and protection which
bound the *seigneur* to his vassal or his tenant. But as, in this
case, one of the parties to the contract was a child of twelve
to fourteen years, every care was taken to reinforce the
protection he was to enjoy, and, while the greatest indulgence
was shown to the faults, the blunders and even the truancy
of the apprentices, the duties of the master were rigidly
set forth; he could take only one apprentice at a time, so
that his training should be profitable, and so that he could
not exploit his pupils by putting part of his work on to
them; he had the right to take on an apprentice only after
plying his trade as a master-craftsman for at least a year,
time enough for his technical skill and moral qualities to be
assessed. 'No man may take an apprentice if he be not wise
and rich enough to teach him and govern him and maintain him for his term of apprenticeship—and this must be
known and declared by two men of integrity and experience
in the trade,' said the regulations. These regulations stipulated precisely the amount to be spent each day by the
master on the food and keep of his pupil; finally, the *jurés*
of the corporation had the right of inspection and could

visit the home of a master to see how the apprentice was being fed, initiated into the trade and looked after generally. The master had the duties and responsibilities of a father towards him and must, among other things, supervise his conduct and his moral behaviour; in return, his apprentice owed him respect and obedience, but a modicum of independence on his part was not looked upon with disfavour: in the event of an apprentice's running away from his master, the latter had to wait a year before he could take another, and during the whole of that year he was bound to receive the truant if he returned. This was in order that all the guarantees should be on the side of the weaker, not the stronger party.

To become a master it was necessary to have completed one's term of apprenticeship, the length of which varied according to the trade, as was normal—the period being usually of three to five years. It was probable that the future master would then have to give proof of his skill to the *maîtres-jurés* of his corporation—this being the origin of the 'masterpiece', concerning which the conditions grew more and more complicated in the course of the centuries; he had, furthermore, to pay a tax (very small, however, usually from three to five *sous*) which was his subscription to the guild; finally, in some trades in which a master was required to give evidence of solvency, a deposit was demanded. Such were the conditions of mastership in the medieval period properly speaking; from about the fourteenth century the corporations, hitherto independent for the most part, became attracted to the central authority and admission to the mastership was made more difficult: in certain trades a probationary period of three years as a journeyman was required and the candidate had to pay a fee varying from five to twenty *sous*, known as the *achat de métier*.

The exercise of every calling was the subject of detailed rules, which tended primarily to maintain a balance between the members of the guild. Every attempt at monopolising a market, every scheme for an understanding between a few masters to the detriment of others, every effort to gain possession of too large a quantity of raw materials, was rigorously curbed. There was nothing more contrary to the spirit of the old guilds than the hoarding of stocks, speculation, or our modern trusts. Severe penalties were imposed on craftsmen who enticed their neighbours' customers by what would to-day be termed defamatory advertising. Competition was not non-existent, however, but was restricted to the sphere of personal merit. The only way of attracting a customer was to do work that was of superior quality, better finished and more careful, than that of one's neighbour, for the same price.

The regulations were intended also to ensure the maintenance of a high standard of craftsmanship, to enquire into fraudulent practices and punish shoddy work: with these aims in view, all work had to be done as far as possible out-of-doors, or at any rate in the light. Woe betide the draper who had piled his poor quality material in the dark corners of his shop! Everything must be displayed in broad daylight, under the awning where the stroller loved to loiter and where Maître Pathelin came to diddle the simple merchant.

The *maîtres-jurés* or *gardes du métier* were there to ensure that members complied with the regulations and they were empowered to make very thorough inspections. Swindlers were put in the pillory and left on view, with their bad wares, for a variable length of time; their fellow tradesmen were the first to point their fingers at them, for men were very sensitive where the honour of their trade was concerned. Those who sullied it earned the contempt of their fellow-workmen, who considered themselves disgraced by the shame which fell upon the trade as a whole. The delinquents were expelled from the association and were regarded rather as perjured knights who had merited degradation. The medieval artisan in general made a cult of his work, as novels written about trades bear witness (for example, those of Thomas Deloney about the weavers and shoemakers of London). The shoemakers called their art the 'gentle craft' and were proud of the proverb: 'Every son of a shoemaker is born a prince.' A medieval poem, the *Dit des Fèvres*, (workers) dwells complacently on the merits of the latter:

> *M'est il avis que fèvres sont*
> *La gent pour qu'on doit mieux prier.*
> *Bien savez que de termoier* (dawdle)
> *Ne vivent pas fèvres, c'est voir* (true)
> *N'est pas d'usure leur avoir*
> *. . . De leur labeur, de leur travail*
> *Vivent les fèvres loyaument*
> *Et si donnent plus largement*
> *Et dépensent de ce qu'ils ont*
> *Que usuriers, qui rien ne font,*
> *Chanoines, prouvères, ou moines.*

This pride in one's calling was a specifically medieval characteristic—and no less medieval was the jealousy with which each corporation claimed its privileges.

The exclusive right of passing judgment on the misdemeanours of its members was perhaps one of the most precious privileges in that era, but the freedom to administer its affairs through its own representatives was also deemed essential. For this purpose a council was elected each year composed of masters chosen either by the corporation as a whole or else by the other masters; the custom varied according to the trade. The councillors took an oath, from which fact their name (*jurés*) derived. They had to see to it that members complied with the regulations, to visit and protect the apprentices, to settle disputes which might arise between masters, and inspect shops for the purpose of uncovering fraudulent practices. To them also fell the task of managing the corporation's funds. Such was their influence in the city that they often played a political role as a result.

In some towns, such as Marseilles, the trades' delegates shared effectively in the administration of communal affairs. They became members of the *Conseil Général* forthwith and no decision affecting the interests of the town could be taken without them; each week they elected '*semainiers*' who assisted the governor and without whom no resolution could be passed. According to the historian of the *commune* of Marseilles, M. Bourrilly, the leaders of the trade associations were the motive power behind municipal life and it might be said that the government of Marseilles in the thirteenth century was based on the corporate system.

The brotherhood, which was of religious origin and existed almost everywhere, even when there was no organised trade *maîtrise* or *jurande*, was a centre of mutual assistance. Among the expenses which fell regularly upon communal funds, pensions paid to aged or infirm masters, and assistance of sick members during the period of their illness or convalescence, figured largely. It was an assurance scheme in which every case could be known and examined individually, which enabled the appropriate remedy to be applied to each situation and avoided duplication and abuses. 'If the son of a master is poor and wishes to learn, the men of integrity and experience in the same trade must pay for his education out of the five *sous* (the corporation tax) and out of their alms,' stated the statutes of the bucklemakers. If need be, the corporation would assist its members when they were travelling or out of work. Thomas Deloney puts into the mouth of a member of the 'gentle craft' some very significant words: Tom Drum, as he is called, has met on the road a young and penniless lord and proposes to accompany him to London. ' ". . . I will beare thy charges, and, Ifaith, at the next towne we will be merry and have good cheere." "Alas" (quoth Harry) "how can that be, seeing you have but one penny?" "I will tell thee what" (quoth Tom) "wert thou a Shoemaker as I am, thou mightest goe with a single penny under thy finger, and travell all England over, and at every good towne have both meate and drinke and lodging of the best, and yet have thy penny in store . . . shoemakers will not see one another lacke, for it is our use if wee know of a good fellow that comes to towne, wanting either meate or money, and that he make himselfe knowne, he shall neede to take no further care, for he shall be sure that the jorneymen of that place will not onely give him kinde welcome, but also provide him all things necessary of free cost: And if he be disposed to worke among them, he shall have a Master provided by their meanes, without any sute made by himselfe at all." ' This short passage is sufficiently eloquent for comment to be unnecessary.

Understood thus, the corporations were a living centre of mutual assistance, worthy of their motto: 'All for each, each for all.' They prided themselves on their charitable works: thus, the goldsmiths obtained permission to open their shops each in turn on Sundays and the feast-days of the Apostles (usually kept as holidays), and all the day's profits went to provide a meal for the poor of Paris on Easter Day: 'Whoever has opened his workshop, puts what he has earned in the box of the Brotherhood of Goldsmiths, and out of the proceeds of the money in this box, a dinner is given for the poor each year on Easter Day in the Paris

Hospital.' In the majority of trades the corporation paid also for the education of its orphans.

All this took place in an atmosphere of harmony and gaiety hardly to be imagined from modern working conditions. The guilds and corporations each had their traditions, their feast-days, their religious rites and their traditional buffooneries, their songs and their badges. According to Thomas Deloney, quoted above, a shoemaker, in order to be adopted as a son of the 'gentle craft,' must always be able to 'sing, or sound the Trumpet, or play on the Flute, or recon up his tooles in rime, or manfully handle his pike staffe, or fight with a sword and buckler'. During the city festivals and in ceremonial processions, the corporations hung out their banners and each sought to win rights of precedence. The corporations were vigorous and extraordinarily active little worlds, which succeeded in stimulating city life and in lending it an unexpected character of its own.

All things considered, one cannot sum up the character of urban life in the Middle Ages better than by quoting the great historian of the medieval towns, Henri Pirenne: 'Urban economy is worthy of the Gothic architecture with which it is contemporary. It created from nothing a system of social legislation more complete than that of any other era, not excluding our own. By suppressing middlemen between seller and buyer, it ensured the advantages of a low cost of living to the *bourgeoisie;* it was merciless in hunting down fraud; it protected the worker from competition and exploitation, regulated his work and pay, looked after his health, provided for his apprenticeship, prevented female or child labour, and, at the same time, succeeded in reserving for the town the exclusive right of supplying the surrounding country districts with its products, and in finding distant outlets for its trade.'[16]

[16] *Les Villes et les Institutions urbaines au Moyen Age.* Vol. I, p. 481.

Chapter Five
The Monarchy

T HE more one studies medieval society from the writings of the period, the more it appears as a complete organism similar, according to a comparison dear to John of Salisbury, to the human body, with a head, a heart and limbs. The three classes, the clergy, the nobility and the third estate, represented an apportionment of strength and a division of labour, rather than any deep-seated inequalities. That, at least, is how they were understood:

> *Labeur de clerc est de prier*
> *Et justice de chevalier;*
> *Pain leur trouvent les labouriers.*
> *Cil paist, cil prie et cil défend.*
> *Au champ, à la ville, au moustier,*
> *S'entr'aïdent de leur métier*
> *Ces trois par bel ordenement.*[17]

There resulted a composite society, reminiscent, in effect, of the human body with its multitude of interdependent organs, all contributing to the harmonious

[17] From the poem *Miserere* by the Reclus de Molliens.

existence of the individual, from which all benefited alike.

This complexity of the social structure was augmented by the great variety of domains and provinces; each had its own strongly marked characteristics. This diversity is complacently—and maliciously—emphasised by the proverbs of the time:

> *Les meilleurs jongleurs sont en Gascogne*
> *Les plus courtois sont en Provence*
> *Les plus apperts hommes en France*
> *Les meilleurs archers en Anjou*
> *Les plus 'enquérants' en Normandie*
> *Les meilleurs mangeurs de raves sont en Auvergne*
> *Les plus 'rogneux' en Limousin, etc. etc.*

Small local traits which become more obvious in the variations of French customs and usages.

Faced with such a piece of patchwork, the task of the central authority proved particularly difficult. It is evident that there was no room in the Middle Ages for either an authoritarian *régime* or an absolute monarchy. The characteristics of medieval monarchy assume a proportionately greater interest for that reason, each of them offering the solution to a problem concerning the ever-thorny question of relations between the individual and the central authority.

What is chiefly remarkable is the multitude of graded intermediaries between the one and the other. Far from being the only two forces in the field, the State and the individual communicated with each other only through a host of mediators. Man was never an independent individual in the Middle Ages: he must, of necessity, form part of a group: a domain, an association or a 'university' of some sort, which ensured both his protection and his moral well-being. The artisan and the trader were both protected and supervised by the masters of their trade, whom they themselves had elected. The peasant was answerable to a *seigneur*, who was the vassal of another, this latter of still another, and so on, up to the king. Thus, a series of personal contacts acted as buffers between the central authority and the ordinary Frenchman who, on that account, could never be affected by general measures arbitrarily applied; neither had he any dealings with irresponsible and anonymous powers such as, for example, a law, a trust or a party.

The sphere of influence of the central power was, moreover, strictly limited to public affairs. In questions of a family nature, which were very important to medieval society, the State had no right of intervention and it could be said of each dwelling that, like the Englishman's home, it was the castle of those who lived there. Marriages, wills, education and private agreements were all settled by custom, as were business affairs and all conditions of private life in general. Now custom was a collection of observances, of traditions and of rules deriving from the nature of things, not determined by an exterior decision: it offered the guarantee of having grown spontaneously in accordance with the evolution of the people—and of not having been imposed by force; it had also the advantage of being infinitely pliable and capable of adapting itself to every fresh development, and of absorbing every change. The respect in which custom was held explains why, during the whole period of the *Ancien Régime*, the king issued no edicts regarding the rights of the individual. Even in the period following the Middle Ages, legislation was passed by the crown upon only the form of acts of private life, never on these acts themselves; for example, on the registration of testamentary bequests, but never on the testament itself. It was decreed that customs should be recorded in writing, but no sort of intervention in customary law was attempted, and nothing that came within its province was dependent upon the king.

These reservations having been made, how then was the royal authority exercised? The theologian, Henri de Gand, saw in the person of the king the head of a family, the defender of the interests of each and every man. Such certainly appeared to be the role of the medieval monarch. The king, placed at the head of the feudal hierarchy, like the *seigneur* at the head of the domain and the father at the head of the family, was at once an administrator and a judge. The sceptre and the hand of justice symbolised these two attributes.

As an administrator he had, firstly, the opportunity of exercising his power directly over his own domain. He knew, therefore, from experience, the details of the management of a fief, and what he could demand from his vassals, since he had the same rights and duties in this fief as they had. This was on many occasions of great value to the realm as a whole. Vassals were tempted, to a certain extent, to imitate their suzerain and the monarchy sometimes set the barons as excellent example. The reforms which were introduced by the king in his own domain, though he did not pretend to the right of forcing them upon others, often spread throughout the whole country. This was so in the matter of the general emancipation of the serfs on the royal domain at the beginning of the fourteenth century. This state of affairs promoted a beneficent emulation from which the monarchy itself sometimes profited. Thus, many great vassals had the right to mint money, but the king finally induced the whole of France to prefer his own to that of anyone else, by seeing that it was always the soundest, and the most reliable; for one must not exaggerate the legend of the royal counterfeiters, which is true only of Philip the Fair and in times of great public distress during the Hundred Years War.

The king possessed only indirect powers over the domains

of the *seigneurs*. The barons who were directly answerable to him were very few, but all men could appeal to the king through their suzerain, and the orders which he gave were transmitted by a series of intermediaries throughout the realm. He exercised what was in essence a right of supervision: he saw to the regular performance of all that custom enjoined and he maintained law and order. He was thus the natural arbiter of quarrels between the vassals. The reply of Saint Louis to those who, according to the *Dit d'Amiens*, pointed out to him that he would do better to let the great barons fight among themselves and weaken each other, is well known: 'If they saw that I allowed them to fight, they might take counsel among themselves and say "The king, out of his malice, allows us to fight." And if it so happened that from the hatred they would bear me, they rose against me, then might I well be the loser—even giving no thought to the wrath of God which I should incur; for he saith: "Blessed are the peacemakers." '

This power might well have remained purely Platonic, for during the greater part of the Middle Ages the resources at the disposal of the king of France, with his very small domain, were inferior to those of the great vassals. But the prestige conferred upon him by his anointment[18] and the high moral standards of the Capets proved singularly efficacious against the most turbulent *seigneurs*. The example of the king of England, who declared that he could not besiege a place occupied by his suzerain, and who also had recourse to the royal arbitration to settle his own differences with his barons, is sufficient proof of this. The

[18] Anointment on the forehead by the Archbishop of Rheims with oil from the Holy Ampulla, kept in that city, did, in fact, represent in essence the investiture of the royal heir. The first of the Capets, in order to ensure the succession, were careful to have their sons anointed during their own lifetime.

royal authority was founded, until the sixteenth century, on moral, rather than military strength.

It was also on this moral strength that the fame of the kings as justiciaries rested. The *Regrets de la mort de Saint Louis* stress this point:

> *Je dis que Droit est mort, et Loyauté éteinte,*
> *Quand le bon roi est mort, la créature sainte*
> *Qui chacune et chacun faisait droit à sa plainte . . .*
> *A qui se pourront mais les pauvres gens clamer*
> *Quand le bon roi est mort qui les sut tant aimer?*

The '*bon roi*', moreover, often refers to the subject in his *Enseignements* to his son: 'Be constant and uncompromising in the upholding of right and justice among thy subjects, and look neither to left nor to right, but go ever straight before thee; sustain the poor man in his dispute until truth shall be established.' Joinville relates on many occasions how Saint Louis puts his principles into practice. The royal justice pervaded the realm to its outermost confines: '. . . and in the valley of the Rhône we came upon a castle known as *Roche de Glin*, which the king had had razed to the ground because Roger, the lord of the castle, had been accused of robbing pilgrims and merchants.' The well-known picture of the oak at Vincennes beneath which he dispensed justice, has become justly famous. Penalties inflicted on culprits might amount to the con-fiscation of their property; that is a notion which is rather difficult to grasp in our own times when the money with which a man buys an estate gives him full rights over it for as long as he continues to have money to pay his taxes and his private debts. This was also the case in Ancient Rome. In the Middle Ages, however, the domain was inalienable and a *seigneur* could keep possession of it during his life-time even if he were up to his eyes in debts; but, on the other hand, it might at any time be confiscated if he proved

F

unworthy of his charge or broke his oath. Thus, all power implied a certain responsibility. The king himself was not exempt from this rule. Henri de Gand, defining his powers, recognised the right of his subjects to depose him if he gave them an order which went against their consciences; the Pope could release the people from their oath of allegiance and did not fail to exercise this right whenever a king was guilty of an unjust act, even in his private life. This was the case when the unfortunate Queen Ingeburge, abandoned by Philippe-Auguste, appealed to Rome from the prison of Etampes. The fundamental principle was, according to St Thomas Aquinas, that: 'The people are not made for the prince, but the prince for the people.'

Men had at this time a very high conception of the duties of a sovereign. Eustache Deschamps, the poet and mirror of his age, recites them thus:

> *Premier il doit Dieu et l'Eglise aimer;*
> *Humble coeur ait, pitié, compassion;*
> *Le bien commun doit sur tous préférer,*
> *Son peuple avoir en grand dilection,*
>   *Etre sage et diligent,*
> *Vérité ait, tel doit être régent,*
> *Lent de punir, aux bons non faire ennui*
> *Et aux mauvais rendre droit jugement*
> *Si qu'on voie toute bonté en lui . . .*

★

The personalities of the Capets were singularly well suited to the medieval conception of royalty; in placing them on the throne their contemporaries made a most fortunate choice, so well did they meet the requirements of their people, given the mentality of the period and the needs of the country. They were, first and foremost, realists. They were very devoted to their domain and never lost sight of their own interests. One might even reproach them with a certain narrowness of vision. When one passes from the last of the Carolingians to Hugues le Grand or Hugues Capet, the difference is striking: the descendants of Charlemagne, even the most decadent, preserved an 'imperial' outlook; they looked to Rome and to Aix-la-Chapelle; they thought as Europeans. The Capets, on the other hand, gave little thought to what happened beyond the boundaries of their own territory; they distrusted the Empire as a dangerous and idle dream; they saw France, rather than Europe. They continued to refuse the imperial crown despite repeated hints from the Papacy, and they frowned severely on their younger brothers—Charles d'Anjou, for example—who went to seek their fortunes abroad.

Their ambitions were limited but practical. Finding themselves at the head of a small domain, but fortified by the prestige of the royal anointment, they sought, with imperturbable tenacity, to strengthen their domain, while at the same time consolidating their moral ascendancy. Even the Crusades were of only secondary interest to them. The first of these, which shook the whole of Europe, did not move the King of France. Philippe-Auguste embarked upon it without conviction—remembering, doubtless, that the Orient had brought no luck to his father, Louis VII, who had both ruined his conjugal happiness there and jeopardised the status of his kingdom; he seized the first opportunity to return home, being of the opinion that his presence was more necessary in Artois or Vermandois than on the shores of Palestine. It needed a Saint Louis to espouse the cause of the Crusades with fervour, but he did so because for him the religious objective was all-important, to the exclusion, in fact, of all worldly ambitions. The imperial dream and the Italian venture were temptations which the Capets did not even pause to consider. Were their descendants well-advised to break with this policy of

sound common sense? The misfortunes of Charles VIII, of
Louis XII and of Francis I, demonstrate clearly enough how
much wisdom was reflected in the moderation of the
Capets.

On the other hand, they strove with amazing consistency
to strengthen their domain. One generation after another
enlarged their precious territory, acquiring here another
comté, there a castle, fighting fiercely for a fortress, staking
their claim to an inheritance, sword in hand if need be.
Intelligent tacticians that they were, they knew the value
of a road or a bridgehead. Louis VI's fame depended on his
having kept control of the road between Paris and Orleans;
he knew that for him the towers of Montlhéry were more
important than a foreign crown. Concerning questions
arising within the boundaries of their realm, the Capets
intervened whenever they could, never missing the
opportunity of reminding a vassal of their presence and
power if he had become too sure of his own strength.
Whether it was to recall a *seigneur* to his senses or to bring
mercenaries such as the Berry *cottereaux* to heel, they were
always on the spot. They knew that justice was the best
policy, and were ready to sacrifice their immediate
interests, if need be to a higher good. One recalls
the amazement aroused among both contemporaries
and later historians by Louis IX, who gave back Agen,
Saintonge and a part of Limousin to the King of England,
after having conquered them from him. This was, however,
as Auguste Longnon has described it, an act of high diplo-
macy, and one which the king himself has explained: 'I
am certain that the predecessors of the King of England lost
their right to that territory, and the land I give him I give not
because I have any obligation towards him or his heirs,
but to foster love between my children and his, who are
cousins; and it seems to me that that which I give him I

put to good use, if he now does me homage, since he was not previously my man.' The result was indeed that he won the fidelity of his most formidable vassal—and ensured peace between France and England for more than fifty years.

Together with this methodical spirit, the good-nature and pleasing friendliness of the kings of France must also be mentioned. It has been observed that no one could have been less autocratic than a medieval monarch.[19] In the *Chroniques* and in narrative accounts, there were constant references to assemblies, deliberations and councils of war. The king did nothing without asking the opinion of his *entourage*. And this *entourage* did not consist, as later at Versailles, of submissive courtiers; there were soldiers, vassals as powerful as the king himself and often wealthier, and monks, scholars and jurists; the king asked for their advice, discussed matters with them, and attached great importance to this personal contact: 'Be sure that thou hast in thy company,' one reads in the *Enseignements de Saint Louis*, 'good, wise and trusty men, who are not covetous—either clergy or laymen—and speak with them often. And if any man shall seem to counsel what is contrary to thy interests, do not think this until thou art sure of the truth, for in this way thy counsellors will judge matters more fearlessly, either for or against thee, but in accordance with truth.' He

[19] The following very pertinent quotation is from A. Hadengue's work: *Bouvines, Victoire Créatrice*: 'Councils of war! They were very common occurrences at medieval military headquarters. The same expressions are penned repeatedly by chroniclers: "First he took counsel"—"then the king took counsel"—"then he took counsel". In the thirteenth century a military leader did not give orders or make decisions like an omnipotent general. His authority rested on collaboration, trust and friendship. If he was at a loss what to do, he would sit down at the foot of a tree, call his great barons to him, lay the facts before them and hear their opinions. His personal judgment did not always carry the day. "Each man gave his opinion," as Philippe Mouskès writes, (p. 188-189).'

himself practised what he preached: there is an account in Joinville (which merits reading in its entirety) of the touching council of war held by the king in the Holy Land when the bad beginning made to his crusade had raised doubts about the whole question and caused the majority of the barons to wish to return to France. The way in which Louis IX tells Joinville that he is grateful to him for having dared to express his opinion is full of that very pleasing friendliness shown by the kings to their *entourage*.

'While the king heard petitions, I went to an iron-barred window and leaned my arms on the bars, and thought that if the king returned to France I would go and join the Prince of Antioch. While I was there the king came and leaned on my shoulder, placing both his hands on my head. And I thought it was Messire Philippe de Nemours, who had annoyed me overmuch that day on account of the advice I had given him. And I spoke thus: "Leave me in peace, Messire Philippe." By accident, as I turned my head, the king's hand fell across my face, and I knew that it was the king by an emerald which he wore on his finger. "Peace," he said to me, "for I would ask how it came about that you, a young man, were so bold as to advocate my remaining here, in opposition to all the great and wise men of France who desired my departure." "Sire," I said, "I should be a dishonest man, were I to counsel you at any price to adopt that latter course." "Do you think," he asked, "that I should be acting wrongly, if I were to leave?" "By my faith, Sire," I replied, "I do." And he said to me: "If I stay, will you stay also?" And I said that I would. "Be of good heart," he said, "for I am very grateful for your counsel." '

This good nature and simplicity were very characteristic of the period. While the Emperor and the majority of the great vassals took pleasure in displaying their ostentatious luxury, the Capets were conspicuous for their frugal way of life. The kings moved freely among the people. Louis VII fell asleep one day alone on the edge of a forest and when his servants woke him he pointed out to them that he could sleep thus alone and unarmed because no one bore him any ill-will. Philippe-Auguste, a few hours before the Battle of Bouvines, sat down at the foot of a tree and ate a little bread dipped in wine. Saint Louis allowed himself to be insulted in the road by an old woman, and forbade his companions to reprimand her. Velvet doublets and ermine coats were kept for festivals and ceremonial processions and a hair shirt was often worn beneath the ermine. The simplicity of the royal suite was a stock joke among German students accustomed to the magnificence of the Emperor's court. This simplicity was emulated very little by the Valois and still less by their successors of the Renaissance period, but, if they gained a brilliant court, they lost that intimate contact with the people which makes a valuable contribution to a king's prestige.

Chapter Six
International Relations

IT looked at first as if the Middle Ages were in danger
of witnessing only chaos and disintegration. The period
should have presented—and at the beginning did, in
fact, present—the most unbelievable lack of cohesion, for
it had been born of a fallen Empire and of successive waves
of invasions, and was composed of ill-assorted peoples each
with their own customs, *milieux* and social orders, all
different from, if not actively hostile to, each other, and
nearly all with a very lively class-consciousness and an
awareness of their superiority as conquerors.

However, in the twelfth and thirteenth centuries Europe,
at first divided and in a state of upheaval, came to know an
era of concord and unity such as she had never previously
experienced and the like of which she may never know again
in the course of centuries to come. At the time of the
first Crusade, princes sacrificed their property and their
interests and forgot their quarrels in order to take the cross
together, and many very diverse peoples banded themselves
into one single army. The whole of Europe trembled at
the words of Urban II or of Peter the Hermit, or, later, at

those of Saint Bernard or of Foulques of Neuilly. Monarchs, preferring arbitration to war, deferred to the judgment of the Pope and that of a foreign king in order to settle their disagreements. It is even more remarkable to find that this Europe of the Middle Ages was organised—not as an Empire, nor as a federation, but as Christendom.

One must recognise here the role played by the Church and the Papacy in the European order, of which they were in fact essential unifying factors. The diocese and the parish, often merging with the domain, were, during the period of disintegration of the Early Middle Ages, the living units from which the nation was reconstituted. The great dates which were to leave their mark on Europe for all time were those of the conversion of Clovis which ensured the triumph of the Catholic hierarchy and doctrine over the Arian heresy in the west—and the crowning of Charlemagne by the Pope, who consecrated the double sword—spiritual and temporal—in which union medieval Christianity was to have its foundations.

From a more general point of view, one must not lose sight of the influence of Catholic dogma, which teaches that all the sons of the Church are members of one body—as the following lines by Rutebeuf remind us:

> *Tous sont un corps en Jésus-Christ*
> *Dont je vous montre par l'écrit*
> *Que li uns est membre de l'autre.*

Uniformity of doctrine, of which men were deeply conscious at that time, favoured the unity of peoples. Charlemagne had understood this so well that, in order to conquer Saxony, he sent missionaries rather than armies—acting, moreover, out of religious conviction and not from mere ambition. History repeated itself in the German Empire with the Otho dynasty.

In point of fact, Christendom can be defined as the

'university' of Christian princes and peoples, who abided by the same doctrine and were animated by one single faith, recognising from that time forward the same spiritual authority.

This common faith expressed itself in a European order which is very baffling to modern minds, very complex in its ramifications, but very imposing when one considers it as a whole. Peace in the Middle Ages consisted precisely in what Saint Augustine has admirably defined as the 'tranquillity' of this order.

One central point remained stable, the Papacy, the pivot of spiritual life. But its relations with the different states varied considerably: some owed special allegiance to the Holy See, as, for example, the Holy Roman Empire, whose head, without coming under the suzerainty of the Pope, as has often been believed, had, nevertheless, to be chosen by him or at least to have his support. This is easily explained if one goes back to the circumstances of the Empire's founding and to the essential part played in this by the Papacy. The Papacy, however, did no more than confer the title and pass judgment on cases of deposition.

Other kingdoms were feudatory to the Holy See, having at one time in the course of their history asked the Pope for protection: they had either presented him formally with their crown, like the kings of Hungary, or else, like the kings of England, Poland and Aragon, had asked him to ratify their laws so that thereafter the seal of Saint Peter upheld and preserved their liberties.

Yet others, France among them, were not dependent in any secular way upon the Holy See, but accepted without question its jurisdiction on matters of conscience and submitted as willingly to its arbitraments.

Such were the broad outlines of the structure of Christendom, as defined by Innocent III at a time when it had existed in practice for many centuries. Essentially it was based on a mystical harmony between peoples. When one examines the basic principles of the balance of European power, as were conceived at the time of the Treaty of Westphalia, one cannot but realise the poverty of that control of nations, that see-saw which took the place of the solid foundations upon which medieval peace had rested.

These relations between Church and State have often been wrongly understood: we are accustomed to see in spiritual and temporal authority two quite distinct powers and sometimes the intrusion of the Papacy into the affairs of princes has been considered intolerable. But everything becomes clear if one recalls the mental attitude of the time: it was not the Holy See which forced its authority on kings and peoples, but these kings and peoples who, as believers, had recourse quite naturally to the spiritual power, whether they wanted their own authority upheld or respect for their rights inculcated, or whether they desired the settlement of their disputes by an impartial arbiter. In the words of Gregory X: 'If it is the duty of those who direct the States to safeguard the rights and independence of the Church, so is it also the duty of those who exercise ecclesiastical authority to do everything possible to ensure that the kings and princes are able to exercise their powers undisturbed.' The two forces, instead of ignoring or fighting one another, offered mutual support.

What may have led to confusion is that it was usual in the Middle Ages to profess a greater respect for ecclesiastical than for secular authority, and to consider the one as superior to the other, in accordance with the celebrated saying of Innocent III, 'as the soul is to the body', or 'as the sun is to the moon'; but this was a hierarchy of values which did not necessarily involve subordination in actual fact.

Further, it must not be forgotten that the Church, the defender of the faith, was also the judge of men's consciences and entrusted with their vows. No one in the Middle Ages would have dreamt of disputing this. When a public wrong had been done, the Church had both the right and the duty of pronouncing sentence, of discharging the accused or of absolving the penitent. The Church was thus only exercising an authority which was universally recognised when she excommunicated Robert le Pieux or Raymond de Toulouse. In the same way, when, as a consequence of reprehensible conduct and unjust acts on the part of Philippe-Auguste and the Emperor Henry IV, she released their subjects from their oath of allegiance, she was performing one of her sovereign duties, for in the Middle Ages every oath took God to witness and, therefore, the Church also, so that she had the power both of binding men on oath and of releasing them afterwards from that oath.

It is undeniable that there were abuses on the side of the Holy See, as on the side of the temporal authority; the history of clashes between the Papacy and the Empire is proof of this. But on the whole it can be said that this bold attempt to unite for the common good the temporal sword with the sword of the spirit showed some success. The moral power to whose decrees a prince could not run counter without incurring certain clearly defined risks —among others that of seeing himself divested of his own authority and of losing the esteem of his subjects—was a guarantee of peace and of justice. As long as Henry II was contending with Thomas à Beckett, no man knew which of the two would prevail; but from the day when the king decided to rid himself of the prelate by murder it was he who was vanquished. The moral stigma and the penalties which accompanied it were more effective then than physical force. Life was no longer bearable for a monarch who had been laid under an interdict: bells remained silent when he passed and his subjects fled at his approach, and that created an atmosphere against which the most hardened character could not hold out. Even Philippe-Auguste yielded finally, although no external compulsion could have prevented him from leaving the unfortunate Queen Ingeburge to languish in her prison.

During the greater part of the Middle Ages the right of waging private war continued to be regarded by both the civil authority and public opinion generally as inviolable: the maintenance of peace both between barons and States therefore presented enormous difficulties and, had it not been for this conception of Christianity, Europe might well have remained merely a vast battlefield. But the system in force permitted a whole series of obstacles to be placed in the way of the wreaking of private vengeance. Firstly, feudal law required that a vassal who swore allegiance to his lord should not bear arms against him; there were lapses, of course, but the oath of allegiance was far from being a mere form or a mockery: when the King of France, Louis VII, came to the help of Count Raymond V, who was threatened in Toulouse by Henry II of England, the latter, although he had vastly superior forces at his disposal and his victory was assured, withdrew, declaring that he could not lay siege to a town occupied by his suzerain; in the circumstances, the feudal bond had rescued the French king from a particularly dangerous situation.

Then again, the feudal system provided a whole series of natural arbiters: the vassal could always appeal for arbitration in a dispute with his *seigneur* to the latter's suzerain. The king played the role of mediator more and more frequently as his authority was extended; and, ultimately, the Pope remained the supreme arbiter. Often

a reputation for justness or saintliness was sufficient in a
person of high standing to cause men to appeal to him thus;
the history of France offers more than one example—for
instance, Louis VII was the protector of Thomas à Beckett
and his mediator during his disagreements with Henry II,
and Saint Louis inspired respect throughout Christendom
when he published the famous *Dit d'Amiens* which settled
the differences of Henry III of England and his barons.

The fact remains, however, that at that time any noble
could, if prompted by either ambition or a thirst for
vengeance, invade the lands of his neighbours, and also
that the central power was not sufficiently strong to replace
private law by its own justice. This is taking no account
of the wars which were always possible between States.
The Middle Ages did not attack the problem of war in
general, but by a series of practical solutions and measures
applied throughout the whole of Christendom the theatre
of war, its cruelties and its duration, were gradually
restricted. Thus it was that, in obedience to well-defined
laws, the peace of Christendom was built up.

The first of these measures was the 'Peace of God',
established at the end of the tenth century:[20] it made the
first distinction in the history of the world between the
weak and the strong, between warriors and civil populations.
In 1023, the Archbishop of Beauvais made the king, Robert
le Pieux, swear the Oath of Peace. It was forbidden to
ill-treat women, children, peasants and clerics; the houses
of agricultural workers were declared inviolable, in the
same way as churches. War was restricted to those who
were equipped to fight. Such was the origin of the modern
distinction between military and non-military objectives—

[20] The Council of Charroux, in 989, anathematised any person who
entered by force into a church and removed any object from it, or
who stole the property of peasants or poor people, either their lambs,
their oxen or their donkeys.

a notion which was totally unknown in the pagan world. The prohibition was not always respected, but whoever contravened this law knew that he was exposing himself to formidable penalties, both secular and spiritual.

Subsequently, the 'Truce of God' was also inaugurated at the beginning of the eleventh century by the Emperor Henry II, the King of France, Robert le Pieux, and the Pope, Benedict VIII. It had already been renewed at the Councils of Perpignan and Elne, in 1041 and 1059, when, during his visit to Clermont in 1095, Urban II defined and formally proclaimed it during the same Council which saw the inception of the Crusades. It restricted the duration of war, as the 'Peace of God' had restricted its objectives: by order of the Church, every act of war was forbidden from the first Sunday in Advent to the octave of Epiphany, from the first day of Lent to the octave of Advent, and, during the remainder of the time, from Wednesday evening to Monday morning. It is hard to imagine these spasmodic, piecemeal wars which were not permitted to continue for more than three days in succession. Here again, there were infractions, but at the delinquent's risk and also to his shame. When Otho of Brunswick was put to flight at Bouvines, contrary to all expectations, by the army of Philippe-Auguste which was vastly inferior in numbers, people did not hesitate to see in this the punishment of a man who had dared to break the truce and engage in combat on a Sunday. The Christian princes sometimes embarked upon enterprises which completed and supported those of the Church. Philippe-Auguste, for example, instituted the '*quarantaine-le-roi*'; an interval of forty days had to elapse between the *casus belli* and the protest duly made by the injured party—and the opening of hostilities. This was a wise measure which allowed time for reflection and amicable settlement. One meets this same interval of forty days in the time granted to the citizens of an enemy city when war broke out to enable them to return to their own country and put their possessions in a safe place. Thus, in the Middle Ages there could have been no question of sequestration or of concentration camps.

But the great glory of the Middle Ages lay in the education of the soldier and the transformation of the trooper into a knight. The man who fought because he had a taste for brute force, for violence and for pillage, became the defender of the weak; he turned his brutality into a useful force, his love of danger into considered courage and his turbulence into fruitful activity; his ardour was both fanned and disciplined. Henceforward, the soldier had a role to play and the enemies whom he was called to fight were precisely those in whom a pagan love of massacre, pillage and debauch still subsisted. Chivalry is the medieval institution which it is most pleasant to remember, and justly so, for it is undoubtedly true that mankind has never had a more noble conception of the warrior. As it existed at the beginning of the twelfth century, it was, in fact, an order, almost a sacrament. Contrary to the opinion generally accepted, it was not identified with the nobility. 'No man is born a knight', runs a proverb. Commoners and even serfs had the distinction conferred upon them, and all nobles did not receive it; but to be armed as a knight was to become a noble; one of the maxims of the time indicates that 'the way to be ennobled without learning is to be knighted.'

Certain specific qualities were required of the future knight, and these were expressed by the symbolism of the ceremony during which his title was conferred upon him. He had to be god-fearing, devoted to the Church and respectful of its commandments. His initiation began with a whole night passed in prayer before the altar, on which was placed the sword he was to carry. That was the eve of battle, after which, as a sign of purity, he took a bath and then heard Mass and received Holy Communion. Then the sword and spurs were formally presented to him, with a reminder of his duties: to help the poor and the weak, to respect women and to show himself valiant and generous; his motto was to be 'Valour and generosity.' Next he was equipped and received the accolade (a stroke on the shoulder with the flat of the sword) and, in the name of Saint Michael and Saint George, he was created a knight.

In order to do his duty he needed to be as skilful as he was brave, so the ceremony continued with a series of trials of physical strength which were tests designed to prove his valour. He entered the lists to 'tilt at the quintain' (that is, to charge on horseback at a dummy), and to unhorse the adversaries who came to challenge him in the tournaments. Days on which new knights were created were holidays, when all men vied with each other in feats of valour, watched by the lords, the seigniorial household, and the working classes massed at the approaches of the tournament field. Skilful and strong, kind and generous, the knight represented the type of complete man, whose physical beauty was combined with the most pleasing qualities:

> *Tant est prud'homme si comme semble*
> *Qui a ces deux choses ensemble:*
> *Valeur du corps et bonté d'âme.*

He was not expected, like the ideal man of ancient times, merely to maintain a golden mean, a sound balance, *mens sana in corpore sano*, but was required to attain a maximum: he was urged to surpass himself, to represent both the best and the most beautiful, while placing his person at the service of others. The tales in which the heroes of the

G

Round Table set out constantly in quest of the most fabulous adventure, are only expressing the stirring ideal presented to the man who had a warrior's vocation. Nothing was more 'dynamic' (to use a modern expression) than the typical good knight.

Knighthood could be lost as well as won: a knight who failed in his duties was publicly degraded and the golden spurs at his heels were cut off as a sign of disgrace:

Honni soit hardement où il n'a gentillesse

it was said—which amounted to asserting that mere warlike valour was nothing without nobility of soul.

Chivalry was, moreover, the great passion of the Middle Ages; the meaning of the word 'chivalrous' which has been handed down to us expresses very exactly the combination of qualities which aroused men's admiration at that time. It is enough to glance through the literature of the period, or to contemplate the works of art which have been preserved for us, to see everywhere, in stories, poems, pictures, sculpture and illuminated manuscripts, the knight of whom the fine statue in the Cathedral of Bamberg represents a perfect example. One has, moreover, only to read the chroniclers of the period to know that this type of man did not exist merely in stories, and that the perfect knight, incarnate on the throne of France in the person of Saint Louis, had at that time a host of emulators.

One can imagine what a medieval war must have been like under these conditions. Strictly localised, it was often confined to a single route march or to the capture of a town or castle. Means of defence were vastly superior then to means of attack: the walls and moat of a fortress guaranteed the safety of the besieged, and a chain slung across the entrance to the port constituted at least a temporary safeguard. In an attack, swords and lances were used almost exclusively. A gallant hand-to-hand fight would draw cries of admiration from the chroniclers, but they had, on the other hand, nothing but contempt for the bow and cross-bow, cowards' weapons, which, while reducing risks, also lessened the number of opportunities for great deeds. In order to lay siege to a place, engines of war were utilised: mangonels as well as siege-trenches and mines. But it was chiefly hunger and the long duration of operations which were relied upon to reduce the besieged. Castle keeps were therefore always well stocked: enormous supplies of cereals were piled up in the great vaults, which romantic legend has made into '*oubliettes*'; [21] and it was always contrived that there should be a well or a cistern inside the fortress. When an engine of war was too deadly, the Papacy forbade its use: gunpowder, whose effects and composition were known in the thirteenth century, did not come into general use until the Papal authority was no longer sufficiently strong and Christian principles were already beginning to crumble. Lastly, as Orderic Vital writes: 'because they feared God, and out of chivalry, men sought to take prisoners rather than to kill. Christian warriors had no desire to shed blood.' It was a common thing to see the victor who had unhorsed his opponent on the battlefield, spare him when he cried quarter. The Battle of Les Andelys has been cited as an example: it was fought by Louis VI in 1119, and afterwards a total of three dead were picked up out of a force of nine hundred.

Did Christian principles stand in the way of patriotism? It has long been believed that the idea of patriotism in France originated with Joan of Arc, but all the facts confute this assertion. The expression '*France la douce*' is found in the *Chanson de Roland*, and no more pleasing description

[21] The mistake is all the more astonishing because these vast vaults serving as store-rooms—with just a circular hole in the middle of the dome through which baskets were passed in order to draw up grain—still exist in certain countries, Algeria, for example.

has ever been conceived. Since then, poets have never
ceased to refer to her thus:

Des pays est douce France la fleur

one reads in *Andrieu contredit*, and, in the *Roman de Fauvel:*

> *Le beau jardin de grâces plein*
> *Où Dieu, par espéciauté,*
> *Planta les lys de royauté . . .*
> *Et d'autres fleurs à grand plenté:*
> *Fleur de paix et fleur de justice,*
> *Fleur de foi et fleur de franchise,*
> *Fleur d'amour et fleur épanie*
> *De sens et de chevalerie . . .*
> *C'est le jardin de douce France . . .*

It would be impossible to write of one's country with more
affection. And if one goes on to examine the facts one finds,
at the early date of 1124, the most convincing proof of the
existence of patriotic feeling: at the time of the attempted
invasion by the armies of the Emperor, Henry V, which were
bearing down on France along the traditional invasion
routes in the North-East of the country in the direction of
Rheims, there was a levy in mass throughout the kingdom.
The most turbulent barons, among them Thibaut de
Chartres, then in open rebellion, forgot their quarrels in
order to take their places beneath the royal standard—the
famous red oriflamme, fringed with green, which had been
taken by Louis VI from the Church of Saint Denis. The
result was that, faced with this mass of warriors who had
arisen spontaneously from all over the country, the Emperor
did not dare to persist and turned back. The idea of patriotism, then, was sufficiently deep-rooted at the time to bring
about a general coalition, and men had, through all the
diversity and lack of cohesion among the fiefs, a feeling of
forming part of a whole. This notion was to be unmistakably

re-affirmed a century later at Bouvines, and the burst of joy which, in Paris and throughout the kingdom, greeted the announcement of the royal victory, is sufficient evidence. Patriotism during this period was rooted in its most solid foundations—love of the land and attachment to the soil— but it could also embrace, if the need arose, France as a whole, the *'jardin de douce France.'*

Chapter Seven
The Church

THE history of the Church is so closely linked with that of the Middle Ages in general that it is difficult to make it the subject of a separate chapter. It would no doubt be better to study the influence she exerted on, or the part she played in, each characteristic of medieval society and each stage of its evolution. [22] It is, moreover, impossible to form an accurate idea of the period without some knowledge of the Church, not only in its broad outlines but even in details such as its liturgy and hagiography; and the first advice given to novice medievalists—for instance, students of the School of Paleography and Librarianship in Paris—is to make themselves familiar with these.

The importance of the role played by the Church will be seen immediately if one goes back to the state of society during the centuries commonly referred to as the Early

[22] To take an example, recent researches have demonstrated the not merely religious, but, properly speaking, eucharistic origins of the medieval associations: the procession of the Blessed Sacrament was the immediate cause of the founding of the trade fraternities. See, in this connection, the fine work of G. Espinas, *Les Origines du droit d'association* (Lille, 1943) in particular, Vol. I, 1034.

Middle Ages, a period of crumbling forces and one during which the Church represented the only organised hierarchy.

In the face of the dislocation of all civil power, the Papacy alone remained stable, radiating in the Western World through the agency of its prelates, and even during the periods of eclipse traversed by the Holy See its organisation as a whole remained unshaken. In France the roles played by prelates, and monasteries were of cardinal importance in the formation of the feudal hierarchy. The impulse which moved the humble people to seek the protection of the great landowners and to commend themselves to their care by those acts of *commendatio* which multiplied after the fall of the Byzantine Empire, could not but favour the growth of ecclesiastical property; men were more willing to gather around the monasteries than around secular domains: 'It is good to dwell beneath the cross' was a popular saying which corresponded to the Latin proverb '*Jugum ecclesie, jugum dilecte*'. Thus, abbeys such as Saint-Germain-des-Prés, Lérins, Marmoutiers and Saint-Victor of Marseilles saw a great increase in their possessions. Bishops often became lay seigneurs of the whole or part of a city which they had made their See and in whose defence against invasions they contributed actively. The attitude of Bishop Gozlin at the time of the attack on Paris by the Normans was far from being an isolated case, and often even the architecture of the churches bore the mark of the military function which was at this time both a duty and a necessity for all who wielded any power. The Saintes-Maries-de-la-Mer and the fortified churches of the Thiérache region are examples of this.

Charlemagne's great wisdom lay in his seeing the advantages of this well-organised hierarchy and in understanding how important a factor the Church could be in the unification of the Empire. In fact, Catholic doctrine

alone could crystallise the possibilities of unity which were
taking shape thanks to the accession of the Carolingian
dynasty. Catholicism alone could unite the scattered groups
of men entrenched on their domains. Charlemagne prepared the way for the coming of Christianity by supporting
the Church, as he had accepted the feudal system, finding it
more to his advantage to make use of the power of the
barons than to struggle against it. His coronation in Rome
by Pope Stephen II remains one of the great dates of the
Middle Ages, linking for centuries the temporal sword with
the sword of the spirit. Pepin's gift had furnished the
Vatican with territorial domains which were to constitute
the basis of its doctrinal empire; and by receiving his crown
from the hands of the Pope, Charlemagne asserted his own
power and the nature of that power, which established the
European order on spiritual foundations. The Papacy had
gained a body, the Empire acquired a soul.

This accounted for the complexity of medieval society,
both secular and ecclesiastical. The spiritual and temporal
domains which, from the time of the Renaissance have been
regarded more and more as distinct and separate, whose
respective limits men have striven to define, and which have
tended increasingly to ignore one another's existence, were
continually overlapping during the Middle Ages. If one
makes a distinction between that which is God's and that
which is Caesar's, the same personages could have represented each in turn, the two powers were complementary.
Bishops and abbots were also administrators of domains
and it was not unusual to see secular and ecclesiastical
authorities dividing the same castellany between them.
Marseilles offers a typical example: the episcopal town
co-existed with the viscountcy, with even an enclave
reserved for the chapter and called the *Ville de Tours*. This
landed power among the clergy was produced by both

economic and social factors and from the general attitude of the period, in which the need felt for moral unity compensated for the lack of centralisation.

Such a system was not without its dangers. The struggles between the priesthood and the Empire prove that the very delicate discrimination needed between the kingdom of God and that of Caesar was not always made to perfection. There were encroachments on either side: the dispute over investitures, in particular, revealed the ambitions of the Emperors to meddle in questions within the jurisdiction of the ecclesiastical hierarchy. France was undoubtedly one of the countries where this synthesis of spiritual and temporal powers was most successfully accomplished, and the Capets down to Philip the Fair managed, on the whole, to reconcile the protection of their own interests with respect for ecclesiastical authority—not by a precarious balance of power, but by that nice sense of proportion and love of justice which, in the twelfth century resulted in the choice of Louis VII as arbiter in the conflicts between the two great opposing forces of Christendom: the Emperor Frederick Barbarossa and the Pope Alexander III.

On her side, the Church was not always able to resist her greatest temptation—cupidity. The medieval priesthood can be seriously reproached with not having set any limit on its wealth. This shortcoming was very much resented at that time. Proverbs abound which demonstrate that the people preferred clerics who practised the Christian virtue of poverty: 'Rich monk merits no praise', 'Crosier of wood, bishop of gold, bishop of wood, crosier of gold.' Tithes paid to the clergy were countenanced: 'Who serves the church, should live by the Church'—but the abuses from which the Church was too often unable to refrain—cupidity in particular—were justly attacked:

Et si ils vont la messe ouïr
Ce n'est pas pour Dieu conjouir
Ains est pour les deniers avoir

So Rutebeuf expresses his feelings and he reiterates his censures on more than one occasion:

Toujours veulent, sans donner, prendre
Toujours achètent sans rien vendre;
Ils tollent (take), *l'on ne leur tolt rien.*

This avarice, according to him, had corrupted even the Vatican:

Qui argent porte à Rome assez tôt provende a:
On ne les donne mie si com Dieu commanda;
On sait bien dire à Rome: si voil impetrar, da,
Et si non voilles dar, anda la voie, anda!

If the attacks stopped short of the Pope's person, the cardinals, on the other hand were often accused of that love of money which resulted in the distribution of prebends and livings to the richest and not to those most worthy of them. And it is well known what vigorous protestations were aroused by the nepotism of both cardinals and bishops:

A leurs neveux, qui rien ne valent
Qui en leurs lits encore étalent
Donnent provendes, et trigalent (amuse themselves)
Pour les deniers que ils emmallent (receive).

Etienne Fougères, the author of these lines gives salutary advice on the subject of those charged with the appointing of pastors for the faithful:

Ordonner doit bon clerc et sage
De bonne moeurs, de bon aage,
Et né de loyal mariage;
Peu ne me chaut de quel parage (origin)
Ne doit nul prouvère ordonner,

Se il moustier lui veut donner,
Que il ne sache sermonner,
Et la gent bien arraisonner.

This wealth was inevitably to bring in its wake both decadence and a slackening in morals, which the Church sought to ward off by a series of reforms. Rutebeuf, for one, protested against the apathy of some clerics who were principally preoccupied with enjoying their material possessions:

Ah! prélats de Sainte Eglise
Qui, pour garder les corps de bise
Ne voulez aller aux matines,
Messire Geoffroy de Sargines
Vous demande delà la mer.
Mais je dis cil fait à blâmer
Qui rien nulle plus vous demande
Fors bons vins et bonnes viandes
Et que le poivre soit bien fort . . .

These weaknesses were at the root of the crises experienced by the Church on several occasions during the Middle Ages and also of the great movements which stirred her. The evolution of the regular clergy reflects very exactly the general evolution of the Church. In the first centuries the Benedictine monks accomplished a practical work: they were the pioneers who prepared the way for the Gospel with their ploughshares; they cut down forests, reclaimed marshlands, acclimatised the vine and sowed corn; their role was largely social and civilising. It was they, moreover, who kept the manuscripts of Antiquity for Europe and founded the first seats of learning. So that they might supply the needs of the society they were evangelising they became both pioneers and teachers, making a powerful contribution to the material and moral progress of this society. The orders which were founded subsequently were quite different in character: the Franciscans and Dominicans had a primarily doctrinal objective: they represented, in fact, a reaction against this abuse of wealth with which the Church was reproached at that time and emphasised the trend of reform which had already been outlined twice by the black friars of Cluny and the white friars of Clairvaux and of the Cistercian order. Thus the Church herself had realised the dangers to which her position in the medieval world exposed her, and she strove to remedy this evil, while at the same time continuing to cope with fresh obligations as they presented themselves. She set the military aid of the Knights Templars and the charitable assistance of the Knights Hospitallers against the perils with which the Holy Land was beset and the difficulties experienced by pilgrims. Each new phase of development roused fresh endeavours through which one can trace the progress of the whole era.

It is more difficult to discern the moral influence exercised by the Church in the institutions of private life, because the majority of the ideas for which she was responsible have been absorbed so completely into current customs that it is difficult to realise the novelty they presented at that time. The moral equality of men and women, for example, represented a conception which was entirely foreign to Antiquity, when the question had not even arisen. Further, in family legislation it was profoundly original to substitute for the conception that might is right, the notion of protection being due to the weak. The role of the father and landowner was altered fundamentally: over against his power the dignity of the woman and the child were proclaimed and the ownership of property was turned into a social responsibility. The way in which marriage was envisaged according to Christian principles was also radically different: until then, only its social utility had been seen and anything had been permitted so long as it did not entail disorders in this sphere; the Church, for the first time in the history of the world, saw marriage in relation to the individual and considered it not as a social institution, but as the union of two beings for the fulfilment of their personal destinies and for the achievement of their purposes in both this world and the next. That involved, among other consequences, the necessity for voluntary consent on the part of both husband and wife, who were made to partake of a sacrament, with the priest as witness—and it also required equality of responsibility for both. Until the Council of Trent, Church formalities were very restricted and an exchange of vows before a priest—'I take thee to husband', 'I take thee to wife'—sufficed for the marriage to be valid. It was in the home that symbolic ceremonies took place: for example, drinking out of the same goblet and eating from the same loaf:

> *Boire, manger, coucher ensemble*
> *Font mariage, ce me semble*

such is the adage of customary law, to which was added in the sixteenth century: 'But the Church must give her blessing.'

The influence exercised by ecclesiastical doctrine on the organisation of labour should be pointed out once again: Roman law recognised only the law of supply and demand in contracts of sale or hire, but canon law, and subsequently customary law, subordinated the will of the contracting parties to moral requirements and consideration for human dignity. This was to have a profound influence on the regulations of the trade associations, which prohibited women from doing work liable to overtire them, high warp tapestry, for example, and was also at the root of all the precautionary measures by which contracts of apprenticeship were hedged in, and of the right of inspection granted

to the *jurés*, which aimed at keeping a check on the working
conditions of the artisans and on the observance of trade
regulations. The fact that the Sabbath-day rest was extended
to include Saturday afternoon—at a moment when economic
activity was increasing with the revival of commerce and
industrial development—should be noted as particularly
significant.

A more far-reaching revolution was to be initiated by the
same doctrine applied to the institution of slavery. It must
be noted that the Church did not protest against slavery as
such, for it was an economic necessity among ancient
civilisations. But she strove to ensure that the slave, who
had been treated hitherto as an object, should henceforward
be considered as a man and have rights proper to human
dignity. Once this result had been achieved, slavery had
been practically abolished: the evolution was facilitated by
German customs which recognised a very mild form of
servitude. The combined result was medieval serfdom
which respected the rights of the individual and entailed,
as a restriction upon his liberty, only the obligation to
remain on the domain. It is curious to note that the para-
doxical fact of the re-appearance of slavery in the sixteenth
century, in the midst of flourishing Christian civilisation,
coincides with a general return to Roman law.

Thus, many notions which belonged to canon law became
incorporated in customary law. The medieval conception
of justice was very significant from this point of view, for
the idea of the spiritual equality of all human beings, which
was foreign to Antiquity, now came to the fore. It was in
this connection that various reforms were subsequently
introduced, for instance, in legislation concerning bastards,
who were more favourably treated by ecclesiastical than
by secular law, since they were not held responsible for
the fault to which they owed their existence. In canon

law, a penalty was inflicted not to avenge the wrong done or as amends to society, but to reclaim the delinquent, and this idea—also entirely new—was not without effect on customary law. Medieval society, moreover, was acquainted with the right of refuge, established by the Church; and the modern mind is nonplussed to find officers of the law being condemned for daring to enter the grounds of a monastery to look for a criminal; that, however, is what happened to the jurist Beaumanoir, among others. It must be added that the ecclesiastical tribunals condemned trial by duel well before its proscription by Louis IX, and they were alone, until the order of 1324, in making provision for damages to be awarded to the injured party. Under the same influence, the Middle Ages became acquainted with free legal aid for the poor, who were, if necessary, allowed a barrister appointed by the court. The accused was not pronounced guilty until his guilt had been proved, which meant that imprisonment pending trial was unknown.

The Church, like all medieval society, enjoyed privileges, the principal being precisely that of possessing its own tribunals. This was the *privilegium fori*, granted to all clerics and to those who by their profession were connected with the clerical world, for instance, students and doctors. The role of the ecclesiastical courts or tribunals in the Middle Ages was the more important because the number of persons directly or indirectly dependent upon the clergy was immense at that time, and as the title of cleric was applied in a very much wider sense than nowadays, there were often disputes and confusion between the law of the king or the *seigneurs* and that of the Church. Clerics were all those who followed a clerical way of life; this rather vague definition had the disadvantage of applying equally well to those who attended the University—masters or pupils—as to monks and priests. Outward signs, such as the tonsure or the habit, were sometimes taken as a basis for definition, but these attributes could be usurped by those who preferred canon law to customary law—whence the proverb: 'It is not the cowl that makes the monk.' Generally speaking, clerics were considered to be those who accepted the obligations of clerical life, in particular with regard to celibacy which, however, applied to only those clerics who took major orders, that is, to deacons and priests. In the twelfth century this rule applied to sub-deacons, but not the minor orders which were not then considered as leading necessarily to the priesthood. Other clerics could enter into holy matrimony provided it was *cum unica et virgine* (with one woman only, a virgin). To marry a widow or to re-marry was, for a cleric, to lay himself open to being accused of bigamy—a term which has often led to confusion.

A series of measures was introduced in the Middle Ages to regulate and restrict the right of the clergy with regard to the system of inheritance. It was, in fact, a matter of preventing the greater part of the land from falling eventually to the Church as a consequence of testamentary bequests to the clergy. Clerics had therefore to renounce their inheritances—at all events in so far as landed property was concerned. This compensated for ecclesiastical privileges. With regard to taxes, the obligations of the clergy were not the same as those of laymen. Parish priests generally received a tithe, which was calculated differently according to the province: it was one sheaf in ten, or every eleventh sheaf, or even, as in Berry, every twelfth or thirteenth. On the other hand, the clergy as a whole were compelled to pay a tithe rent-charge to the king. A number of embassies to the Vatican were made for the purpose of requesting authorisation for the levying of an 'extraordinary tithe rent-charge'

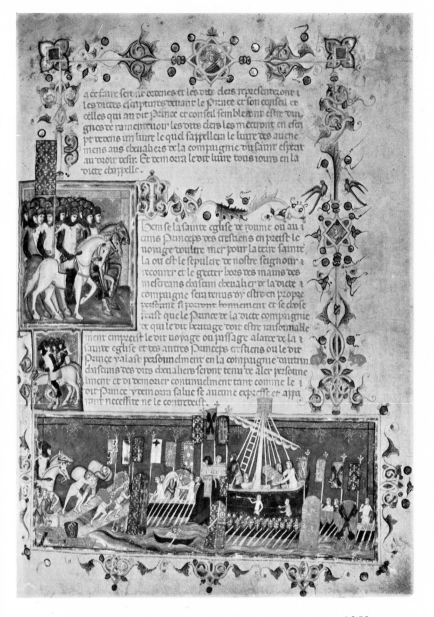

CRUSADERS EMBARKING FOR THE HOLY LAND, 1352

—for instance, on the occasion of some expedition. This corresponded to the taxes levied on the peasants and represented their contribution to the wars of the country.

One of the functions of the Church and its tribunals was to combat heresy. Here we meet with an essential characteristic of medieval life and one which often caused a great deal of feeling in later years. In order to understand the matter it is necessary to realise that the Church was at that time the guarantor of the social order and that all that threatened the Church also attacked secular society. Thus, heresies often drew more violent censure from the laity than from the clergy. To take an example, it is difficult nowadays to imagine the profound anxiety caused among society generally by the Albigensian heresy simply because it rejected the oath of allegiance. This was to attack the very essence of medieval life: the feudal bond. The foundations of the feudal system were shaken as a result[23]—and this accounted for the vigorous and sometimes excessive reactions which were provoked. Should these excesses be attributable to the Church? Luchaire, who can scarcely be suspected of indulgence towards the Papacy, sees in it an 'essentially moderating influence' in the struggle against heresy. That is, in fact, what appears from the relations between Innocent III and Raimond de Toulouse, and from the correspondence between the Pope and his legates. Moreover, the examination of particular cases reveals plainly that the pillage and massacre which took place were the work of an excited minority who were afterwards severely reprimanded by the Church. The letter of Saint Bernard to the burghers of Cologne after the massacre of heretics which took place in 1145 has already been quoted:[24]

[23] The remark was made by M. Belperron in his work *La Croisade des Albigeois* (p. 76).
[24] Ibid, p. 115.

H

'The people of Cologne have gone too far. We may approve of their zeal, but we do not in any way approve of that which they have done, for faith is born of persuasion and cannot be thrust upon men.' The fact was that, as often happens, laymen were much less moderate and more pitiless than the clergy in their judgments and that in this case material considerations also combined to aggravate doctrinal anxieties. The first sovereign to order the burning at the stake of heretics who were sentenced to be handed over to the secular authorities was the Emperor Frederick II; this seems surprising when one thinks how little this man cared for orthodoxy. Did he not show himself on many occasions to be one of the most 'modern' spirits, inclined to scepticism, far from anxious to heed the objurgations of the Pope, and a man who, when he went on a crusade, perpetually flaunted the deepest contempt for his co-religionists, combined with the most lively sympathy for the Moslems. Consequently, it is very probable that the prevention of heresies interested him in only a very second degree. But, as a far-sighted politician, he had sensed the peril in which the heretics were placing secular society. In the same way, the massacres of Jews during the first crusade were not perpetrated by the armies of Peter the Hermit or of Gautier Sans Avoir, but were ordered in Germany by a lay *seigneur*, Count Ennrich of Leiningen, after the crusaders had set out. The banishments of Jews were, moreover, at least in France, many fewer than has been alleged, since there were only three on a large scale—one under Saint Louis at the time of his crusades, and two others under Philip the Fair and ordered by him for financial reasons.

It was as a result of similar action on the part of the secular authorities in turning the measures for defence taken by the Church to their own advantage and in using these as an instrument of power—sometimes, it must be allowed, with the connivance of certain individual ecclesi-astics—that the Inquisition acquired its unfortunate repu-tation. However, it was only from the beginning of the sixteenth century and in Imperial Spain that it assumed a really bloody and ferocious nature. During the whole of the Middle Ages it was merely an ecclesiastical tribunal for the purpose of 'exterminating' heresy, that is, of extirpating it by driving it outside the boundaries (*ex terminis*) of the realm; the penances which were imposed did not exceed ordinary ecclesiastical penances ordered at confession, such as alms, pilgrimages and fasts. Only in very serious cases was the accused handed over to the secular authorities, which meant that he incurred civil punishments such as imprison-ment or death—for the ecclesiastical tribunal had not in any case the right to impose such penalties itself. Moreover, authors of no matter what persuasion who have studied the Inquisition from writings of the period are agreed that it had, as Lea, the Protestant writer, says, 'but few victims.'[25] Out of the nine hundred and thirty convictions recorded by the Inquisitor Bernard Gui during his career, those involving the death penalty totalled forty-two. As for torture, one finds only three cases when it was applied for certain, during the whole history of the Inquisition in Languedoc; that is to say that its usage was far from general. It was necessary, moreover, that before it could be applied there should be some proof at least of guilt; it could only serve to effect the completion of confession already begun. It must be added that, like all ecclesiastical tribunals, that of the Inquisition did not recognise imprisonment pending trial, and left the accused at liberty until his guilt should be proved.

★

It is interesting, in studying the Church during the Middle

25 Lea, *History of the Inquisition.* Vol. I, p. 489.

Ages, to devote some attention to the characteristics of medieval faith, on which subject many erroneous judgments have been passed. One is apt to see it as a period of 'simple faith', when men accepted all ecclesiastical precepts and prescriptions blindly and without question, when fear of hell kept credulous populations in a state of terror so that they were the more easily exploited, when, finally, rigorous discipline and fear of sin precluded all temporal pleasures.

It was, in fact, during the Middle Ages that one of the greatest and most audacious syntheses ever known in the history of philosophy was made. This reconcilement of the wisdom of Antiquity with the dogma of Christianity, which culminated in the great works of the theologians of the thirteenth century, surely represents a magnificent intellectual achievement, quite apart from any religious considerations. The quarrel about the Universals and the passionate discussions on Nominalism and Illuminism which absorbed all the thinking world of that time, bear witness to the intense intellectual activity of which the Universities of Paris, Oxford and elsewhere were the centres. The theological contests and the disputes of Abélard or Siger de Brabant, ardently followed and discussed by all young students, were surely proof that in such matters, more, perhaps, than in any others, men found plenty of opportunities for the exercise of their critical faculties. When the Crusade against the Albigenses was decided upon, it was after the murder of the legate Pierre de Castelnau, but it was also after twenty years of discussion between the Papal envoys and the upholders of Catharism. One can hardly conclude from this that faith was unquestioning. It seems, on the contrary, that religion as it was understood then was the concern of the intellect as much as of the heart, and a concern whose different aspects were the subject of increasingly profound study. There was no trace of naïveté in this attitude—any more than in anything it inspired, whether cathedrals or crusades. One might make the objection that this was not so among the people: but it was, however, from the people that these monks and these fervent students of dialectic and theology sprang. In the *fabliaux* of the time it was the people who launched attacks against the riches of the clergy and they, too, who set out on crusades and built cathedrals. In obeying the precepts of the preachers men were not acting without reflection or in a spirit of pure submission. The songs and poems of the Crusades which were current throughout the period relied on persuasion in order to convince—on that persuasion which is a part of Catholic doctrine and which offers man the love of God as his ultimate good—but this persuasion was dialectical and not based on sentimental appeals:

> *Vous qui aimez de vraie amour*
> *Eveillez vous, ne dormez point.*
> *L'alouette vous trait le jour*
> *Et si vous dit en son latin:*
> *Or est venu le jour de paix*
> *Que Dieu, par sa très grand douçour*
> *Promet à ceux qui pour s'amour*
> *Prendront la croix, et pour leur fair*
> *Souffriront peine nuit et jour.*
> *Or verra-t-il les amants vrais . . .*

The result of the Crusades—the founding of the Latin states in the Orient—proves that there was no question there of unreasoning exaltation; certainly all the knights who built fortresses and framed laws for the use of their new principalities did not give an impression of either frivolousness or fanaticism; nor did they allow events to carry them out of their depth. As Lavisse himself has observed: 'Our knights were able, if necessary, to combine the glory of conquest with that of organising the lands they had conquered and of setting up a government there. But it is possible that, had the Church not collaborated with them in their work, their success would not have been so great.'[26] If their faith was naïve, it must be admitted that it did not rule out sturdy common sense. And the achievements to which it led also make one realise that it consisted of more than the cult of relics, as it has been sometimes described. The Middle Ages loved relics as they loved all that was a visible sign of an invisible reality. This was not sentimentality, but realism. The relic corresponded to the *traditio*, the handing over of a token which constituted an act of sale, or the investiture of a count. This was a general characteristic of the period as a whole and not of its religion alone.

This is not the place to discuss belief in hell, which belongs to Catholic dogma and is not, therefore, peculiar to the Middle Ages. It is a moot point whether the vision of hell, evoked with such mastery by painters and poets, engendered the paralysing terror one is apt to imagine, and if the mortification of the passions, advocated by the Church, robbed our ancestors entirely of the joys of life. It certainly seems that the mainspring of medieval faith was not fear, but love: 'Without love no man can serve God.' it was said. And, again:

Sans amour nul ne peut à honneur parvenir
Si doit être amoureux qui veut grand devenir.

It is not a little surprising to find eight capital sins enumerated in the treatises on ethics of the period, instead of the seven we know to-day. Now the eighth was, strangely enough, sadness, *tristitia*. The theologians defined and denounced it, and set forth the *remedia tristitia*, to which a man should have recourse when he felt himself a prey to melancholy:

Car irié, morne et pensis
Peut l'on bien perdre Paradis,

26 *Histoire de France.* Vol. II, 2, p. 105.

Et plein de joie et envoisié—
Mais qu'on se gard d'autre péché—
Le peut-on bien conquerre aussi.

At the basis of the medieval conception of the world,
however, one finds a sturdy optimism. Rightly or wrongly,
men started from the principle that the world was fundamentally good, that if sin was man's ruin, redemption was
his salvation, and that there was nothing—whether joy
or affliction—which was not for his good, or from which
he could not derive instruction and profit:

Car maintes fois aller à l'aventure
Et ce qu'on craint, avoir peine et douleur
Vient à effet de douce nourriture:
Je tiens que Dieu fait tout pour le meilleur.

Dieu n'a pas fait chacun d'une jointure,
Terres ni fleurs toutes d'une couleur:
Mais rien n'advient dont fleur n'ait ouverture.
Je tiens que Dieu fait tout pour le meilleur,

thus wrote Eustache Deschamps, a poet who has depicted a
complete and most exact panorama of the life of his time.
Faced with writings of this nature, and without even
considering the gigantic carousals for which religious
festivals furnished an opportunity, one is certainly obliged
to concede that if ever there was an epoch of joy in the
history of the world, it was the Middle Ages. We must
conclude with this very sound observation by Drieu la
Rochelle: 'It is not in spite of Christianity, but through
Christianity, that the joy of life is so plainly and fully
revealed, the joy of having a body and a soul in that body,
the joy in existing.'[27]

[27] Article on *La Conception du Corps au Moyen Age* in the *Revue
Française*, No. I, 1940, p. 16.

Chapter Eight
Education

THE child, in the Middle Ages as in every period, went to school—generally to his parish school or to that of the nearest monastery. All the churches, in fact, had a school attached, the Lateran Council of 1179 having made this a strict rule. It was quite common then— and still is in England, a more conservative country than France—to find church, cemetery and school combined. Often, too, seigniorial endowments assured the education of the children: Rosny, a little village on the banks of the Seine, had a school from the beginning of the thirteenth century, endowed by its *seigneur*, Guy V Mauvoisin, about the year 1200. Sometimes, too, there were purely private schools: the inhabitants of a hamlet would join together to pay for a master who was charged with the education of the children. An amusing little document has preserved for us the petition of some parents, demanding the dismissal of a master who, not having been able to inspire respect among his pupils, had been plagued by them to the point where *eum pugiunt grafionibus*, they pricked him with their *grafiones* (the stylets with which they wrote on their waxed tablets).

But the privileged persons were obviously those who could take advantage of the instruction in the episcopal schools or those of the monasteries, or else of the chapters, for the cathedral chapters also were obliged to give instruction as stipulated by the Lateran Council,[28] mentioned above. Some of these schools won quite extraordinary renown in the Middle Ages—for instance, those of Chartres, Lyons and Le Mans where the pupils performed the ancient tragedies, that of Lisieux where at the beginning of the twelfth century the bishop was pleased to come and teach in person and that of Cambrai; a document quoted by the learned Pithou tells us that they were founded with the especial object of assisting the people in the management of their temporal affairs.

The monastery schools were perhaps even more celebrated, and one thinks naturally of names such as Le Bec, Fleury-sur-Loire where the King, Robert the Pious, was educated, St. Géraud d'Aurillac, where Gerbert learned the rudiments of the sciences which he was himself to bring to such a high degree of perfection; and, also, of Marmoutiers, near Tours, Saint-Bénigne of Dijon, and so on. In Paris in the twelfth century one finds three types of scholastic institution: the Notre-Dame schools, or the group of schools where the precentor was in charge of the elementary classes and the chancellor reponsible for the more advanced instruction; the abbey schools such as Sainte-Geneviève, Saint-Victor and Saint-Germain-des-Prés; and, finally, the private institutions opened by masters who had obtained a licence to teach, as, for example, Abélard.

Children were taken at the age of seven or eight and the

[28] 'In each diocese,' says Luchaire, 'apart from the rural and parochial schools already in existence . . . the principal chapters and monasteries had their own schools and their own masters and pupils.' (*La Société Française au temps de Philippe-Auguste*, p. 68.)

course of instruction which prepared them for the University continued, as in our own times, for about ten years (these figures are given by the Abbot Gilles le Muisit). The boys were separated from the girls who generally had their own establishments, less numerous, perhaps, but where studies were sometimes very advanced. The Abbey of Argenteuil, where Héloïse was educated, instructed girls in Holy Scripture, literature, medicine, and even surgery, not to mention the Greek and Hebrew taught there by Abélard. Generally speaking, the small schools taught their pupils elementary grammar, arithmetic, geometry, music and theology, which allowed them to proceed with the sciences studied in the universities. It is possible that a few of them included a sort of technical training—the *Histoire Littéraire* cites, for instance, the Vassor school in the diocese of Metz, in which, as well as studying literature and Holy Scripture, the pupils worked in gold, silver and copper.[29] The masters were almost always assisted by the eldest and most advanced students, as in mutual improvement centres in our own time.

C'étoit ce belle chose de plenté (many) *d'écoliers:*

Ils manoient (lived) *ensemble par loges, par soliers,*

Enfants de riches hommes et enfants de toiliers (workers),

writes Gilles le Muisit, recalling his youthful memories. In those times, children of all classes of society were in fact educated together, as the famous anecdote testifies, which tells of Charlemagne dealing severely with the barons' sons who had proved slothful—in contrast with the sons of serfs and poor people. The only distinction lay in the fees asked, as education was free for the poor, but not for the rich. Education might remain free for the entire period of instruction, even up to graduation, since the Lateran

[29] Book VII, Chap. 29, quoted by J. Guiraud, *Histoire partiale, histoire vraie*. P. 348.

Council forbade persons charged with the directing or supervising of schools 'to exact any payment from candidates for mastership when they take their degree.'

There was, moreover, very little difference during the Middle Ages in the upbringing of children in varying walks of life. The sons of the humblest vassals were reared on the baronial domain with those of the suzerain; those of wealthy citizens had, if they wished to run their father's business when their turn came, to serve the same apprenticeship as the meanest artisan. This is doubtless why there are so many examples of great men who sprang from families in humble circumstances: Suger, who governed France during Louis VII's crusade, was the son of serfs; Maurice de Sully, the bishop of Paris who built Notre-Dame, was born of a beggar; Saint-Pierre Damien minded pigs in his childhood, and one of the brightest stars of medieval science, Gerbert d'Aurillac, was a shepherd; Pope Urban VI was the son of a small shoemaker in Troyes and Gregory VII—the great Pope of the Middle Ages—of a poor goatherd. On the other hand, there were many great *seigneurs* who were scholars and whose education cannot have been very different from that of the clerics: Robert the Pious composed hymns and Latin sequences; William IX, prince of Aquitaine, was the first of the troubadours; Richard Coeur de Lion left poems, as did the lords of Ussel, Les Baux, and many others—not to mention more exceptional cases such as that of Alphonso X, the Astronomer, the King of Spain who wrote poems and works on law alternately, who contributed outstandingly to men's knowledge of astronomy at that time by the compiling of his Alphonsine Tables, who left a comprehensive Chronicle of the Origins of the History of Spain, and a compilation of canon law and Roman law which became the first code his country knew.

The most gifted scholars proceeded naturally to the

University: they made their choice according to the branch of learning which attracted them most, for each University was inclined to specialise. At Montpellier, it was in medicine: in 1181, Guilhem VII, the *seigneur* of the town, granted to every person, whoever he might be or whencesoever he came, the right to teach this art, provided he could offer adequate proof of knowledge. Orleans specialised in canon law and Bologna in Roman law. But already 'nothing could compare with Paris', where the teaching of theology and the liberal arts drew students from every land—from Germany, Italy, England and even from Denmark and Norway.

These universities were founded by the Church and were, in a sense, the continuation of the episcopal schools, differing from them in that they were directly dependent on the Pope and not on the local bishop. The bull, *Parens scientiarum*, of Gregory IX, can be considered as the first charter of the medieval university, with statutes enacted in 1215 by the cardinal-legate, Robert de Courçon, acting on behalf of Innocent III; these statutes explicitly accorded the right of association to masters and pupils. The University, founded by the Papacy, had an entirely ecclesiastical character: the professors all belonged to the Church, and the two great names which did her such honour in the thirteenth century, the Franciscans and the Dominicans, were soon to win great renown with Saint Bonaventure and Saint Thomas Aquinas. The students, even those not intending to take orders, were called clerics and some submitted to the tonsure. This, however, did not mean that only theology was taught, for the syllabus covered all the great scientific and philosophical disciplines, from grammar to dialectic by way of music and geometry.

This 'university' of masters and students formed an independent unit. Philippe-Auguste had withdrawn its

members from the sphere of secular jurisdiction in the year
1200—in other words, from the authority of his own
courts. Masters, pupils, and even their servants, were
dependent on only the ecclesiastical tribunals. This was
considered a privilege, and established the autonomy of
this body of *élite*. Masters and students were therefore
completely exempted from duties towards the central
power; they administered their own affairs, made decisions
among themselves on matters which concerned them, and
managed their own finances without interference from the
State. That was the essential feature of the medieval
university, and probably the one which distinguishes it most
markedly from the university of to-day.

This independence promoted a rivalry between the
various cities which would be hardly imaginable to-day.
For years the masters of canon law of Orleans and those of
Paris wrangled over their pupils. The records of the
Faculté de Décret, published in the *Collection des Documents
Inédits*, are full of recriminations against the Parisian
students who went off without leave to sit for their degrees
in Orleans, where the examinations were easier. Threats,
expulsion and proceedings at law were all useless, and the
disputes continued interminably. There was rivalry also
over professors of greater or lesser reputation, and the
various theses were heatedly discussed by students who
took up the cudgels for them, sometimes to the extent of
going on strike. The University was an even more turbulent
world in the Middle Ages that it is to-day.

It was also a cosmopolitan world: the four 'nations',
between which the Parisian clerics were distributed, are
sufficient indication of this. There were the Picards, the
English, the Germans and the French. The students from
each of these lands were sufficiently numerous to form an
autonomous group, with its own representatives and its

own activities. Apart from that, one frequently finds in the records, Italian, Danish, Hungarian and other names. The professors also came from every part of the world: Siger de Brabant and John of Salisbury are significant names; Albert the Great came from the Rhineland, and Saint Bonaventure and Saint Thomas Aquinas from Italy. There was nothing then to hinder exchanges of thought and a master was judged on the breadth of his learning. This motley world had a common language—Latin—the only one spoken in the Universities. This certainly was what saved them from becoming new Towers of Babel. In spite of the heterogeneous groups of which they were composed, the use of Latin facilitated relations and permitted communication between scholars from one end of Europe to the other; it avoided the possibility of linguistic confusions and safeguarded unity of thought. The problems which absorbed philosophers were the same in Paris, Edinburgh, Oxford, Cologne and Pavia, although each centre and each man made an individual contribution. Thomas Aquinas, who came from Italy, was able to elucidate and formulate in Paris a doctrine whose first principles he had conceived while listening to the teaching of Albert the Great in Cologne. Nothing, obviously, was less of a closed world than the Sorbonne in the thirteenth century.

> *Clercs viennent à études de toutes nations*
> *Et en hiver s'assemblent par plusieurs légions.*
> *On leur lit et ils oient* (listen) *pour leur instruction;*
> *En été s'en retraient* (return) *moult en leurs régions.*

is how Gilles le Muisit sums up the student's life in his times.

Their comings and goings were indeed unceasing: they left to go to the University of their choice, returned home for vacations, set out between-whiles to take advantage of lessons given by a master of renown, or to study a subject in which a certain town specialised. We have already mentioned the 'flits' to Orleans of the candidates for examinations in canon law; this was a frequent occurrence, sometimes between cities which were much further apart. Students and professors were regular travellers along the highways; either on horseback or, more often, on foot, they would cover many a league, sleeping in barns or inns. It was they, together with the pilgrims and merchants, who contributed to that extraordinary bustle on the roads of France in the Middle Ages, which was not seen again until the century of the motor-car, or, rather, until the development of the outdoor sports habit. The fraternity of scholars was an itinerant one—to such an extent that, with some, travel became a necessity, a mania; in our own time one meets students in the Latin Quarter who have grown old in Bohemia, who have not been able to settle down to a normal life nor to make any use of the studies whose load they have borne for years. In the Middle Ages this type of individual was to be found on the road; he became the wandering scholar or *goliard*, a typically medieval figure, inseparable from the 'atmosphere' of the period; 'always in the taverns and after the wenches,' he would wander from one inn to another in search of a free meal and, particularly a glass of wine; he frequented places of ill-repute, still retained a few scraps of learning which he used to astonish the good folk to whom he recited a few lines of Horace or some fragments of the *chansons de geste*; or he would perhaps embark on a discussion of some theological question with a chance acquaintance. He generally ended by being swallowed up in the crowd of wandering minstrels, good-for-nothings and beggars—if not by getting himself hanged for some misdemeanour. His songs travelled the length and breadth of Europe, and students still know the *chants goliardiques*:

Meum est propositum in taberna mori,
Vinum sit appositum morientis ori
Ut dicant cum venerint angelorum chori:
Deus sit propitius huic potatori!

The Church was often obliged to take severe measures against these *clerici vagi*, who encouraged sloth and dissolute living among the students.

However, they remained the exception: on the whole, the students of the thirteenth century did not lead a life very different from that of twentieth century students. Letters to parents and friends have been kept and published [30] which show that their concerns were much the same then as to-day: studies, requests for food and money, examinations. The rich student lived out with his valet; those in humbler circumstances lodged with townspeople in the Sainte-Geneviève district and had all or part of their entrance fees remitted; one often finds a marginal note in the records to the effect that such and such a student had not paid, or had paid only half the fees, *propter inopiam*, because of poverty. The student who was without resources often did small jobs in order to live: he would become a copyist or a book-binder with the booksellers in the Rue des Ecoles or the Rue Saint-Jacques. But, apart from this, he could obtain free board and lodging in the established colleges. The first of these had been set up in the Paris Hospital by a Londoner who, on his return from a pilgrimage in the Holy Land towards the end of the thirteenth century, had the idea of doing a charitable work by promoting learning among people of small means. He left an endowment in perpetuity for the purpose of providing free board and lodging for eighteen poor students who were required only to take it in turns to watch over the hospital's dead and to

[30] Cf. Haskins: *The Life of Medieval Students as illustrated by their letters* in the *American Historical Review* (III, 1892, No. 2.)

THE HOLY GRAIL APPEARS TO THE KNIGHTS
OF THE ROUND TABLE
(*Fourteenth Century*)

carry the cross and the holy water at funerals. A little later
the Collège Saint-Honoré was also founded and that of
Saint Thomas du Louvre, followed by many others.
Gradually the habit developed of organising communal
study sessions in these colleges, as in the German *Lehrer-
seminar*, or like the 'study groups' which have existed for
several years in French universities; masters came to give
lessons; some settled there and sometimes the college was
better attended than the University itself—that is what
happened in the case of the college of the Sorbonne.
There was a general scholarship system, not officially
organised, but existing in practice, which resembled that
of the Ecole Normale Supérieure without the entrance
examination, or the custom in English Universities
whereby the scholarship student receives not only free
tuition but free board and lodging and, sometimes,
clothing.

Instruction was given in Latin and was divided into
two branches: the *trivium*, or the liberal arts—grammar,
rhetoric and logic—and the *quadrivium*, that is, the sciences
—arithmetic, geometry, music and astronomy; these,
together with the three faculties of theology, law and
medicine, formed the total of human knowledge. The
method of teaching most commonly employed was com-
mentary. A text was read, the *Etymologies* of Isidorus of
Seville, the *Maxims* of Peter the Lombard, or a treatise by
Aristotle or Seneca, according to the subject; it was then
expounded and all questions to which it might give rise
were commented upon from the grammatical, legal,
philosophical and linguistic angle. This instruction was
thus primarily oral, and emphasised the importance of
discussion; the *Questiones disputate*, the set questions, were
commented upon and discussed by candidates for the
licence before an audience of masters and pupils, and

I

sometimes complete philosophical and theological treatises were produced as a result; certain famous written glosses were themselves commented upon and expounded during lectures. The theses maintained by candidates for the doctorate were not then mere expositions of a written work, but *theses* properly speaking, propounded and upheld before a whole lecture hall of doctors and masters, while everyone present was at liberty to speak and raise objections.

One can see that such an education was liberal in form; each branch taking its place in a whole where it assumed a proper value corresponding to its importance to human thought. To take an example, in our own times a degree in philosophy is equivalent to a degree in Spanish or English, although the culture presumably derived from these different subjects is each on a very different plane; but in the Middle Ages one could be a master of philosophy or of divinity or of law—or a master of arts, which implied the study of the sum or essence of all knowledge relative to humanity—the *trivium* representing the sciences of the mind and the *quadrivium* those of bodies and the numbers governing them. The whole course of studies was therefore designed to give a general culture and there was no real specialisation before leaving the University. That is the explanation of the encyclopædic knowledge of the scientists and scholars of the period: Roger Bacon, John of Salisbury and Albert the Great covered, in fact, the whole range of knowledge available in their age, and could devote themselves to the most varied subjects one after the other, without fear of dissipating their powers of mind, because their fundamental outlook was all-embracing.

When he came out of his classes at the University and College, the medieval student liked outdoor exercise. He was well able to do a day's march of several leagues, or

to handle a sword—(the public records complain vigorously
of this). Brawls sometimes broke out among this turbulent
population around Sainte-Geneviève and Saint-Germain-
des-Prés, and it was because he was too good a swordsman
that François Villon was obliged to leave Paris. The student
was as familiar with athletics as with libraries, and his life,
more even than that of members of other fraternities,[31] was
brightened by feasts and amusements which enlivened
the Latin Quarter. Even without counting the *Fête des Fous*
and the *Fête des Sots*, which were exceptional occasions,
every time a student was successful in obtaining his doctor's
degree there were burlesque ceremonies in which the
dignified masters at the Sorbonne took part; Ambroise de
Cambrai, chancellor of the *Faculté de Décret*, who took his
role very seriously, left an account in the detailed records
he kept while he held this office. A man educated in this
way was prepared for action as well as for intellectual
activity, and that, doubtless, is why one sees men adapting
themselves successfully to the most varied situations during
this period: fighting prelates, like Guillaume des Barres or
Guérin de Senlis at the Battle of Bouvines, jurists capable
of organising the defence of a castle, like Jean d'Ibelin,
Seigneur of Beyrouth, merchant-explorers, architect-ascetics,
and so on.

The University was, moreover, the great pride of the
Middle Ages: the Popes spoke with satisfaction of the
'stream of knowledge whose many branches water and
make fruitful the lands of the universal Church.' It was
pointed out, not without some complacency, that the crowd
of students in Paris was so large that they exceeded in

[31] It must be noted that the Middle Ages made no distinction between
manual trades and liberal professions, and the terms employed in this
connection are significant: the clothier who had completed his apprenticeship was described as a 'master' in exactly the same way as the
student of divinity after he had taken his degree.

numbers the ordinary population.[32] Much indulgence was
shown to the students in spite of their high spirits and
practical jokes which often caused the people inconvenience;
they were universally liked. Some scenes from student life
have been recorded by one of the sculptors of the Saint-
Etienne portal of Notre-Dame-de-Paris: the students are
to be seen reading or studying; a woman comes and
disturbs them, tearing them from their books, and as
punishment she is placed in the pillory by order of the
authorities. The kings set an example of this habit of
treating the *'écoliers'* as spoilt children: Philippe-Auguste sent
a messenger to announce his victory first to the students of
Paris.

Everything connected with learning was honoured in
the Middle Ages: 'Who loves not books, he justly dies
dishonoured,' ran a proverb,[33] and it is enough to consult
the documents of this time to find evidence of measures by
which every desire for knowledge was encouraged and
gratified; for instance, in 1215 a chair of theology was
founded for the express purpose of enabling the priests
of the diocese to pursue and complete their studies—which
showed men's anxiety to maintain a high standard of
education even among the ordinary clergy. The *'prud'homme'*
the type of complete man who was the ideal of the thirteenth
century, had to be a scholar:

> *Pour rimer, pour versifier,*
> *Pour une lettre bien dicter,*
> *Si métier fut* (if need be), *pour bien écrire*
> *Et en parchemin et en cire,*
> *Pour une chanson controuver.*[34]

[32] This statement cannot be taken literally, but it is interesting that
the population of Paris at this time numbered rather more than forty
thousand inhabitants.

[33] Renart, Prov. franç. II, 99.

[34] Quoted by the *Histoire Littéraire*, Vol. XX.

One may well ask if, under these circumstances, the people were as ignorant in the Middle Ages as is generally believed. There is no doubt that they had the means of educating themselves within their reach, and poverty presented no obstacle since tuition was free, if necessary, from the village or parish school right up to the University. And the people took advantage of this, for there are numerous examples of humble folk who became great scholars.

Is that to say that education was as widely disseminated then as in our own time? It seems there is some confusion on this point: culture and literacy have now become more or less synonymous, and an illiterate is, for us, inevitably an uneducated man. Now the number of illiterates was undoubtedly greater in the Middle Ages than in our own time. [35] But is this point of view quite right? Can one make knowledge of the alphabet the criterion of culture? Can one assert that, because education has now become primarily visual, man can be educated by visual means alone?

In a section of the municipal statutes of Marseilles, dating from the thirteenth century, the qualifications required of a good lawyer are enumerated and it is added: *litteratus vel non litteratus* (whether he be literate or not). That seems very significant. One could be a good lawyer, then, and not be able to read or write—one could know customary law and Roman law and the use of language, and not know the alphabet. This is an idea we find difficult to accept, but one which is, nevertheless, of cardinal importance in the understanding of the Middle Ages. One learned then more by listening than by reading. Honoured though they were, books and writings held a position of

[35] Although smaller than has been alleged, since the majority of witnesses to deed signatures were able to sign their names and there is, besides, the example of Joan of Arc who, though only a little peasant-girl, was able to write.

only secondary importance; it was to speech, to the spoken word, that the chief role fell. This was the case in all circumstances of life: in our time, officers and civil servants draw up reports; in the Middle Ages they took counsel and deliberated; a thesis was not a printed work, but a discussion; the making of a contract depended not on a signature appended to a written document, but on the act of handing over, or on a verbal agreement; to govern meant to enquire and investigate and then have the measures which had been decided upon proclaimed by a crier.

Preaching was an essential feature of medieval life. To preach, in this period, was not to deliver a sermon in chosen phrases before a silent congregation and one already convinced. Preachers spoke anywhere, not only in churches but in the market place, on the fair grounds, at the cross-roads—and with much animation, fire and ardour. The preacher spoke to his audience and replied to their questions, even suffering them to contradict and upbraid him, and to make disturbances. A sermon could sway the crowd enormously and might unleash a crusade, propagate a heresy or whip up a revolt on the spot. The didactical role of the clergy was very great at that time: it was they who taught the faithful their history and their legends, their science and their faith—they who announced great events, spreading the news of the capture of Jerusalem or the loss of Acre from one end of Europe to the other. They gave counsel to some and guidance to others, even in their temporal affairs. In our own days, those who are lacking in visual memory—which is, however, rarer and more mechanically exercised than aural memory—are handicapped in their studies and in their lives. In the Middle Ages this was not so at all—one learned by listening and speech was golden.

It is a curious fact that our own era is witnessing a return of the importance of the spoken word and a revival of the auditory faculty which had been almost lost. It is possible that for future generations radio will take the place formerly occupied by preaching; it is to be hoped, in any case, that it will play an equally valuable part in the education of the people.

For, if the expression 'latent culture' has ever had a meaning, it was certainly in the Middle Ages. Everyone had at least a colloquial knowledge of spoken Latin, and could modulate plainsong, which implied, if not the understanding, at least the habit, of accentuation. Everyone had some knowledge of myths and legends—and fables and tales teach more about the history of mankind and its nature than a good part of the prescribed subjects on the official syllabi to-day. In the novels about trades published by Thomas Deloney, one finds the weavers alluding to Ulysses and Penelope, Ariadne and Theseus in their songs. If stained-glass windows have been called 'the Bible of the illiterate,' was it not because through them even the most ignorant were able to make out the stories with which they were familiar—the same work of interpretation which now gives so much trouble to the archæologist was then accomplished quite simply!

Apart from this, there was technical knowledge assimilated during the years of apprenticeship. Neither arts nor crafts were unskilled—if they were to be exercised to advantage, it was necessary that they should become second nature; that, doubtless, is why so many local artists whose names we shall never know were able to attain that mastery revealed by works such as the *Christ* of Perpignan and the *Crucifixion* of Vénasque. Has one the right to consider as ignorant a man who knew his trade thoroughly, no matter how humble? And it must be borne in mind that there was, in addition to technical knowledge, a whole collection of folklore: the *Compost des Bergiers*, which a happy curiosity re-discovered not long ago, offers us an example of the little *Epitomes* of traditional learning—astronomy, medicine, botany, and meteorology—which could be acquired within a trade—varying with each of them—and which constituted the basis of a culture undoubtedly wider and certainly better adapted to local needs than one might believe.

Chapter Nine
Literature

IN spite of the large number of modern works devoted to the subject, we have yet to succeed in gaining an accurate idea of medieval literature and in appreciating it as it deserves. It remains a curiosity for the scholar or, which is more dangerous, serves to conjure up quite artificial notions. An important step has been taken, however, in that it has been found possible to convince the public of the existence of medieval literature. The great difficulty which stands in the way of further progress is the language problem. It is to be regretted that among the mass of miscellaneous knowledge heaped on our adolescents, no place, or an absurdly insignificant one, should have been found for Old French—which undeniably constitutes a part of the national heritage and one which is estimated less meanly as it becomes better known. [36] Views such as those of

[36] It must be said that this indifference extends more to the Middle Ages in general than to its literature in particular. For months, students study the Oriental question in the nineteenth century or ministerial changes from MacMahon to Jules Grévy; but how many university graduates have even a vague notion of the principal events of the Crusades or of the manner in which French unity grew up during the centuries which represent the foundation and the epitome of French history.

Gustave Lanson and Thierry Maulnier, who saw in all the 'versified literature' of the Middle Ages 'only a hotchpotch of jabbering preciosity', destined to sink into 'kindly oblivion', cannot stand up to an even superficial examination of medieval poetry.

There is only a single era during which France possessed a national literature of exclusively French inspiration, and that period is the Middle Ages. After the fifteenth century, a strange craze for imitation resulted in strict literary rules and limitation of literary styles, and throttled individual inspiration in favour of an immutable prototype: Antiquity. There is no question here of belittling the achievements of Antiquity, or its indisputable masterpieces, nor, above all, of failure to recognise the individual mastery of men such as Racine and Molière who were able to dominate the derivative art imposed on them by their age. Account must also be taken of the non-conformists who, without being honoured by the text-books, yet made an important contribution to French Literature. The fact remains that, until the end of the nineteenth century, generally speaking both classicists and romanticists in France were willing to subject themselves to disciplines which derived from either the Greeks or the Romans, or from later foreign writers. To find, outside our own twentieth century, a true blossoming French genius, a pure and individual literature free from any borrowed element, one must look to the Middle Ages. If one insists on not looking farther back than the Renaissance, one cuts oneself off from the most authentic manifestation of French genius. Further, one knows nothing of a period during which French civilisation was copied throughout Europe, and one is deprived of an incomparable treasure of poetry, verve and grandeur—one of the richest, most colourful and most moving that exists.

A large part of the literary production of the Middle Ages

is still in manuscript form, hidden away in libraries (while other works are re-published again and again). This does perhaps show a lack of curiosity, but the fault lies more in the methods employed in the study of the history of literature—when these methods have been applied to medieval literature they have hampered us considerably. Men have exercised their wits to discover the sources of medieval works, the sources of the *Roman de Renart*, the sources of the *fabliaux*, and so on, as if it were a matter of the classical tragedies, taken from the plays of Sophocles or Seneca. Precious time has been wasted in this way. Investigations into sources, useful where French literature from the sixteenth century onwards is concerned, were no more than a hindrance to the study of the Middle Ages and have proved, in most cases, futile if not childish. Bédier has rendered an immense service to literature by demonstrating the importance of human themes which belong no more exclusively to India or China than to Europe or Africa: the theme of the biter bit, the fable of the fox and the grapes, and many others, which have been the subject of endless arguments terminating in the establishment of complicated filiations which, however, collapse automatically as soon as one perceives that men in every latitude react similarly to the same phenomena, and that if French medieval folklore has features in common with those of certain ancient races, it is because it has drawn from the eternal wellsprings of humanity. Rhythms similar to those of old French pastorales have been recognised in Czech shepherd songs—but this is not because the French are derived from the Czech, but because the same life and the same habits inspired identical cadences. In the same way, sailors in every latitude and of every race have, in order to transmit orders and synchronise their efforts, made use of *tropes* and rhythms and poetic modulations of voice dictated by their work and harmonising with the roll of the sea and the ship. A certain knowledge of mankind would have been more valuable in the gaining of an understanding of medieval literature than research into its sources, in the venerable Sorbonne tradition.

That does not mean that the Middle Ages were unaware of Antiquity. Horace, Seneca, Aristotle, Cicero and many others were studied and frequently quoted, and the principal heroes and heroines of ancient literature, Alexander, Hector, Pyramus and Thisbé, Phædra and Hippolytus, have all inspired medieval authors in their turn. Ovid's *Metamorphoses* and *Heroides* were translated several times; Virgil, especially, was greatly loved in the Middle Ages, which gave proof of impeccable taste, for Virgil was undoubtedly the only Latin poet worthy of the name. But if men were conscious of its store of imagery, stories and maxims, they did not go so far as to hold up Antiquity as a model, or as to see there the criterion for every work of art; they assumed that it was possible to do as well or better; they admired Antiquity, but refrained from imitation.

On the contrary, French medieval literature sprang in its entirety from the soil of France, reproduced faithfully its slightest shades and contours. Every social class, every historical event, all the characteristics of the French genius lived again in its dazzling fresco; for poetry was of great significance in the medieval period and one of the greatest passions of the age. Everywhere it held sway; in church and castle, at feasts and on public squares, there was no celebration without poetry, no rejoicing in which it did not have a part, no society, university, association or fraternity from which it was excluded; it had its place at the most solemn functions. Some poets governed counties, as, for instance, William of Aquitaine or Thibaut of Champagne; others governed kingdoms, like King René of Anjou or

Richard Coeur de Lion; others, again, like Beaumanoir, were jurists and diplomats; there was even the incident of Philip of Novara, besieged in the Tour de l'Hôpital with thirty companions, writing in haste to ask for help, only writing not a cry of distress, but a poem; and the legend of Blondel finding his imprisoned master, thanks to a song they had composed together, was merely the expression of a commonplace truth in those times. To recite verses or to listen to them appeared then as one of humanity's inherent needs. One would hardly be likely, nowadays, to see a poet stand up on the boards before a fair booth and there declaim his work—but this was a common spectacle in the Middle Ages. A peasant would leave his plough, a trades-man his shop and a *seigneur* his falcons, to go and hear a *trouvère* or a minstrel. Never, perhaps, except in the greatest days of Ancient Greece, was such an appetite for rhythm, cadence and the beauties of language manifested.

Poetry now belongs more or less to an *élite*. The Middle Ages knew no *élite*, either in the intellectual domain or elsewhere, for each man in his own sphere could become a member of an *élite*. The enjoyments of the mind were not reserved to the privileged or to scholars, and one could, without knowing Latin or Greek, or even A from B, savour poetry's most refined delights. Among the some five hundred *trouvères* and *troubadours* whose names have come down to us, one finds great *seigneurs* such as the Castellan of Coucy, the Seigneurs des Baux and the princes already mentioned, as well as villains and clerics like Rutebeuf, Peire Vidal or Bernard de Ventadour. Contrary to what happened in, for example, the seventeenth century, when a literary work was destined exclusively for the Court or the *salons*, there was a fruitful exchange between the social classes; the poetic sap flowed freely and was enriched by all the vigour the people could contribute and by all the refinement of high society. Moreover, in the fifteenth century a single poetic theme was treated at the same time by Charles d'Orléans, Alain Chartier, Jean Régnier, François Villon and others—men who differed from each other in education, rank and profession, but whose works, nevertheless, were not unalike—poetry being so much of a common ground for both princes and beggars. *La Forêt de Longue Attente* and the refrain of the ballads for the famous competition at Blois are well known:

Je meurs de soif emprès de la fontaine.

Some types of literature were cultivated for preference by the nobility: for instance, the romances of chivalry; but the villains had the *Roman de Renart*, the principal characters of which still live and have remained familiar to us after travelling across Europe and captivating even Goethe, who adapted them. The *fabliaux*, whose sturdy, truculent verve inspired writers such as La Fontaine and Molière, corresponded to the lays and fables which delighted the courts of England and of Champagne.

Some literary forms remained common to all medieval society: the epic, for example, and the drama. French *chansons de geste* excited as much admiration in the inns where pilgrims and travellers stopped on their way to Rome or Santiago, as in the baronial halls. As for the drama, which was at once religious and popular, it attracted the entire population and aroused the enthusiasm of the clerics, equally with that of the nobility and the working classes. References in the Middle Ages to popular literature, clerical literature and the literature of the nobility must be understood as applying more to the prevailing theme, for, in so far as their creators and public were concerned, all works, generally speaking, were common to all classes, with scarcely any pronounced leaning towards one or the others.

This literature was as volatile as it was vast. One runs up against grave difficulties when one attempts to produce a critical edition of a *chanson de geste* or a medieval poem. There, too, it seems that it was wrong to apply to the study of medieval works a system which was useful only for works of Antiquity or for modern writings. There were always, in fact, not one, but many forms of a single work. Bédier, in collecting the various episodes of the story of Tristan and Iseult, which had been scattered among several poems, produced a work which was excellent both for its authenticity and for its accessibility—and much closer to the Middle Ages than an irreproachable edition of each of these poems would have been.

For us, a literary work is a personal and unchangeable thing, fixed in the form given it by its author. Whence our obsession with plagiary. But, during the Middle Ages, anonymous works were common. It must be realised that an idea, once it had been put abroad, immediately became public property, passing from one person to another, becoming embellished by a thousand fancies and suffering every imaginable adaptation; it did not sink into oblivion until its multiple forms had been exhausted. The poem lived a life of its own, independent of its creator; it was a mobile thing, repeatedly regenerated; every lucky find was revived, re-shaped, amplified and rejuvenated, and was characterised by the protean quality and the animation of life itself. The explanation of the mistake made by the German critics, who saw in the *Chanson de Roland* a collective and impersonal work, is obvious if one considers this fluid character, if one can call it that, of the great epics and of literary creations in France generally during the Middle Ages. Originally there was certainly a specific creative act, but constant evolution took place, dependent on poets who quickened the original works with fresh life or, quite simply, on the minstrels who recited them in their own way, grafting on to them episodes out of their own imagination. Thus it was that the Breton romances were transformed over and over again and were eventually found in the fifteenth century in a form very far removed from the original, in the Amadis cycle.

Sometimes, moreover, a literary work represented the completion of an evolution—as, for instance, in the case of the wonderful trade novels already mentioned, whose atmosphere has been well rendered into French by Abel Chevalley. Their subject-matter consisted of workshop songs, stories handed on from journeyman to apprentice, tales of the adventures of a master or his wife or servant, and the legends of the patron saints of the guilds; and all this finally constituted a veritable mine of material for any writer with a modicum of talent; Thomas Deloney [37] made very good use of it for England at the beginning of the sixteenth century. The trades of France were not so fortunate, but it is not impossible that such works might still be found in manuscript. In another *genre*, Bédier has given a brilliant description of the birth of the French epic poems on the roads taken by pilgrims, and of the role of the clerics who taught and of the minstrels who entertained, in the formation of the great French epics. This constant act of creation which drew its inspiration from the life of the people or, more precisely, from the life of a whole district, from the masses as much as from the 'privileged' classes, was, moreover, one of the manifestations of the fecundity of medieval life. Poetic themes with romantic heroes spread and multiplied in the likeness of humanity. Roland, Charlemagne and Guillaume au "Courb-Nez" were a part of the European heritage, in the same way as the Gothic style.

[37] Cf. *The Gentle Craft, Jack of Newbury* and *Thomas of Reading*, novels about the shoemakers and weavers of the City of London.

KINGS AND PROPHETS
(*early Thirteenth Century*)

It was only local differentiations and the character of each province, each dialect and each country, which gave an individual aspect and a fresh savour to each of their reincarnations. There, as elsewhere, French influence or, more precisely, Anglo-French influence, dominated the entire known world. French *trouvères* had an international reputation—Wolfram von Eschenbach, Hartmann von Aue, Walter von der Vogelweide, and the other *Minnesinger* imitated them and Breton romances were translated in Italy, Greece and even in Norway.

Volatile and lively as it was, medieval literature had another characteristic which belonged to the Middle Ages as a whole: love of life. Endowed with an extraordinary faculty for assimilation, the authors of the period treated their heroes as actual living beings who would not have been out of place in the society in which they themselves moved. They did not need to create an artificial setting in order to establish their reality; they described their characters as they felt them to be. In other words, the literature of the Middle Ages dispensed with local colour and historical documentation. Such incidents as the dwarf Oberon being called the son of Julius Cæsar or Alexander behaving as a Christian knight, have been regarded as examples of the famous medieval *naiveté*. But, far from being a defect, did not this talent for transposing the heroes of romance from their dead past into a living present testify to a prodigious power of imaginative representation? In the Middle Ages men had no difficulty in imagining Aristotle, Aeneas or Hector in medieval society; the vitality of the period triumphed over notions of time and space. And that is why, without showing the slightest *naiveté*, the sculptors represented Castor and Pollux on the spandrels of the cathedrals as two knights of their own time. This disregard of local colour in favour of fundamental truth could not be understood better than in our own time, when historico-documentary methods are being discarded more and more in favour of vividness of representation. It is infinitely more agreeable to see the Jeune Fille Violaine in a conventional 'medieval period' setting, unrelated to historical truth but very close in spirit to the real medieval period, than to watch a reconstruction, no matter how skilful, of the *Vray Mistère de la Passion*. And it has become a truism to say that it is preferable to act Œdipus in a pullover and flannels than to tolerate a revival of *Les Burgraves* or *Salammbô*.

Medieval literature is closely bound up with its period and is inseparable from the realities which made up the everyday life of that time. All the topics of those days— military expeditions, the prestige of a king, the misdeeds of a vassal, religious wars, and so on—were rhymed and set to rhythm, amplified and assimilated into the great poetic world of humanity by the tireless tellers of tales and their public, eager for poetry. The exploits of Charlemagne inspired the great French epics, the crusades were sung by the *trouvères*, Peire Cardinal expressed in his verse all the bitterness of the Albigensian Midi, and Guillaume le Breton sang of the renown of Philippe-Auguste. The institution of chivalry gave birth to the vast literature of romance and gallantry, and the disasters of war left their mark on, for instance, the works of Jean Régnier or Charles d'Orléans. The relations between *seigneurs* and their vassals, respect for the feudal link, the work of serfs and peasants, the reading of the clerics and the prayers of the monks, all are found in medieval poetry, and anyone acquainted with no more than the literature of the period would know enough to dispense with any study of its history. It bears the stamp of the land of its birth and reflects faithfully her joys and woes. If, during the centuries which followed, literature was sometimes no more than an exercise done by good pupils of Horace and Theocritus, or merely the pastime of scholars, if its links with the people were forgotten and it became a speciality of the well-bred, during the whole of the Middle Ages at least it remained true to itself, a national creation as much as a human one, popular as much as personal, collective as much as individual, drawing its material from the soil of France, from the adventures of the barons, the wiles of the women, the fertile countryside and the noisy towns, among which Paris already stood out—the Paris of Rutebeuf, of Eustache Deschamps and of François Villon.

But it is not only because it sings of France and her story that medieval poetry represents France's most precious national heritage. This poetry which inspired all Europe and travelled across the whole of the known world was French in its very fibres. France could not deny it without denying her own nature and personality. It is imbued with the spirit of France and is its most genuine creation. The verve, the unceasing flow of irony, of trenchant witticisms, of sarcasms which did not respect even the most sincere beliefs, the resounding laughter, the laughter of the *fabliaux*, of the farces, of the joyous sermons, of the *Fêtes des Fous* and other buffooneries, the laughter which found no further echoes in literature except in the plays of Molière—was not this laughter peculiarly characteristic of the French with their gift for repartee, their sense of the ridiculous, their taste for a good story and a rather *risqué* joke. It is probable that the majority of the French *fabliaux* and certain scenes from the *Jeu de Saint Nicolas* or *Maître Pathelin* could be played by our contemporaries before a popular audience with complete success; the *Quinze joies de mariage* is still read with as much pleasure as ever, and the medieval jokes about women's chatter and deceived husbands are the same as those one hears every day.

This comedy, whose gaiety and exuberance cannot be denied, is reproached with one great fault: its vulgarity. The authors of textbooks on literature throw up their hands in horror at these 'common' characters, these indecent farces and this vocabulary in which gentility suffers some rather rough treatment. These criticisms are just: a great part of medieval literature—and the most successful, too—is strewn with very vulgar jokes. That is, moreover, very French—very Gallic, to use the traditional expression. In the Middle Ages they called a spade a spade, and even vulgar jokes, were found vastly amusing as long as they were funny. One can take offence or emulate the attitude of Francisque Sarcey in leaving his seat at the opening lines of *Ubu Roi;* but the fact remains that, penned by the medieval story-tellers, as well as by Rabelais or Alfred Jarry, or in the mouth of a man of the people, this vulgarity is nearly always so apt, so expressive and so racy, that one cannot help laughing. It must be noted, moreover, that it was not accompanied by indecency, it remained spontaneous and was never premeditated or the outcome of an attitude, as among certain intellectuals in our own days. As for the 'immoral' tales and the 'common' characters with which medieval literature abounds, they were generally based on very sound observation of life and are no more immoral than, for instance, the fables of La Fontaine. Their gusto, far from being shocking, cannot but rejoice a mature mind —all the more because it is accompanied by that subtlety and talent for repartee which are inherent in the France race.

★

By a curious chance—or perhaps chance is not entirely responsible—the first two important works in French literature are a perfect illustration of its dual character: they are the *Chanson de Roland* and the *Pèlerinage de Charles.* In the first poem, the purest sentiments of French chivalry predominate: fidelity to the Emperor, love for sweet France, the friendship of two heroes, the grandeur of death, valour and wisdom; the second is a gigantic buffoonery, in which Charlemagne is merely a merry fellow (before turning into the old fogey of *Huon de Bordeaux*), who indulges in the most bewildering and fantastic activities with his peers: monstrous gags, Gascon boasting, extravagant tipsy conversations; Roland wagers that he will sound his horn with so much force that his breath will blow down all the city gates; Oliver offers to seduce the daughter of King Hugon in record time. The unbridled vitality of the Middle Ages was given free play in this first example of the French epic, which was already a parody of the epic and proves that men were far from taking themselves too seriously or from being deceived by fine phrases and high-flown sentiments. A sense of humour always came to the rescue in time to counteract grandiloquence and avoid bombast— as the following lines from the *Jeu de Saint Nicolas* show, for they have both nobility and comedy:

Seigneur, si je suis jeune, ne m'ayez en dépit
On a veü souvent grand coeur en corps petit
Je ferrai cel forceur, je l'ai pièça élit:
Sachez je l'occirrai, s'il avant ne m'occit.

Such contrasts of noble sentiments and whimsical humour were popular: a work entitled *Dialogue de Salomon et de Marcoul* constantly opposes proverbs based on the highest wisdom and others derived from sturdy common sense:

Qui sage homme sera
Ja trop ne parlera
(ce dit Salomon)

Qui ja mot ne dira
Grand noise ne fera
(Marcoul lui répond)

Le Pèlerinage de Charles, of which *Ubu Roi* is the direct
descendant, is set around the Abbey and fair of Saint-
Denis. The clerics addressed their purely secular or edifying
stories to the people through the medium of the
minstrels but the people, amid the bustle of the market,
the laughter and the good-humoured drunkenness,
transformed them into racy stories—while, simultaneously,
the most noble of French epics was being produced, based
on the same legends.

For France, the home of laughter and sparkling vitality,
was also the native land of chivalry: the word must be
understood in its medieval sense: the cult of honour and
respect for women.

The Frenchman, as revealed in literature, from the
Chanson de Roland to the *Roman de la Rose*, had an innate
horror of treachery: to break the feudal oath of allegiance
or to fail in the undertakings which bound him to his
seigneur was for him the worst kind of transgression.
'Everyone must conduct himself loyally,' is the way in
which Eustache Deschamps sums up the obligations of
'*prud'homie*'. Launcelot, the lover of Queen Guinevere, and
Tristan, of Iseult the Fair, suffered ceaseless pangs of
remorse at their betrayal of their king; there lies all the
tragedy of their lives and of their loves. An unshakeable
sense of loyalty to a pledged word is manifested in all
medieval French poetry, whether it concerns the feudal
link, as in the romances of chivalry, or, as in the songs of
the troubadours, troth plighted to a lady. Gawain had to
endure the most terrible ordeals because he broke his
tryst.

The true lover had, besides, to be prepared to dare anything for his love: trials of physical prowess, moral torments,
the anguish of separation—nothing must seem too difficult
if it was a matter of winning the lady he loved:

Pour travail ni pour peine
Ni pour douleur que j'aie
Ni pour ire grevaine (bitter wrath)
Ni pour mal que je traie (which I bear)
Ne quiers que me retraie (leave)
De ma dame un seul jour.

He never addressed her without boundless respect:

Dame, de toutes la nonpair
Belle et bonne, à droit louée

or else:

Belle plaisant, que je n'ose nommer.

Woman appeared as half-goddess. With her 'sweet body', fair face, 'shining like the gold of the sun,' and her charming graces, she represented for the knight the ideal of all perfection:

Dame, dont n'os(e) dire le nom
En qui tous biens sont amassés
De courtoisie avez renom
Et de valeur toutes passé

Oeuvre de Dieu, digne, louée
Autant que nulle créature
De tous biens et vertus douée
Tant d'esperit que de nature.

It is easy to visualise the medieval type of feminine beauty from the literature of the time:

Elle a une chef blondet.
Yeux verts, bouche sadette,
Un corps pour embrasser,
Un gorge blanchette . . .

Je ne vis oncques fleur en branche
Par ma foi, qui fût aussi blanche
Comme est votre sade gorgette;

Les bras longuets, les doigts tretis (slender) . . .
Les pieds petits, orteils menus
Doivent être pour beaux tenus . . .
Vos yeux riants, à point fendus
Qui frémissent comme l'estelle
Par nuit emmi la fontenelle . . .

The charming wiles which the writer describes for us by many delicate touches (an art at which Chrestien de Troyes excelled) made of her an adorable being, all refinement, distinction and subtlety: the ruses of a shepherdess to avoid an encounter with her swain, the artifices of a lady in feigning anger or pride in order the better to allure the knight who courted her.

And, to enhance still further the charm of such pictures, the dual nature of the eternal feminine was emphasised more strongly during the Middle Ages than in any other period: besides the Virgin, the woman who was honoured and respected, whom one could not approach without trembling, and for whom one died of love, there was Eve, the temptress, Eve by whom the world was lost. Story-tellers, poets and writers of *fabliaux* were not sparing in their sarcasms:

Femme ne pense mal, ni nonne, ni béguine
Ne que (no more than) *fait le renard qui happe la géline*

She displayed her charms only to make her subsequent betrayal more dastardly:

La douce rien qui fausse amie a nom.

Coquettish and corrupt, her smiles served only to torment the simple soul who allowed himself to be deceived by them:

Trop est fou qui tant s'y fie
Qu'il ne s'en peut departir

Nothing but grief and disillusionment were in store for him for:

Femme est tôt changée

. . . *Ci rit, ci va pleurant*

. . . *Pour décevoir fut née.*

Cruel and merciless, she was not moved by any entreaties or any suffering, and like *La Belle Dame sans Merci*, she gave only cold indifference in return for the most impassioned stanzas. She was greedy and selfish:

Femme convoite avoir plus que miel ne fait ourse:
Tant vous aimera femme comme avez rien en bourse.

In the home she made life unbearable for her unfortunate husband, and deceived him shamelessly. If she ran away he was only too glad to assist her—as was the poet Vaillant:

Bonnes gens, j'ai perdu ma dame
Qui la trouvera, par mon âme
De très bon coeur je la lui donne
. . . *Car, par Dieu, la gente mignonne*
Est à chacun douce personne.

However, pure or corrupt, scoffed at or adulated, woman dominated French literature during the Middle Ages as she dominated society:

Pour femme donne l'on maint don
Et controuve mainte chanson;
Maints fols en sont devenus sages,
Homme bas monté en parage,
Hardi en deviendrait couard,
Et large qui sut être avare.

It was she who inspired songs and fired the heroes of romance, she who moved the troubadours to sighs and passion. Poems were dedicated to her; for her, beautiful and richly illuminated manuscripts were limned. She was the sun, the rhyme and reason of all poetry.

Women were, moreover, poets themselves. Fables and lays written by Marie de France delighted the barons of

Champagne and of England. Women sometimes earned a livelihood by writing, as in the case of Christine de Pisan. They did not have to overcome the contempt aroused in recent times by the 'blue-stockings', perhaps because they avoided the faults of the latter and were able to retain a truly feminine charm. The Middle Ages was the great period for women, and if there was one sphere in particular where their influence was apparent, it was in the literary field.

That again was very French. The French had already gained a reputation for being the most gallant of peoples, and French manners were the model for all Europe. No civilisation placed the feminine ideal higher, or showed itself more anxious to honour this ideal. In the Germanic countries, man always played the leading role, from Siegfried to Werther; doubtless women such as Kriemhild did not have what was needed to captivate a knight and arouse in him those sentiments of mingled love and gallantry which originated in France and which were called chivalry.

All the great distinguishing features of French literature are essentially French, but this literature is, besides, a mirror of the country's many provinces. Picards with their bluff vigour, natives of Champagne with their shrewd smiles, wily Normans, Provence folk and men from Languedoc with their warm speech, melodious as their poetry—all the subtle diversity of the land found expression. There is an infinite variety in this literature which the text-books offer us in one solid shapeless mass. Every provincial could find his soul somewhere in it, and his familiar countryside and the accent of his part of France—this sometimes quite literally, as in this little piece by Conon de Béthune, where the poet complains that people have been laughing at his Picard accent:

Encor ne soit ma parole françoise
Si la peut-on bien entendre en françois
Et cil ne sont bien appris ni courtois
Qui m'ont repris, si j'ai dit mot d'Artois,
Car je ne fus pas nourri à Pontoise . . .

After the sixteenth century, more or less, French literary works wore a uniform which, however magnificent, cannot obliterate the memory of the dazzling patchwork of medieval poetry. The *langue d'oc* and the *langue d'oil*, the dialects of Poitou and Provence, Norman and Burgundian *patois*—all these were translated into poetry, each found its own Mistral, capable of revealing their richness and of expressing the spirit of the homeland in its own dialect. It is important to see medieval literature in the light of those thousand different aspects of the French provinces, to understand these thousand aspects and to realise all that literature can reveal of the French genius; Joinville or Gace Brulé on Champagne, Jean Bodel or Adam de la Halle on Artois, Beaumanoir on the Ile-de-France, the troubadours on the Midi of Languedoc and Provence.

★

In the inexhaustible multiplicity of its forms and in its very marked individuality, medieval poetry drew its inspiration primarily from humanity itself and contained the eternal themes of all poetry.

Wonderingly it had gazed at the world and the creatures therein, the song of birds, the murmurings of forest trees, gushing streams and the magic of moonlit nights:

> *En avril au temps pascour*
> *Que sur l'herbe nait la flour,*
> *L'alouette au point du jour*
> · *Chante par moult grand baudour*

Pour la douceur du temps nouvel.
Si me levai par un matin
J'ouis chanter sur l'arbrissel
Un oiselet en son latin.

Such awareness of nature and its perpetual miracle, such
tender yearnings at the re-birth of the trees in spring, at
the freshness of the morning dew and the splendour of the
sunset, quickened medieval literature with the great breath
of life:

Le nouveau temps et mai et violette
Et rossignol me semont de chanter.

Kindly and ever astonishing Nature, the wildflowers
wreathed by Nicolette, the branches of honeysuckle to
which Tristan compared his love, the green groves to
which the despairing lover of *La Belle Dame Sans Merci*
betook himself—those fields, those gardens and those
streams, exquisitely depicted by the limners, were not less
deeply appreciated by the story-tellers and the poets. With
a word they could evoke landscapes, seasons, the shade of
an olive tree, the tender grass which 'grows green when
the rain falls.'

Et la mauvis qui commence à tentir
Et le doux son du ruissel sur gravelle.

Their vision was direct, their style simple but always evocative; even La Fontaine appears not to have had any more
happy inspiration than the writers of the Middle Ages,
those passionate devotees of nature and the open air.

After them, this tremulous consciousness of universal
life disappeared from French literature. Ronsard's lament
for the forests of Gastine was inspired only by the nymphs
with which Antiquity had peopled them, and ended with
philosophical reflections; and if the Fountain of Bellerie
inspired a poem, it was only because Horace had addressed
an ode to the Fountain of Bandusia. Save for very rare

exceptions, we have to wait for the Romanticists in order to find—this time accompanied by a rather irritating sentimentality—similar excursions into the vast realms of nature. In our own time, Apollinaire and Francis Jammes have rediscovered this sharpened awareness of the life which surrounds us; it is a contact which was lost, but in modern French literature this breeze laden with the scents of forest and plain, mountains and sea, blows once again—a fresh wind which has come to France, thanks largely to foreign novelists, Knut Hamsum among others; and this same sense of landscape and atmosphere is regained for us in *Le Grand Meaulnes*. For it is not lofty philosophisings in the manner of Jean-Jacques Rousseau, or Lamartinian effusions, which constitute a love of nature—but rather direct observations of everyday life, factual jottings on a day of fine rain or a glorious morning spent on the edge of a stream—simple descriptions of a particular detail—a wall covered with ivy, a rose in a bouquet, the flight of a raven above a field of corn, a lilac grove in a Touraine garden—which remain linked in the memory with hours of joy or anguish, which lend an individual character to events in a human life, which perfect the harmony of an instant of beauty.

But the great theme of medieval poetry was love. All the aspects, all the shades of human love were evoked in turn, from the most brutal passion to the subtleties of amorous rhetoric so dear to the troubadours. One can say, without hesitation, that no other literature had such riches or lent such wings to the human heart. From the very noble love of Guibourc, which could not tolerate that the loved one should be inferior to itself for even an instant, to the shameful love of La Belle Heaulmière, there is not a sigh, not a kiss, not a desire which poets and novelists did not catch in mid flight and render faithfully in writing.

There were the simple fresh loves of the shepherds and shepherdesses, of Robin and Marion, which, however, were soon to lose their sincerity and become a purely literary theme:

> *Chevalier, par Saint Simon,*
> *N'ai cure de compagnon.*
> *Par ci passent Guérinet et Robeçon*
> *Qui oncques ne me requirent si bien non.*

But, as malicious wit was never absent in the Middle Ages, many a shepherdess, after threatening a knight with her staff, finally allowed herself to succumb to his charm:

> *Ma belle, pour Dieu merci!*
> *Elle rit, si répondit:*
> *Ne faites, pour la gent!*

There was the glory of conjugal love, as sung by Villon in the splendid ballad to Robert d'Estouteville, where all that makes up the nobility and beauty of marriage is to be found expressed with simplicity and facility, and a mastery of language and thought which approaches perfection:

> '*Princesse, oyez ce que ci vous résume:*
> *Que le mien coeur du vôtre désassemble*
> *Jà ne sera; tant de vous en présume,*
> *Et c'est la fin pour quoi sommes ensemble.*'

Besides these serene and gentle pages, the accents of desire are heard as in this poem by Guiot de Dijon, where there is expressed, with burning sensuality, all the anguish of unassuaged desire:

> *Sa chemise qu'ot vêtue*
> *M'envoya pour embracier.*
> *La nuit, quand s'amour m'arguë,*
> *La mets avec moi coucher*
> *Moult étroit à ma chair nue.*

And sometimes, too, separation, no less bitter, is felt more chastely; never has the poignant pain of a distant love been more movingly described than in these lines of Jaufre Rudel; a solution to the enigma of these verses was long sought, yet they are in reality very clear: they are bursting with repressed yearnings and impossible desires and the bitter consciousness of a past beyond recall which suddenly tarnishes all the joy of a summer's day:

> *Si que chants et fleurs d'aubespis*
> *N'om platz plus que l'hiver gelatz.*

Each of these poems must be savoured word by word, if one is to understand what riches were extracted from this wealth of material. Generally, when one thinks of the Middle Ages, one's mind turns to chivalrous love, which is visualised in the form of a 'gentle lady', a knight fighting in tournaments and a few additional embellishments. Nothing could be farther from the period than such insipidity. Without doubt, flirtation was known and appreciated —flirtation in the French style, pleasure in saying and hearing pretty things, sweet nothings and romantic phrases, the delicious banter of light-hearted courtship and half-serious refusals:

> '*Surpris suis d'une amourette*
> *Dont tout le coeur me volette* . . .
> *Hélas, ma Dame et si fière*
> *Et de si dure manière*
> *Ne veut ouir ma prière*
> *Ni chose que je lui quière*
> *Ayez merci douce amie*
> *De moi qui de coeur vous prie.*

Jean le Seneschal, in his ballads which present a panorama of love, does not fail to mention these conceits of chivalry:

Jà votre coeur ne s'ébahisse
Si priez damoiselle ou dame
Qui raidement vous escondisse:
Tôt se rapaisera, par m'âme,
Donnez en à Amour le blâme
En lui priant que vous pardonne . . .
Puis l'embrassez secrètement . . .

Thibaut de Champagne, Guy d'Ussel and many others wrote charming works of this type, where nothing mattered but the graceful sentiment and the easy flow of the verses; people found delight in flirtations, in feminine wiles, or in the awakening of a heart to coquetry. Chrestien de Troyes showed an incomparable skill in describing the thousand little intrigues, tricks and jealousies of women who wished to captivate men and deceive each other; with some writers this developed into a literary and purely verbal device, which is, moreover, not without interest:

Qui n'auroit d'autre déport
En aimer
Fors Doux Penser
Et Souvenir
Avec l'espoir de jouir,
S'auroit-il tort
Si le port
D'autre confort
Voulait trouver.
Car pour un cœur saouler
Et soutenir,
Plus quérir
Ne doit mérir
Qui aime fort.
Encor y a maint ressort:
Remembrer,

THE FALL OF BABYLON
(*early Thirteenth Century*)

Imaginer
En doux plaisir,
Sa dame veoir, ouïr,
Son gentil port,
Le recort
De son parler
Et de son doux regarder
Dont l'entr'ouvrir
Peut guérir
Et garantir
Amant de mort.

This chivalry was, without doubt, one of the beauties of the Middle Ages—chivalry which knew only nobility of heart, delicacy of sentiment and mystical respect for Woman. But to believe that in such a period of intense life no more profound or more passionate notes were sounded, would be pure absurdity. Sometimes in the very midst of amorous rhetoric there is expressed with a poignant sincerity all the anguish of a heart in despair. *La Belle Dame sans Merci* by Alain Chartier is a striking example of this—a poem where the principal theme recurs constantly, where the rejoinders follow one another with relentless cruelty and which is as much a lament as a dialogue. This poem is one of the masterpieces of poetry of all time, by its restrained passion, its lucidity in grief and by the implacable logic of a love without hope:

A.   *Vos yeux ont si empreint leur merche*
En mon cœur, que, quoiqu'il advienne,
Si j'ai l'honneur où je le cherche
Il convient que de vous me vienne.
Fortune a voulu que je tienne
Ma vie en votre merci close:
Si est bien droit qu'il me souvienne
De votre honneur sur toute chose.

L

D.   *A votre honneur seul entendez,*
        Pour votre temps mieux employer;
        Du mien à moi vous attendez
        Sans prendre peine à foloyer;
        Bon fait craindre et supployer
        Un cœur follement déceü
        Car rompre vaut mieux que ployer,
        Et ébranlé mieux que cheü.

A.   *Pensez, ma dame, que depuis*
        Qu'Amour mon cœur vous délivra
        Il ne pourroit, ni je ne puis
        Etre autrement tant qu'il vivra:
        Tout quitte et franc le vous livra;
        Ce don ne se peut abolir.
        J'attends ce qu'il s'en ensuivra.
        Je n'y puis mettre ni tollir.

D.   *Je ne tiens mie pour donné*
        Ce qu'on offre à qui ne le prend;
        Car le don est abandonné
        Si le donneur ne le reprend.
        Trop a de cœur qui entreprend
        D'en donner à qui le refuse,
        Mais il est sage, qui apprend
        A s'en retraire, qu'il n'y muse.

A.   *Ah! cœur plus dur que le noir marbre,*
        En qui merci ne peut entrer,
        Plus fort à ployer qu'un gros arbre,
        Que vous vaut tel rigueur montrer?
        Vous plaît-il mieux me voir outrer
        Mort devant vous par votre ébat
        Que pour un confort démontrer
        Respirer la mort qui m'abat?

D.   *Mon cœur ni moi ne vous feïmes*
Oncq rien dont plaire vous doyez
Rien ne vous nuit fors que vous-mêmes:
De vous-mêmes juge soyez.
Une fois pour toutes croyez
Que vous demeurez escondit.
De tant redire m'ennuyez
Car je vous en ai assez dit . . .

And what literature offers a more perfect or more moving example of tragic lovers than Tristan and Iseult? Has there ever been a more powerful or more exquisite conception of two beings vowed to each other without hope, living only through their mutual love? 'Neither you without me, nor I without you'—heart-breaking passion, soberly expressed, violent contrasts, Tristan reduced to a clown's role, Iseult sure of her lover, but tortured by jealousy; wild chaste loves, pangs of remorse and separation:

Je suis Tantris qui tant l'aimai
Et aimerai tant com vivrai
—Anuit fûtes ivre au coucher
Et l'ivresse vous fit rêver!
—Voir est: d'itel boivre suis ivre (it is true: I am drunk of
          a wine such that I think I will never recover)
Dont je ne cuide être délivre . . .
Le roi l'entend et si s'en rit,
et dit au fol: Si Dieu t'aït,
si je te donnais la reïne
en hoir, et la mette en saisine,
or me dis que tu en ferois
ou en quel part tu la menrois? (take)
—Roi, fait le fol, là sus en l'air
ai une salle où je repair(e);
de verre est faite, belle et grand;
le soleil va parmi rayant,

en l'air est, et par nuées pend,
ne berce et ne croule pour vent.
Delez la salle a une chambre
faite de cristal et de lambre;
le soleil, quand main (in the morning) *lèvera,*
céans moult grand clarté rendra . . .

Never did a poet's inspiration range so widely, never has human love found truer or more heart-felt expression.

Many other lovers too, such as Launcelot and Guinevere, retain amid the transports of their pleasure, a sense of honour, of uprightness, and of respect due to their sovereign whom in spite of themselves, they are betraying. How human, too, are those sudden wild moments, revealed, for example, in the strange story of *La Fille du Comte de Ponthieu*, in which a young woman, violated before the eyes of her husband, turns on him when her torturers leave her and tries to kill him before he can free himself of his shackles—being unable to bear seeing him after the great shame she has undergone in his sight. The Middle Ages are typically represented in these cries of grief and passion, in the violent emotions of the sensitive soul—here too is the ardent, direct and unforgettable poetry which, once one has tasted of it, holds one in its enchantment like the love-potion drunk, inadvertently, by its two most moving heroes.

Other themes—primarily war—lent a virile note to inspiration. The man who claimed that the French did not have any talent for the epic did not know the Middle Ages. No literature is more epic than the French. Not only does it begin with the *Chanson de Roland*—one of the summits of epic poetry and one whose beauty, it seems, has not yet been fully appreciated—but it includes more than a hundred other works which are its peers and which are also an El Dorado yet to be explored. All, or nearly all, show the same simplicity in greatness, and the same sense of imagery which made the author of the *Chanson de Roland* one of the great poets of all time. This simple, unadorned style of the Middle Ages is characteristic of the French epic, in which a hero was not half god, but a man, whose warlike valour did not preclude human weaknesses. Despite all Virgil's art, Aeneas seems a pale figure and his psychology very sketchy beside Roland or Guillaume d'Orange—human beings, full of contradictions, whose courage led them sometimes to inordinate conceit, sometimes to humility; sometimes to overconfidence, sometimes to despondency. This accuracy of observation saved the French epic from becoming what it might otherwise have been: a monotonous parade of heroic individuals and marvellous exploits. Valour was esteemed above all things, even in one's enemies or in traitors, and, with it, a sense of honour and fidelity to the feudal bond; but so much high-mindedness might well have become wearisome without the lights and shades which enriched the characters and brought them to life. That is why, however little one knows the *Chanson de Roland*—the only French epic poem honoured in the school-books—its heroes leave so vivid an impression on one's imagination. Roland, valiant but rash, Turpin, the pious archbishop and warrior, Oliver the Wise and Charles, the great and powerful Emperor who is, nevertheless, full of pity for his murdered barons and, sometimes, overcome by the burden of his 'troublous' life. The storyteller evoked all his characters by means of pictures, of actions, one might say, not by descriptions. His story comes straight to the point and his stage directions are confined to a bare minimum, to details which one can see and which stimulate visually: Roland's white banner, with its gold fringe descending to his knees, fixes him more firmly against the background of the resplendent beauty of his retinue than would any minute descriptions in the modern manner. The deeds and exploits of the heroes, their thoughts and pre-occupations, are thus expressed by visual notation, by clear swift touches with an infinite artistry in the choice of vivid detail. In the same way, in real life it is not the general order and composition of a procession which impresses one, but a certain silhouette, one predominant colour, the gleam of brass or the sound of a drum; it is the sparks that fly from the bright helmets during the fray, the carbuncles glittering on the mast trucks of the Saracen fleet or the glove which Roland offers to God in repentance and which is taken by the Archangel Gabriel—that conjure up a picture.

What has disconcerted literary circles in the medieval epics is the total absence of the analytical methods to which classical literature has accustomed us: no narrative accounts but direct action; no development of character but encounters; no dissertations but deeds, colours, 'snapshots.' Only lack of imagination has been seen in what was in fact a great power of evocation. Some modern techniques—for example, that of the cinema—have made us familiar with this translation of thought into terms of pictures, and we can savour these masterpieces which now belong to the spirit of the times. Hitherto, their intrinsic beauty had been resolutely ignored in favour of the discussion of problems which did not in fact arise, and which would have appeared very trivial to medieval minds: in particular, the question of the sources of the epics and their historical value. Were there originally one or several poems on the *Coronation of Louis?* Who was, in reality, Guillaume d'Orange?—and so on. It is surely time to take these masterpieces for what they are: stories in which the historical inspiration was no more than a pretext, and the sole aim to charm or to stir the audience, according to the fancy of the author or the taste of his public. The essential was that they should be beautiful, and that they are. Beautiful and marvellously varied: we have already pointed out how, of the two oldest French epics, one was sublime and the other comic. Elsewhere, in the *Charroi de Nîmes*, for example, these two types overlap; and nowhere does humour not have its place, the grandeur of certain scenes being always enhanced by the burlesque or comic fantasy of others. Here is Shakespeare, before the printed word.

Besides epic poetry, war has also inspired a number of literary works, troubadours' songs, chronicles, narrative poems, not to mention the innumerable duels and tournaments of romantic literature. Everywhere it was evoked with the same simplicity; everywhere the same admiration was manifested for valour and skill and a sense of what we call fair play, which made of it a fine game in which hitting below the belt was prohibited or at least frowned upon, where courage, even misguided courage, was always respected, and where chivalry was esteemed above all else. Launcelot, triumphant, bows before his suzerain whom he has unseated and assists him to remount; Joinville makes a shield of his own body for his king, Saint Louis. There was always some act of mercy, some echo of pity to redeem the excesses of war and its scenes of carnage and cruelty which were, however, not lacking.

The men of the Middle Ages looked on death in much the same way. There is no doubt that in no other period has death been considered with so much sober courage or such unembittered lucidity. Villon's lines on this subject come immediately to mind:

> *La mort le fait frémir, pâlir,*
> *Le nez courber, les veines tendre*
> *Le col enfler, la chair mollir*
> *Joinctes et nerfs croître et étendre*

> *Et meure Pâris ou Hélène*
> *Quiconque meurt, meurt à douleur;*
> *Celui qui perd vent et haleine*
> *Son fiel se crève sur son cœur*
> *Puis sue: Dieu sait quelle sueur* . . .

Many other poets have spoken with this sharp realism, this gift of powerful evocation and this same impressive calm:

> *Mort qui saisis les terres franches*
> *Qui fait ta queuz* [38] *des gorges blanches*
> *Pour ton rasoirr affiler,*
> *Qui l'arbre plein de fruits ébranches*
> *Que le riche n'ait que filer,*
> *Qui par long mal le sais piler,*
> *Qui lui ôtes au pont les planches,*
> *Dis moi à ceux d'Angivillers*
> *Que tu fais t'aiguille enfiler*
> *Dont tu leur veux coudre les manches* . . .

A great serenity in suffering was shown in the deaths in battle of warrior-heroes, in the harrowing death of Tristan and the pious death of Vivian—though these are described with force enough to make one shudder.

Besides these universal themes, there are others, peculiar to the literature of the Middle Ages. For example, the supernatural. There is a superabundance of imaginative creation: the real world and its treasures were not enough for the storytellers' energies: they had to draw on phantasmagoria and strew the lives of their heroes with prodigies. Often these imaginary details were merely masks concealing great truths. Allegory comes within this class: one can consider these evocations of abstract qualities as artificial—for instance, the fashion of holding debates between Sweet Thoughts and Insincerity, or of invoking Hope and inveighing against Doubt and Treason. It was, in any case,

[38] Grindstone

a sign of the wonderful life which animated medieval literature and gave a soul, a body and a tongue to all things, even the most abstract. We have already observed the taste of the period for everything concrete, personal and visible. The allegorical form, which is so curiously allied to the worship of images, is yet another manifestation of this preference. Should it be despised *a priori?* Allegory seems to be no more than the transposition of an invisible world to a newly selected position. For it is, in fact, not very far from the '*débats*' in which the Middle Ages delighted, to the tricks of the subconscious to which in our own time we attach names which are more precise but less poetic: repressions, guilt complexes, the sub-conscious reflexes and reactions of the human organism.

The element of the miraculous had no less deep a significance: enchanted fountains which gushed forth at the feet of the knights, magic words to subdue the forces of nature, mysterious powers which led men to their destiny and which they obeyed without pausing to consider the consequences of their actions. There are numerous examples of this type of romantic literature—a style to which Chrestien de Troyes gave its most lofty expression. The greatness of Gawain and Perceval owed much to this fairy-tale sense of the miraculous which is, nevertheless, so human.

But there was, above all, deliberate imaginative creation— pleasure in heaping up marvels and in creating an impossible world, the taste for nonsense and burlesque, the magic horse of Cleomades, the comic jests and exploits of the peers in the *Pèlerinage de Charles*, the adventures of Merlin and Vivian, or of the dwarf Oberon. There, no obstacle was placed in the way of the fantastic, and half-joking, half-wondering creations followed on one another's heels at the whim of imagination run riot. It seems that no other period has brought forth so many strange imaginative productions or so many endless and incredible stories; the Middle Ages thoroughly enjoyed such things, and made full use of this faculty peculiar to man, of creating out of his brain a topsy-turvy world as far removed as possible from material reality; this was a mental exercise at which the Middle Ages excelled.

This taste for the absurd was combined with a concern for the most noble and sometimes the most moving themes: that of a search, for example, a 'quest,' which is one of the most fascinating subjects the literary domain has known, and one of the most significant for the understanding of a period which, in this respect, bears a striking resemblance to our own. The obsession of setting out in search of hidden treasure, the need to make discoveries, the burning desire to regain a lost love—all this is at once very medieval and very modern. Perceval is the forbear of Le Grand Meaulnes; and if many 'Petits' Meaulnes have since disgusted us a little with childhood dreams, the fact remains that this theme of a paradise lost, of a sacred mission to accomplish, a thirst to assuage, an uncertain groping towards a mysterious destination, finds a true echo in modern thought and literature. The Holy Grail, the goblet of a substance unknown to mortals, which all men sought but which only a pure heart could bring back, is still one of the most fascinating treasures of the Middle Ages. Its story has, of course, given rise to incredibly silly interpretations; firstly, the inevitable historical researches: analysis of origins, influences, etc.—when it is a matter of human verities not of an historical enigma. Some critics have gone so far as to show surprise at Perceval's behaviour in gazing speechless as the mysterious Grail passed, without daring to ask for any explanation concerning it. In this dread—which is, however, very natural and very true to life, the dread that seizes a man when he attains his goal, when the unhoped-for happens, when reality exceeds his ambitions and desires—critics have seen a poetic device to pad out a story which might otherwise have ended there! It is to be supposed, however, that such lack of understanding would not be possible in our own time, for the secret reactions of the human soul are more familiar to us and its inner workings have been more clearly revealed now than in the rational and romantic periods which preceded our own. Occultism and, to a certain extent, psycho-analysis, have rendered us a great service in this respect, despite the exaggerations and errors of both occultists and psycho-analysts. To see in Perceval or in Galahad mere novelette heroes, whose author has padded out his story by piling up the most complicated adventures possible, is to misunderstand one of the great creations of the human mind, one which incarnates that profound wisdom and that disconcerting boldness which are the attributes of the single-hearted.

In their own way, the quests of the knights errant also express this tendency which characterised the Middle Ages. It was natural that the wander-lust of those times should leave traces in the literature. Apart from the works of Chaucer, which are its most direct expression, it is to be found in the tales of adventure and in the literature of chivalry. The youth who is satisfied with familiar landscapes and feels no need to explore fresh horizons should have his eyes put out, roundly declares Philippe de Beaumanoir. The Middle Ages sang of the joy of setting out on journeys, as well as of the pain of separation:

> *N'en puis ma grand joie celer*
> *En Egypte vais aller*

runs an anonymous anthem of the twelfth century. Pilgrimages in all forms were as familiar in literature as in life itself, and provided, like everything else, material for jesting: the way in which they were sometimes abused inspired the author of the *Quinze joies de mariage* with a highly entertaining chapter.

Finally, there is one universal theme which became a medieval one: God. In direct opposition to the theory which the *Art Poétique* and the classics were subsequently to uphold, the Middle Ages drew on its faith as the purest source of all poetry. And, in fact, how could a believer, steeped in religious feeling, leave his very substance out of account in his poetic creation—which, more than any other, demands the participation of all man's faculties? To have disregarded religious feeling in poetry during this period of sincere faith would have amounted to nothing less than a mutilation of the man and a resulting abstraction and negation in the essentially positive realm of poetry —which was subsequently condemned to artificiality and insincerity. The thought of God is, moreover, inseparable from medieval poetry. From Roland's companions, calling on God as they fell in battle, to the knights of the *Jeu de Saint-Nicolas*, whose guardian angels welcomed them with great joy after their massacre by the Saracen army, from Beaumanoir's *Ave Maria* to the *Ballade que fit Villon à la requête de sa mère pour prier Notre-Dame*, it can be said that all forms of medieval piety passed one by one into literature.[93] As the Middle Ages had a special predilection

---

[39] The singular opinion expressed in this connection by M. Thierry Maulnier in his *Introduction à la poésie française* (in which, incidentally, the medieval period is totally misunderstood and neglected) causes one some surprise. According to this work, all French poetry instinctively followed Boileau's advice and knew no divinities other than those of mythology. M. Maulnier is compelled, however, to admit certain exceptions: 'Villon, d'Aubigné, Corneille and Racine,' he says, 'have produced Christian poems, but this was to pay for or to buy the right to produce others which were not.' It must be pointed out that it is hard to believe that Villon wrote the *Ballade des Pendus* solely to ensure that *La Belle Heaulmière* was accepted, or that Corneille wrote *Polyeucte* only to win forgiveness for *Horace*. It seems difficult, also, to eliminate all those who have spoken of a very Christian God

for the worship of the Virgin Mary, her gracious image—
'sweeter flower than the rose,'—was an inspiration in all
poetry, secular as much as religious. Does not Thibaut de
Champagne seek from her a cure for his love-sickness?

Quand dame perds, Dame me soit aidant!

Thus it is a fact that the medieval poet felt and thought
quite naturally as a Christian, even in his misdeeds and his
pleasures.

The Church, moreover, was a very great source of
inspiration at that time. It produced the first dramatic works
and stirred the crowds by incidents of the Passion of Christ
or the Miracles of Our Lady; it provided the minstrels with
the legends on which their stories were based—not to mention the countless liturgical prose works, sequences and
hymns which emanated directly from the clergy and which,
by the variety of their cadences and the richness of their
rhythms, hold a place of honour in the French poetical
heritage. Take, for example, the Whitsuntide sequence
attributed by some to Pope Innocent III and by others to
King Robert the Pious:

Veni sancte Spiritus
Et emitte celitus
Lucis tue radium . . .
In labore requies
In estu temperies
In fletu solacium . . .

or this admirable Traveller's Prayer, written in simple prose
yet cunningly cadenced:

. . . esto nobis, Domine,
in procinctu suffragium

(even if only to blaspheme his name) and to cross off with a single
stroke of the pen, not only all the Romantics, but Baudelaire, Rimbaud,
Verlaine, Péguy, Claudel, Francis Jammes and many young modern
poets. In any case, medieval poetry as a whole flatly contradicts this
theory.

in via solacium
in estu umbraculum
in pluvia et frigore tegumentum
in lassitudine vehiculum
in adversitate presidium
in lubrico baculus
in naufragio portus
ut, te duce, quo tendimus/prospere perveniamus
ac demum incolumes/ad propria redeamus . . .

The very great art of liturgical poetry (the verses composed by Saint Thomas Aquinas for the Feast of the Holy Sacrament are true masterpieces) is completed by the Gregorian Chants which give to the Latin phrases and syllables their full value, bringing out their sonorous quality. The monks of Solesmes, in making these treasures of sacred music known to the public by means of recorded versions, also revealed to the world a very pure fountain of poetry.

A simple outline of medieval literature permits one to correct certain prejudices on the subject of French writing. The alleged poverty of French lyrical production is more a reality than the alleged poverty of the French epic. If the poetic vein was sometimes found to be exhausted, as a result of the shackles by which inspiration was bound, it is none the less true that the first centuries of French literature produced a galaxy of lyric poets who can bear comparison with those of any other nation and are inferior perhaps only to those of England, the chosen land of the lyric until modern times. But the best French lyrical poets are unknown to the public and will remain so until the people make an effort to understand and until publishers and educationalists attempt a work of adaptation.[40]

[40] An *Anthologie de la poésie lyrique du Moyen Age* (Editions du Chêne) attempts to make some of these poets accessible to the public by lessening the linguistic difficulties.

Only an effort of this nature would allow us finally to become aware of the past and its glories—glories of thought and of expression. For medieval literature is as rich in literary forms as it is in literary themes. Every imaginable poetical form is represented: the drama, the novel, history, the epic; above all, lyrical poetry presents unbelievably varied aspects: narrative and romantic tales, the lays for which Marie de France was renowned, stories in mingled verse and prose as, for example, the delicious *Aucassin et Nicolette*, pastoral poems and *rondeaux*, tensons and virelays, songs for dancing, weaving songs, anthems and ballads; the variety of form is equalled only by the variety of rhythm and verse. This was adapted to the type of writing: for the epic the decasyllable was usually employed, but in lyric poetry lines of twelve, ten, eight or seven syllables were used in turn, with refrains of four or six feet. It can be said that only the cadence demanded by the general tone of the poem and the sentiments to be expressed governed the writing of verse, and the framework of the lines, the caesura, and the accentuation were more important than the end-syllable, rhyme or assonance.

In fact, this apparent liberty concealed great technical knowledge and, generally, great technical skill. We have not yet been able fully to appreciate the art of the old French poets and the ease with which they worked in the midst of difficulties. The facile rhythms represented, in fact, masterly composition. Certain of the troubadours' poems, with verses made up uniformly with the same end-syllables, testify to an astonishing virtuosity, which one finds in Villon, in Alain Chartier and, in general, in the poets of the fifteenth century who brought this technique to perfection. Such are the ballads with re-echoing rhymes of which Christine de Pisan has left more than one example:

Fleur de beauté en valeur souverain
Raim de bonté, plante de toute grâce,
Grâce d'avoir sur tous le prix à plein
Plein de savoir et qui tous maux efface,
Face plaisant, corps digne de louange,
Ange au semblant où il n'a que redire . . .

Et j'ai espoir qu'il soit en votre main
Maints jours et nuits, en gracieux space,
Passe le temps, car jà bien hautain
Atteint par vous, et Amour qui m'enlace
Lasse mon cœur qui du vôtre est échange . . .

These are mere rhyming gymnastics, but they reveal
surprising skill. In the same way, the refrain is taken up
again from one verse to the other:

. . . Si te supplie sur toute chose
Prie le qu'il ait de moi merci.

Merci requiers à jointes mains
A toi, trésorière de grâces . . .

In another class there are the countless acrostics, anagrams,
and various other pastimes which, while not belonging to
the poetic heritage properly speaking, yet reveal that love
of verbal perfection and fine language which was common
to all the Middle Ages. Charles d'Orléans proved himself
a prince of poets in this art by his impeccable mastery of
both language and rhyme which was achieved under cover
of a seeming nonchalance. Every one of his exquisite little
pieces, alternately melancholy, gay or jovial, gives proof
of a highly refined artistry.

It must be said that, in these technical matters, the
exceptional flexibility of the French language in the Middle
Ages was of assistance. It was much richer than to-day, for
it had not yet undergone those unfortunate purges of which

it has since been the victim and it lent itself admirably to poetic devices and elegances. As in our own days, there was no distinction between the aristocratic style and the vernacular. The language was especially enriched by the whole gamut of technical terms which formed an inexhaustible reservoir of images of which later centuries have been deprived. It was easy to form compound words, to employ infinitives as nouns and to make use of dialect and local expressions. Thus, an abundantly vigorous language was evolved, capable of being adapted with felicity and daring to the subtleties of the poetic art. The Middle Ages, in particular, made the most of verbal enchantment and the value of a well-chosen word or a happy linguistic discovery was fully appreciated. One finds also pure conjuring with words, when they are strung together haphazard as, for instance, in the extraordinary *Fatras* which were produced by no other process than the 'automatism' to which modern surrealists have had recourse: each word suggests another and the poet allows himself to be led by the successive pictures and sounds, uninfluenced by coherent thought or logic:

> *Le chant d'une raine*
> *Saine une baleine*
> *Au fond de la mer*
> *Et une sirène*
> *Si emportait Seine*
> *Dessus Saint-Omer.*
> *Un muet y vint chanter*
> *Sans mot dire à haute haleine* . . .

These are merely verbal gymnastics, but are not devoid of a certain contemporary interest for us.

This sense of word values, moreover, and this feeling for the cadence of a sentence, extended beyond the literary domain. In the Middle Ages all language—the Paris street

M

cries equally with the sailors' shanties—showed an appreciation of rhythm which has reappeared in our own time in the form of the advertising slogan. Laws, judicial formulæ and proverbs—for example, those collected by Antoine Loisel—all showed a feeling for a striking phrase, and a spontaneous and direct character which prove clearly that this felicity of expression sprang from a natural ability, attributable, perhaps, to the fact that the intellect had not yet absorbed the other faculties to its own advantage, or classified verbal statement, along with everything else. All the expressions which have come down to us and which are still current, though their noble origin is seldom realised—'*neiges d'antan*,' '*être comme l'oiseau sur la branche*,' or '*comme chien et loup*,' '*manger son blé en herbe*,' '*ni chair ni poisson*,' etc.—turns of phrase which, whether used poetically or colloquially are always expressive, testify to a very lively instinct for the value of words.

OUR era, which has finally rid itself of the last vestiges of classical prejudice and over which the dogma of antiquity has no further hold, is better equipped than any other to understand medieval art: no one to-day would think of objecting to the green camels of the *Psautier de Saint-Louis,* and modern artists have made us understand that, in order to give an impression of harmony, a work of art should not ignore geometry and decorations should be in keeping with architecture.

Medieval art is easier for us to appreciate than the literature of the same age, because we can enjoy it directly: we have learned to examine its traces stone by stone in cathedrals and museums scattered over Europe. Technical progress in photography has allowed us to know wonders which were hidden away in illuminated manuscripts and which, until recently, only a few of the initiated could enjoy; it has even proved possible to reproduce the colours with extraordinary fidelity—in, for instance, such admirable publications as the review *Verve,* or those of the Editions du Chêne or de Cluny, among others. As our knowledge of medieval art has grown, so we have lost our taste for the pseudo-medieval: Gothic art of the eighteenth century, such as Orléans Cathedral (unfortunately extolled by the Romantics as a model of the style), over-enthusiastic restorations and the chimeras and gargoyles which were abused so deplorably in the ornamentation of the last century, or sentimental theories culled from the *Génie du Christianisme* on the origins of the cathedrals of France. Our present vision is at once truer and more æsthetically genuine.

What stands out most clearly is the synthetic character of medieval art: its scenes, personages and monuments appear to have been created in one piece, for they vibrate with life and express forcefully the feeling of action they are required to interpret. Every work at this time was, in its own way, a whole, a powerful unity, but one in which under cover of what appeared to be pure fantasy, a host of elements played a part, each cleverly subordinated to the other: its strength derived primarily from the sense of order which governed its creation. Art, even more than genius, was the reward of long patience.

Contrary to what one might believe from the imaginative fancy which seemed to rule his inspiration, the artist was far from free; he obeyed exterior and technical requirements which governed his work step by step. The Middle Ages were not acquainted with Art for Art's Sake, and every artistic creation was then determined by the use to which it was to be put. It was, in fact, in the usefulness of such works that the chief source of their beauty lay, for this consisted of a perfect harmony between the object and the purpose for which it was designed. Thus, the most common-place objects of that time now appear to us as clothed in veritable beauty: ewers, cauldrons and tankards which are now given a place of honour in museums, have often no other merit than that of being perfectly suited to the need they supplied. On another plane, also, the medieval artist was concerned primarily with the purpose of his creations. A church was a place of prayer and if the architecture of the medieval cathedrals varied according to times and provinces, this was because it was bound up so closely with the requirements of the local worshippers. Not a chapel, not a window was placed haphazardly, or added out of pure caprice. In the same way, in civil and military architecture all the details of a turret or of a battlemented tower were designed to facilitate defence and were modified as offensive weapons evolved. It might be said that the chief factor in art was expediency.

Next, there were technical requirements. Materials, first of all, were the objects of minute research: the wood, parchment, alabaster and stone which the artist was to use were all subjected to the appropriate preparation. Thus it was that only the heart-wood—the strongest part—was employed in medieval buildings, which were, for this reason, extremely light and yet strong enough to stand up to any strain. French forests could not provide such fine wood at the present time and it is strange to pass from the old part of, for example, Notre Dame, where the light beams support the roof of the building with ease, to the new part where one finds very heavy beams which are, nevertheless, more vulnerable to the havoc wreaked by the passing of time and by insects. It has been pointed out that there were no spiders in these ancient buildings because neither worms nor flies could settle there. The sculptor, according to the use he wished to make of the stone, either fashioned it straight away in the quarry or, on the other hand, left it to give up its moisture before going to work on it. The tapestry-maker took great pains in the choosing of his wools and silks and the painter in the selection of his colours. Work was thus preceded by meticulous preparation, by a veritable genesis, in the process of which the creation was rehearsed and adapted exactly to suit the style chosen. The position of the work of art also became a matter for similar consideration. A sculptor was always concerned with the angle from which his statue was to be seen—those placed on the top of Rheims cathedral, which are strangely ugly when they are brought down from their pedestals, take on all their beauty when they are seen in perspective from the foot of the building.

There were, moreover, traditional obligations which the artist could not allow himself to disregard and which formed a very rigid framework for his inspiration. In religious art, for example, certain unvarying attributes were assigned to every scene: the Angel and the Virgin of the Annunciation, the Holy Family and the animals of the Nativity, the apostle, the two disciples and the women of grace of the Descent from the Cross; the Christ of the Last Judgment always wore a halo and was surrounded by the symbols of the four evangelists; Saint Paul held a sword in his hand and Saint Peter the Keys of Heaven. None of these subjects allowed the artist much latitude and yet, by a strange feat of genius, there are not two faces among the countless procession of medieval Virgins which are alike. Artists were able, within the narrow limits assigned them, to avoid stereotyped creations and conventional classical poses. Their workmanship, which generally remained anonymous, was always highly individual. In order to obtain this originality in the interpretation of the most commonplace scenes, and to create real beings where it would have been so easy to be satisfied with types, an extraordinary vigour of temperament and imagination was necessary. Academism made its appearance in art at precisely the same moment when inspiration seemed to be hemmed in no longer, when religious art was becoming less and less traditional and liturgical and secular art was ranging more and more widely.

Apart from technical requirements properly speaking, there was the particular visual approach peculiar to each art form and this was highly specialised in the Middle Ages. A certain order, a characteristic harmony, belonged to each branch of activity: a tapestry was not the same as a picture, a stained-glass window was different from a painting, the laws of perspective were different in each case. Directly the tapestry-makers and master glass-workers began to imitate painters and to try to work in multiple planes, by means of colours or by copying architectural forms, the decadence of their art set in. Similarly, the goldsmith should not imitate the worker in ivory or the enamellist the limner. Each should be aware in planning his work, of the beauty inherent in the material with which he is working, and conform to its individual perspective, composition and idea, instead of tending towards uniformity and imitation. Subsequently a certain confusion was introduced among the different art forms and this explains the decadence of the minor arts. Sometimes also it was excessive zeal in the attaining of technical skill which precipitated decadence. An example of this is provided for us by the evolution of the stained glass window: in those of the twelfth and thirteenth centuries, primary colours were used, the panes of glass were thick and uneven, full of blisters and impurities through which the light played, and they were held in place by leads which were thicker than they were broad and set off the designs without making them appear heavy; but when this mosaic of coloured glass was replaced by painting on glass, when, instead of a red-hot iron a diamond was used for cutting, which gave a cleaner, more regular edge and demanded much wider leads, then windows ceased to be vivid marquetry: the light showed uniformly through the thinner, better-made panes and soon they were no more than dull, lustreless coloured glass. This corresponded, moreover, to the prevailing tastes of the different periods: the eighteenth century, in its hatred of colour, went so far as to replace the beautiful stained-glass windows of the Middle Ages, which had almost all remained intact, with panes of clear glass.

The medieval artist acquired the visual approach proper to his art in the course of a long apprenticeship. Raoul Dufy has pointed out that there was nothing dramatic then between inspiration and its expression; he adds: 'Is it not true that our problems have their roots in a loss of balance between mind and matter; should we not, instead of seeking for æsthetic solutions, look for our remedy in craftsmanship?'[41]

It was, in effect, in the exercising of his craft that the medieval artist gained both that mastery over his materials and that originality of expression which still astonishes us. His technical skill was very great because he continued to be a craftsman, besides whom, in spite of modern specialisation, present-day artists would too often seem mere amateurs or semi-dilettanti. The painter and the worker in stained glass knew all the secrets of the mixing of colours and the making of glass; they prepared their colours themselves or had them prepared in their workshops according to the trade secrets which were painstakingly handed on from master to apprentice and perfected in the process. The architect continued to be a foreman on the job, mingling with his workers, taking a direct share in their tasks, of which no detail escaped him, for he had himself passed through every stage of the craft.

All these elements made up the personality of the artist

[41] From an article in *Beaux Arts*, 27.12.37.

and it was his personal genius which united them. But whatever degree of talent he possessed, it is amazing to see what care he took in the composition of his work. When one studies any of the primitives, one is surprised to discover a rigid sense of order beneath the imaginative or haphazard appearance of the whole. In the admirable *Pieta* of Villeneuve-les-Avignon, for instance, there is not one unessential line or detail among the figures surrounding the body of Christ: everything is subservient to the pale stiff corpse which lies in the foreground of the scene; the other figures serve merely to frame the body, whose contours are repeated exactly by the folds of their apparel, like the widening wake of a ship on a stretch of water. Other pictures are constructed in circles, in the shape of rose-windows, but their geometrical regularity, which can be detected by a practised eye, does not betray itself by any stiffness; certain of Angelico's frescoes are very remarkable from this point of view. The grouping of the figures in the Vénasque Crucifixion is also very skilful: the penitent thief and the women of grace on the left balance the enemies of Christ, the Pharisees, soldiers and the impenitent thief on the right. In the Wilton Diptych, the attitudes of the tutelary saints and their gestures on the left-hand match those of the young king, while, on the right, the angels spread their wings in a sort of corolla which frames the figure of the Virgin. And yet one cannot reproach any of these works, which are so moving in their perfection, with the slightest academic prejudice.

If one examines in more detail the mediæval conception of plastic beauty, one sees that, contrary to what might be imagined, medieval artistic vision was infinitely superior to that of Antiquity. In the representation of the human body, as in all the arts, generally speaking, Antiquity had adopted a static viewpoint: painters, sculptors and architects obeyed certain fixed canons—and not, as in the case of the medieval artists, the dictates of empirical knowledge or practical requirements. They were guided by geometrical considerations and the proportions of the different parts of the face, the laws on the equilibrium of bodies, and so on—and generally arrived at an idealised type, a monotonous perfection which constantly repeated the same model or the same style. The Middle Ages were also acquainted with geometrical data, and the proportions of the various parts of the body; none of the laws of plastic beauty was unknown during this period; in the album of Villard de Honnecourt, the nudes sketched there are broken down into segments which the cubists would not have disowned: triangles, cones and parallelepipeds; groups of wrestlers are portrayed first in broken lines, in curves drawn with a compass, and so on. But the artist, once this preparatory study was completed and once he had mastered his method and his technique, grasped the man as a whole and animated the bodies he created with the breath of real life: distorted by passion, twisted with pain, exalted in ecstasy. Man was caught unawares by the medieval artist in his most human, most natural and most impressive attitudes. This was, to use Claudel's fine expression, 'the movement which creates the body.' It is enough to have seen in the Musée des Augustins the figures, palpitating with joy, contorted with anger or tortured by grief, which adorn the ancient capitals of Saint-Sernin-de-Toulouse— King Herod leaning towards Salome or Christ baring his pierced side to Saint Thomas with a gesture charged with truth and strength—to understand the secret of medieval art: it discovered human beauty in the vitality of human life, in the complete expression of the individual, in interpreting not only his external appearance but his inmost reality. To convince oneself of this one has only to contemplate the tumultuous, vibrating forms which decorate the spandrels of Vézelay or Moissac, or the delicate and infinitely varied figures which, on every page of the Psalter of Saint Louis or that of Blanche of Castile, furnish an inexhaustible source of fresh surprise and delight. Sincerity was their most reliable rule for attaining true beauty; sincerity in their inner vision and in their external observation, and fidelity in interpretation, together with a faculty for combining inspiration and method, genius and craftsmanship, into a harmonious whole.

★

The most complete expression of French medieval art is to be found in the architecture, in the cathedrals where nearly every technique was used. This does not mean that secular art was non-existent: there are many allegorical scenes, and even more portraits, battle-scenes, pastoral scenes and idylls in which nature was always a source of inspiration. But the men of the Middle Ages put their hearts into the cathedrals.

Medieval architecture flourished more vigorously in France than in any other country and this was not fortuitous. There are few French villages which have not retained some vestiges, sometimes in the form of a simple porch lost among modern buildings, or sometimes in the shape of a magnificent cathedral quite out of proportion with the cluster of houses now surrounding it. The rather massive serenity of the Roman buildings was enlivened by restless, turbulent decorations with scenes of dizzy grandeur taken from the Apocalypse and still impregnated with Oriental influences. The evolution of this art gave rise to the ogival transept and to Gothic architecture in general, of which France and particularly the heart of the country, the Ile-de-France, was perhaps the cradle. The Gothic arch enabled architects to show bold initiative and made possible the perfect flowering of French medieval art in its Golden Age, the twelfth and thirteenth centuries.

As has been pointed out on several occasions, the ancient temples clung to the earth: their massive columns, their absolute regularity of design, the traditions which determined their position, their decorations and their horizontal lines—everything in them was in contrast to the Gothic cathedrals where the line was vertical, where the spire pointed to the sky, where symmetry was scorned, but not to the detriment of harmony; where, finally, technical requirements were wedded to the imaginative creation of the master workman, with disconcerting facility. When one examines a Gothic cathedral closely one is always tempted to see it as somehow miraculous: miraculous in its columns which, though never standing in regular lines, yet support the whole weight of the building; miraculous in the arches which turn and twist and revolve and overlap; miraculous in the glazed walls in which there is often more glass than stone; one tends, in fact, to see a miracle in the whole edifice, in the wonderful synthesis of faith, inspiration and piety.

In the case of ancient monuments the finding of a single capital enables one to reconstruct a whole temple, but if three-quarters of a Gothic cathedral were found it would still be impossible to reconstruct the other quarter. And yet, despite this apparent lack of order, no work imposed more rules and obligations on the architect than the building of a church. The planning of its aspect, the lighting, the requirements of the ceremonies, the material necessities arising from the nature of the soil and from the site—all these were problems which the foreman generally appears to have taken in his stride. Some cathedrals, for instance that of Strasbourg, are built on marshland or subterranean rivers; others, for example Les Saintes-Maries-de-la-Mer, or some churches in Languedoc, are fortresses in which the work of art itself had to form a means of defence. The widespread knowledge of liturgy facilitated the task of the artist who complied almost instinctively with its requirements; thus, in our own time the altar is usually raised to allow the congregation to follow the service visually, but formerly they participated in ceremonies more by singing and vocal prayers—whence the very careful attention paid to acoustics: the placing of the columns, the contriving of the arches, and so on. Above all, there was the lighting problem. In some periods men liked dark churches which, they thought, were conducive to meditation. But the Middle Ages loved light: the great concern then was to have ever brighter sanctuaries; and it can be said that all technical discoveries in architecture tended to allow more free space in the building so that the immense stained-glass windows could let in more sunshine to light up the splendour of the religious services ever more brightly: at Beauvais, for example, the stone served merely to frame the walls of glass, giving an impression of alarming and even excessive fragility, for the stone building was never extended beyond the transept.

And yet the aim was solidity even more than beauty; one understands nothing of a Gothic cathedral until one realises that the volume of the stone foundation buried in the ground exceeds that which stretches towards the skies. Beneath the apparent fragility there is a powerful framework of stone, an enduring and robust work supporting the slender pillars and the delicate spires. Every medieval work of art has this solid framework which is not at first apparent because the creator knew how to veil it in delicate fantasy.

In decoration too, beauty was derived solely from utility. There was no detail of ornamentation which was not subservient to architectural detail, nothing was left to chance though it may appear to be merely the product of exuberant imagination. In some churches, the sculptured panels followed precisely the architectural design of the building as a whole. This is very obvious at Rheims in the famous bas-relief of the *Communion du Chevalier*. Some people have been amused at the stiffness, the naïveté (one is always hearing about this naïveté!) of certain statues, such as those ornamenting the door of Chartres Cathedral. But in fact this was deliberate and not in the least naïve, the statue being intended exclusively as decoration for the shaft and its lines being designed to harmonise with a straight, cramped row of columns.

One might be tempted to see in the grey stones of the cathedrals and their sculptures the triumph of line alone, but in reality colour burst through everywhere; not only in the paintings and the stained glass, but also on the stone itself. It is not correct to speak of a time when the cathedrals were 'white', for brilliant colours were reflected in the sunlight both outside and in the interior; it was an iridescent world where everything seemed alive. The colours were of course skilfully contrived: sometimes they covered now drab expanses with vast vivid and exuberant frescoes: an edifice such as that of Saint-Savin or the traces of the paintings of Saint-Hilaire de Poitiers are enough to give some idea of the effect produced. In other cases, colour served to emphasise the curve of an arch with a simple fillet, or made a groin or rafter stand out more clearly. Sculptures were also adorned in this way: not by the pallid shades which are precisely what has given modern religious statuary its poor reputation, but by fresh hues which became an integral part of the stone and of which the traces, unfortunately only too rare, demonstrate the mastery with which it was used; in its cathedrals too, the medieval world was a world of colour. Unfortunately it is rare to find the pictures and painted statues which formerly decorated them anywhere but in museums, that is to say, removed from their setting and placed in conditions quite other than those for which they were created. Only the stained-glass windows—those of Chartres or of Saint-Denis, for example—and the illuminated manuscripts kept jealously—too jealously, perhaps—by the libraries—allow us to visualise the brilliancy and the perfection of medieval colours.

Apart from the strictly religious themes of decoration: biblical scenes demonstrating the correspondences between the Old and New Testaments, details of the life of the Virgin and the Saints, awe-inspiring pictures of the Last Judgment and the Passion of Christ—painters and sculptors turned to good account all that nature offered for their contemplation: all the flora and fauna of the country lived again, re-created by their brushes and chisels, the precise observation of the naturalist being combined with their own imaginative creations. It has been possible to study the different species reproduced on the cathedral doors and to find flowers and ferns of the Ile-de-France, here in bud, there in full flower, elsewhere—in particular in the flamboyant period—in the withering leaves of autumn foliage. With equal facility they used geometrical motifs of decoration, foliated scrolls, tracery and stylised animals modelled on Oriental originals to which the Irish monks had given new and singularly vigorous life in their illuminated manuscripts.

The symbolism of the cathedrals still escapes the modern intellect, although great advances have been made during recent years, thanks chiefly to the admirable work of M. Emile Mâle. We have not yet grasped fully the reasons for the details of their architecture and ornamentation; we know merely that these details all have a meaning. Not one of the praying, grimacing or gesticulating figures was placed there without reason: all have their significance and constitute a symbol, a sign. The symbolism of the Egyptian pyramids has been discovered recently and—even allowing for the exaggeration of certain occultists—one is forced to recognise there the evidence of very profound learning, veritable monuments of geometry, mathematics and astronomy: it remains for us to discover the symbolism of the cathedrals, of these familiar churches which are an exhortation to prayer, to meditation and to what is, perhaps, the most miraculous of all human emotions: wonder. We have not completely fathomed their secrets—far from it. Scholars to-day have not yet been able fully to interpret these windows which simple peasants used to read like a book; we are not always able to identify faces which formerly a child could have named. We know that the cathedrals were given a certain aspect, that their transepts represented the two arms of the Cross, but we are still ignorant of a whole host of notions which are essential before we can fathom the mystery. The science of numbers played a part in their construction: the numbers which are the harmony of the world and which have been hallowed by Catholic liturgy. Three is the number of the Trinity, of the three theological virtues, the pre-eminently divine number which brings all things to oneness. Four is the number of matter, that of the four elements, of the four cardinal humours, the four evangelists, the interpreters of the word of God, and of the four cardinal virtues, those which man must practise during his life on earth. Seven unites the human and the divine, and is the number of Christ and, subsequently, of redeemed mankind; of the four physical humours, combined with the three mental faculties: the intellectual, emotional and instinctive. Another combination of three and four gives twelve, the number of the universe, of the twelve months of the year, the twelve signs

THE CLERK, THE ASTRONOMER AND THE MATHEMATICIAN
(*Thirteenth Century*)

of the zodiac, the symbol of the cycle of the universe. The metric system has not taken these key-numbers into account, but it must be noted that its rather abstract and rudimentary numeration has not succeeded in adapting itself to, for example, the phases of the sun and the moon; and its place is still taken, in nearly all country districts, by methods which are at once more simple and more learned. This permits one to guess at the existence of an occult science much deeper than had been supposed up to the present, and iconography, which is, in scientific form, still in its infancy, may soon open up vistas as yet unrevealed to us.

For the moment we must be content to marvel at the way in which medieval artists managed to make their houses of prayer into both the epitome and the acme of their lives and their activities. They represent not merely secular and religious knowledge and liturgy, but are also the reflection of their everyday pursuits: beside a masterly Last Judgment, the living epitome of the divine majesty and of the final purpose of man, one sees peasants binding sheaves, warming themselves by their firesides and slaughtering a pig. One also finds evidence of the robust sense of beauty possessed by the men of the Middle Ages, their love of life, their serene souls, enamoured of work well done, their roving imaginations, always inventing new forms (have two identical foliated scrolls ever been seen side by side in medieval decoration?)—and their high spirits which they could not hold in check even in church—some of the faces on the stained-glass windows are pure caricatures and certain statues neither more nor less than good jokes.

How can one not be amazed at this frenzied desire to build which was manifested during the twelfth and thirteenth centuries and which abated hardly at all during the two following centuries: these enormous masses of stone which were carried from the quarries to the building site,

N

this host of sculptors, stone-hewers, carpenters, painters, labourers, jobbers and the ever-increasing activity of the glass-makers? Chartres Cathedral, for instance, has no less than one hundred and forty-four windows: all artistic considerations apart, one must reflect upon the gigantic amount of labour represented by this enormous surface of glass, or, rather, of pieces of glass fitted together; the work of the draughtsman, the lead-workers, the glass-cutters, all the host of anonymous artists whose united efforts produced this riot of colour which illuminated the interiors of the buildings and which was enhanced by the play of the light and shadows on the groins of the arches or the deeply hollowed grooves of the capitals, on the cylindrical or diamond-shaped tori, and on the skilfully placed columns, arranged alternately in order to contrive an uninterrupted medley of lights and shades. Contrary to what one might think, such masterpieces were built quickly and men had no hesitation in demolishing them in order to build better. Maurice de Sully pulled down the church which had been built only seventy years previously in order to re-build Notre-Dame; at Laon, Bishop Gautier de Mortagne built a Gothic church about 1140 in the place of a Roman church which dated only from 1114.

The continuity—the consistency, one might say, of this immense effort on the part of the builders, is no less amazing. Successive generations all made part of a whole; trade traditions and secrets were handed down freely and in the course of building or partial reconstruction no one hesitated to make use of any technical advances which had been made: fourteenth-century flying-buttresses rubbed shoulders with naves of the thirteenth century, without the harmony of the whole being at all impaired—although it would be impossible to conceive a Le Corbusier window, for example, in a 1900-style building—though less than thirty years

separate them. But in the Château de Vincennes one can
see two windows side by side which were made at an
interval of one hundred years and which seem to have been
designed to be neighbours, although they are completely
dissimilar both artistically and architecturally. That is why
some over-conscientious restorations have only defaced
the monuments which have been restored because excessive
zeal to remake the whole in one style has resulted in the
work being hampered by rules and canons which never
existed in the minds of the original builders; consequently,
only uniformity has been achieved where previously effort-
less harmony was attained. The evolution of medieval art
can almost always be explained by advances in technical
skill, and the details of decoration are attributable to
architectural requirements: gargoyles would not have been
sculptured if they had not served as water-spouts; likewise,
the straight-edged designs of the Gothic-style rose-window
were modified into curves and the windows took on the
characteristic form of the flamboyant style in order to
facilitate the draining of rain-water which, by freezing in
the corners where it lay, had often caused the stone to
crack. Thus there is, throughout medieval art, a harmony
which is illustrated with startling aptness by the following
example: in the infancy of Gothic Art the bud was a common
motif of ornamentation; that was the period of narrow
arches and small rose-windows; then the bud seemed to
open and to germinate, with the period of lanceolated
arches and large rose-windows; finally, in the fifteenth
century the bud became a flower and while sculpture was
being twisted into superhuman forms, tortured and agonised,
the arches grew broader and the curves softened until the
flamboyant arch completed the evolution.

One could write many pages about medieval music which
has been brought into honour once more by scholarly and

discerning efforts made recently. What more eloquent tribute could one invoke than that of Mozart: 'I would give all my own work to have written the Preface of the Gregorian Mass."

Chapter Eleven
The Sciences

MEDIEVAL science presents itself beneath disconcerting exteriors—so disconcerting that one has difficulty in taking it seriously. In contrast to our exact sciences, it did not belong to the intellect alone; its domain was allied to that of the imagination and of poetry. This, moreover, had been the case from Antiquity. The legend was the original form of History, and, until modern times, there was scarcely any scientific discovery which did not pass into folklore in one form or another, in the guise of either poetry or religious rites or trade secrets. We still find examples of truly scientific ideas being concealed behind a screen of poetry: for instance, certain African peoples, it is said, know about immunisation from small-pox and practise it during a ceremony which has all the appearances of an initiation; what we call vaccination they call 'driving out the evil spirit' or something of that nature; but the process is the same.

Medieval science conserved these characteristics of folklore and that explains many of its contradictions. At the time of the *Exposition des plus Beaux Manuscrits Français*

which was held in the Bibliothèque Nationale in 1937, a
thirteenth century bestiary[42] showed, side by side and facing
each other, two miniatures, one representing an elephant
reproduced exactly, correct both in drawing and in proportions, and the other a dragon with outspread wings: a
striking picture of natural science in the Middle Ages. This
was not a sign of ignorance. It was simply that imagination
and observation were placed on the same plane. The 'tissue
of absurdities' of a work such as the *Imago Mundi* by
Honorius d'Autun has shocked many people for a long
time: for instance, the Scinopodes with only one leg and the
Blemyes with their mouths in the middle of their bellies.
It is hard to say whether the author believed in them any
more than we do, or whether, regarding nature as a vast
reservoir of wonders, he deliberately gave his imagination
free rein, convinced that he would still not surpass reality.
When one thinks of the superabundance of strange things
contained within the Universe, does not a title like *Pictures
of the world* justify any flight of fancy. We know now that
pygmies exist and giraffe-necked negresses whose necks
have an extra vertebra. Surely these are no more extraordinary than the 'men with big ears' sculptured on the
tympanum of the cathedral at Vézelay? We know that
humming-birds, phosphorescent butterflies and carnivorous
flowers exist, not to mention incredible creatures such as
the giant spiders and the fantastic poulpes of marine flora
and fauna. So what was there against inventing the unicorn
or the dragon?

One must also take into account the very medieval
aptitude for seeking the hidden meaning in things, and for
seeing in nature 'forests of symbols.' For the people of the
Middle Ages, natural history was of only very secondary
interest, but they found every manifestation of spiritual

[42] Latin MS. 3638. Folio 80-81.

truth extremely fascinating; and their vision of the outside world was often only a simple prop to support moral precepts: such are the bestiaries in which, while describing animals—the most familiar as well as the most fantastic— the authors saw a higher reality in their actual or supposed habits. The unicorn which only a virgin could take captive was for them the Son of God made man in the womb of the Virgin Mary; the cock crowed to proclaim the passing hours; the onocentaur, half-man and half-donkey, was man led astray by his evil instincts; the nycticorax, which thrived on excrement and darkness and flew only upside down, was the Jewish people who had been cursed for abjuring the Church; the phœnix, the single bird, purple in colour, which was burned to death and rose again from its ashes on the third day, was Christ victorious over death. The whole gives, with a sombre poetry, an exact indication of what the men of the Middle Ages liked to see in nature: not a system of laws and principles, the classification of which would probably have bored them, even if they had known it, but a world vibrating with beauty and with a secret life— not very different from that revealed in our laboratories to-day. Rightly or wrongly, they saw factual and spiritual truth on the same plane—preferring the latter if need be. Take for example the legend of Saint George and the Dragon, so popular in the Middle Ages: the question of what this monster could, in fact, have been, or of the degree of authenticity which could be ascribed to it, never entered their heads; what was important was the example of courage given by this legendary struggle which was to inspire the knights of Christendom. By an analogous process, the preachers of the period attributed much miraculous detail to the saints about whom they preached, and borrowed indiscriminately from one or the other; if we are to believe what they said, Saint Denis carrying his head under his arm had many 'imitators.' But neither the public nor the preachers were fooled by any of this and it would be very naïve to take such things literally: the essential was not accuracy of detail, but the truth of the whole and the moral it pointed.

Is that to say that there was no scientific curiosity? A mere catalogue of the manuscripts contained in the great libraries would be sufficient answer to that question: a complete list of the treatises on medicine, mathematics, astronomy, alchemy, architecture, geometry, etc. has not yet been compiled, and these manuscripts have remained for the most part unpublished. Efforts in this direction have so far been very restricted and do not afford us a general conspectus of medieval science. But all that we do know precisely enables us to realise that it ranged much more widely than had been imagined, and was akin in many ways to modern science. As early as the thirteenth century, Roger Bacon knew about gun-powder and the use of convex and concave lenses. Albert le Grand made researches in acoustics and sound-tubes, which led to his construction of a talking-machine—eight hundred years before Edison. Arnaud de Villeneuve, who taught at Montpellier, discovered alcohol, sulphuric acid, hydrochloric acid and nitric acid. Raimond Lulle presaged organic chemistry and knowledge of the functions of mineral salts in organised bodies. Through the Arabs, the Middle Ages profited by the scientific discoveries of the Persians, the Greeks and the Jews, and were able to make a synthesis of all these, including Syro-Chaldean knowledge of astronomy and Hebrew medicine. Oxford, where Robert Grossetête, Roger Bacon's master taught, was for students of mathematics what Montpellier was for medical students and great figures such as the King of Spain, Alphonse X, the Emperor Frederick II and Roger, the Norman King of Sicily, following

Charlemagne's example, maintained scientists at their courts—geographers, physicists and alchemists—just as they had their philosophers and their poets.

Strangely enough, the types of research which fascinated men in the Middle Ages and which provoked only contemptuous smiles as long as modern science had got no further than the Encyclopædists and their successors of the nineteenth century, are among those which the most recent discoveries are now restoring to a place of honour. What was, precisely, the philosophers' stone which Nicolas Flamel claimed to have discovered? It was defined as a tenuous substance 'which one finds everywhere,' a 'glowing sun', a 'body existing in itself, different from all the elements.' According to Raimond Lulle, it was a 'mysterious oil, penetrable, beneficient and miscible with all bodies, whose effect it will augment beyond measure, in the most secret way conceivable.' If translated into modern scientific language, these data define Radio-activity. The scientists of the Middle Ages glimpsed intuitively what modern scientists have achieved by method. As for the transmutation of substances, which was the great dream of the alchemists, is this not a reality to-day? Avicenna speaks of an 'elixir which, when applied to a body, changes its own natural substance into another substance,'—in the laboratories to-day scientists are able by 'bombardment' with electrons, to make for example, phosphorous out of aluminium and there seems to be nothing to prevent base lead from being changed into pure gold by atomic experiment. The apparatus exhibited at the Palais de la Découverte during the 1937 Exhibition did credit to the genius of the research workers of the thirteenth century. By methods which were certainly vague and vitiated by errors which would have made the practical application of their discoveries impossible, they did nevertheless attain a standard in science which was very much higher than that of ensuing centuries. The nineteenth century scientist, steeped in the physical and natural sciences and in the discoveries of chemistry, shrugged his shoulders when confronted with medieval beliefs in the homogeneity of matter; but the scientist of the twentieth century, thanks to discoveries in biology and electro-chemistry, has re-established the same belief by recognising that every atom is composed in the same way of a proton around which electrons gravitate.

We are, moreover, taking a fresh interest in occultism and astrology. If these are not exact sciences, strictly speaking it seems more and more as if a certain value should be assigned them—a human, if not a scientific value. No one contests the influence of the moon on the tides and peasants know that cider should not be bottled nor vines pruned except at times determined by the phases of the moon. Is it therefore entirely impossible that other more subtle influences should be exercised by the stars? Because these matters lend themselves to exploitation by charlatans, does it follow that all such things must necessarily be charlatanry? Our twentieth century, the century of research into the occult sciences, will perhaps prove the scientists of the Middle Ages to have been right on this point as on so many others.

In another domain, that of exploration and geographical knowledge, activity was no less great. To regard the Renaissance as the period of the first great voyages is more than an injustice: it is an error. The discovery of America has caused men to forget that the curiosity of medieval geographers and explorers towards the East was no less than that of their successors in the West. At the beginning of the twelfth century, Benjamin de Tulède journeyed as far as India; some hundred years later Odéric de Pordenone reached Tibet. The voyages of Marco Polo and those, less well-known, of Jean du Plan-Carpin, Guillaume de Rubruquis, André de Longjumeau and Jean de Béthencourt, are enough to give an idea of the activity devoted to the exploration of the Earth during this period. Asia and Africa were infinitely better known then than subsequently. Saint Louis established relations with the Khan of the Mongols and with the Old Man of the Mountains, the terrible chief of the sect of the Assassins. In 1329, a see was established at Colombo to the south of India and the Dominican Jourdain Cathala de Séverac was appointed incumbent. The Crusades provided an opportunity for the Western World to make and keep up contact with the Near East, though in fact relations had never been completely severed, but had been maintained by pilgrims and merchants. In the direction of Africa, exploration was extended as far as Abyssinia and the banks of the Niger, which was reached at the beginning of the fifteenth century by a citizen of Toulouse, Anselme Ysalguier. One cannot, in fact, be sure that America was not, if not 'discovered', at least visited, during this period. It is certain that the Vikings crossed the Northern Atlantic and established regular relations with Greenland. Icelanders settled there; a see was founded and in 1327 the Greenlanders responded to an appeal to join the Crusade of Pope John XXII by sending him as a contribution towards expenses a cargo of seal-skins and walrus teeth. It is not impossible that they had by that time explored a part of Canada and sailed up the Saint Lawrence, where Jacques Cartier was to discover to his stupefaction some centuries later, that the Indians made the sign of the cross and declared that they had been taught to do so by their ancestors.

This is not at all surprising if one remembers that in the Middle Ages the French had relations, at least indirectly, with India and China through the Arabs, and profited from their knowledge of astronomy and geography. A planisphere dating from 1413, made by Mecia de Viladestes and preserved in the Bibliothèque Nationale, gives the nomenclature and exact position of the roads and oases of the Sahara, across the whole desert as far as Timbuctoo. A traveller could, in the Middle Ages, plan his route exactly across this immense expanse of sand which was subsequently to remain blank on our maps until the middle of the nineteenth century, and he could know what would be the stages of his journey from the Atlas mountains to the Niger. The disasters of the Hundred Years War, the Oriental Schism, and, later, the breach with Islam and the Turkish invasions, all had a direct influence on the relations of Europe with the East and, consequently, on geographical knowledge. It must be added that, contrary to what has been believed, the scholars of the Renaissance revealed a retrogressive spirit in comparison with that of their precursors in basing their studies on the works of Antiquity.[43] Aristotle and Ptolemy had been far surpassed in this sphere, and in neglecting the lessons of experience in order to revert to their theories they deprived themselves of a whole sum of knowledge which the modern world has gradually regained, vindicating medieval science on this point also.

[43] Cf. in this connection the very pertinent and well-documented article by R. P. Lecler, entitled *La Géographie des Humanistes* in the first number of the review CONSTRUIRE, (1940).

Chapter Twelve
Daily Life

AT the beginning of the Middle Ages, since men were seeking security above all else, life was concentrated almost entirely within the estate; this produced a régime of feudal or, rather, family self-sufficiency, under which each *mesnie* strove to provide for its own immediate requirements. The position of the villages revealed how necessary it was to form a group in order to gain security; they clustered on the slopes leading up to the seigniorial manor, where the serfs took refuge in times of danger; the houses were huddled together and concentrated in a small area; they took up the smallest possible morsel of land and did not spread beyond the escarpments of the eminence on which the keep stood. Such an arrangement is still to be seen around castles such as that of Roquebrune, near Nice, which dates from the eleventh century. But, as soon as the period of the invasions was past, the peasants' dwellings were dispersed over the countryside and the town broke away from the castle. It was out of necessity and not from choice that the earliest cities had only narrow alleys, because it was essential that, whether they liked it or not, the people should remain within the ramparts; but this was not so in the case of the suburbs which began to multiply at the end of the twelfth century. In the same way, the alleys were winding because they followed the curve of the ramparts, which was determined by the natural lie of the land. But it must not be imagined that the choice of the position of the houses was left entirely to the whim of the inhabitants; most ancient cities were built to a very clear plan. In Marseilles, for example, the principal streets, for instance, the Rue Saint-Laurent, run strictly parallel to the quayside, to which the small transversal roads lead. When these roads are very narrow one can be certain that it is for a definite reason—as a protection against the wind, or the sun in the Midi. This was a prudent arrangement, as was realised in Marseilles when the disciples of Baron Haussmann made the unfortunate Rue de la République, a vast icy corridor which disfigures the old Butte des Moulins.

In Languedoc the central plan was often employed as a protection from the terrible *Cers:* for example, in the little town of Bram, where the roads run in concentric circles round the church. But whenever they were able, and when they were not handicapped by the climate or by external conditions, architects preferred a rectangular plan similar to that of the most modern cities, those of America or Australia, for example: wide thoroughfares intersecting at right angles with a site provided in the interior of the rectangle for the public square on which were situated the church, the market and the town hall, if there was one— and secondary roads running parallel to the major ones. It was in this way that most of the new towns were planned: Monpazier in Dordogne was very characteristic in this respect, with its perfectly straight roads dividing blocks of houses with absolute regularity: towns such as

Aigues-Mortes, Arcis-sur-Aube, and Gimont in the Gers region, all show the same symmetry of design.

This arrangement of the streets was very important for the men of the Middle Ages for they lived out-of-doors a great deal. It is rather curious to note that until this time, following the customs of Antiquity, day-light had been admitted to houses at their centre, and they had had few or no openings on to the street. This, then, was the sign of a veritable revolution in men's habits. The street became a feature of daily life—as the market-place had been earlier, or the gynæceum. Now people liked to go outside. All the shop-keepers had an awning which they rolled down each morning, beneath which they displayed their wares in the open air. Lighting had been one of the great problems of existence until the century of electricity, and in the Middle Ages, when people loved light, they solved this problem by making the most of the daylight. A draper who led his customers into the back of his shop acquired a bad repu-tation: if bad workmanship had not betrayed itself in his materials he would not have feared to display them in the road like anyone else. The customer wanted to be able to loll beneath the awning and examine at leisure the lengths of cloth from which he was going to make his choice, with the assistance of his tailor who often accompanied him for the purpose of advising him. The shoemaker, the barber and even the weaver, worked in the road or looking out on it; the money-changers set up their tables on trestles out-of-doors, and all that the municipal authorities could do to avoid obstructions was to limit the dimensions of these tables according to a fixed scale.

Thus, the streets were extraordinarily animated. Each district of the town had its own peculiar character, since the trade guilds were generally grouped together, as the names of the streets remind us: in Paris, the Rue de la

Coutellerie, the Quai des Orfèvres, the Quai de la Mégis-
serie where the tanners worked and the Rue des Tonneliers,
are a sufficient indication of which guilds were grouped
there. The booksellers were nearly all to be found in the
Rue Saint-Jacques, the Saint Honoré district was that of
the butchers. But all were very lively because the shops,
which were used as both workrooms and sales counters,
overflowed on to the roadway, resembling the markets of
Tunisia and the Ponte Vecchio in Florence; in the Paris of
to-day it is only the quays on the Left Bank with the second-
hand booksellers and their boxes and their clientèle of
idlers and regular customers which can give one some idea
of the scene. But the 'background noises' which were very
different in the Middle Ages from those of our own time,
must not be forgotten: the carpenters' sawing, the black-
smiths' hammering, the shouts of the bargees who hauled
their barges laden with foodstuffs along the river, and the
cries of the merchants—instead of taxi-horns and the
rumbling of buses. Everything in the Middle Ages was
'cried': the latest news, police regulations, and judicial rulings,
tax levies, auction sales which took place in the open air
on the public squares, and also—and more universally—
goods for sale; advertising was not displayed on the walls
in the form of gaudy posters, but was 'spoken' as it is on
the radio in our own days; the local authorities had frequently to put a stop to abuses and prevent shopkeepers from
'giving tongue' with undue vehemence. The most popular
of these advertisers was the tavern-crier: every innkeeper
had his wine 'cried' by someone with a powerful voice who
stood behind a table and superintended the drinks. Passers-
by who were attracted would order a glass of wine, and
for those who had no time to go inside the tavern this
took the place of the '*zinc*' in Paris cafés. In the *Jeu de
Saint Nicolas* the crier plays a large part:

SECTION OF THE BAYEUX TAPESTRY
(late Eleventh Century)

Céans fait bon dîner, céans
Ci a chaud pain et chaud hareng
Et vin d'Auxerre à plein tonnel.

He serves the king's messenger with a glass of wine, saying:

Tiens, ci te montera au chef (to the head)
Bois bien, le meilleur est au fond!

All this must be pictured in the medieval streets of which the old districts of Rouen and Lisieux still allow us to form an idea: one can see the wooden-beamed houses with their sculptured stylobates, from which hung signs in wrought iron, and beside which the bold arch of the church door rises unexpectedly, so that, by lifting one's head one can see the spire, jutting upwards like a mast among the roof-tops. For at this time, far from being dwarfed and isolated by the great open spaces with which it is now usual to surround them, churches were not separated from the houses which clustered about them as if anxious to dwell right beneath their bell-towers. This may still be seen around Saint-Germain-des Prés. Thus, even their situation in the town expressed the intimacy which existed at that time between the people and the church. The Gothic cathedrals were, moreover, planned to be seen thus, in vertical perspective—very unlike the temples of Antiquity—and it is in this way that they are seen to the best advantage. At the time of the reconstruction of Rheims Cathedral it occasioned great surprise when, among the gems of medieval sculpture, astoundingly ugly statues with deformed features were found; but they had only to be replaced in their niches, almost at the top of the building, for the mystery to be solved; they had been sculptured so that the deliberately exaggerated features retained their natural expressions and took on a singular beauty for anyone looking up at them from below; this was as much the

o

product of geometrical calculation as of artistic method. Blocks of buildings such as those of Salers in Auvergne and Peille near Nice, with their multitude of arcades, their carriage-gateways, their rows of windows on the upper stories of the houses and the covered bridges thrown across the road to join two blocks, that is, two groups of houses— also allow one to reconstruct the appearance of a medieval town with fair accuracy.

It is permissible to wonder, in face of this irrecusable evidence, what could have suggested Luchaire's strange opinion that medieval houses were no more than 'damp hovels, and the roads no better than cesspools.'⁴⁴ It is true he cites no document or any sort of building in support of his assertion; it is hard to see why, if they were accustomed to living in hovels, the people of the Middle Ages went to such pains to adorn them with mullioned windows and open arcades resting on delicately sculptured pillars which often imitated the ornamentation of neighbouring chapels, as can be seen at Cluny in Burgundy and Blesle in Auvergne, or in the little Gascon town of Saint-Antonin—to mention only houses dating from the Roman period, that is, from the eleventh, and the first years of the twelfth centuries.

As for the roads, far from being 'cesspools,' they were paved at quite an early date. Paris roads were paved in the first years of the reign of Philippe-Auguste and by a process similar to that employed in Antiquity: the paving stones were placed on a bed of concrete mixed with broken tiles. Troyes, Amiens, Douai and Dijon were also paved at different times, as were nearly all the towns of France. These towns also had sewers—generally covered; in Paris these have been found beneath the Louvre and the former Hôtel de la Trémoille, dating from the thirteenth century, and it is known that two hundred years later the University

⁴⁴ *La Société Française au temps de Philippe-Auguste*, p. 6.

and the suburbs of the Cité had a drainage system comprising four sewers connected with a main sewer. In Riom, Dijon and many other towns also evidence has been found of the existence of covered sewers which prove that public health was not neglected. Where main-drainage did not exist, public night-soil dumps were used whose contents were afterwards emptied into the rivers—as is still the case in our own time—or burned. Many of the regulations publicly proclaimed at this time related to the cleanliness of the roads, and the police of those days, the '*banniers*', had the task of ensuring that these regulations were observed. Thus the municipal bye-laws of Marseilles directed each house-owner to sweep in front of his own house and to see to it that refuse could not be carried by rain-water down the streets which sloped towards the harbour. At the end of the roads which came out at the quays, moreover, barriers were erected, designed to protect the harbour-water, which the local authorities wished to keep clear. No less than four hundred *livres* a year were allotted for the upkeep of the harbour, and for the periodical cleansings a contrivance was invented consisting of a barge to which an overshot wheel was attached, whose buckets dredged the bottom one by one and deposited the mud they collected in the barge which was afterwards emptied at sea. Special regulations protected places which public interests required should be particularly safeguarded against uncleanliness, for example, the meat and fish markets, which had to be thoroughly washed down every day and the tanneries whose evil-smelling waters had to be emptied into a drain dug expressly for this purpose.

From all this it would appear that concern was certainly shown for sanitation in the Middle Ages, as it is to-day. The greatest obstacle in the way of cleanliness was caused by the number of domestic animals, which was greater than at the present time; it was not rare to see a herd of sheep or goats or even of cattle making their way among the stalls, overturning them and creating disorder; a line was fixed on the outside of the town which they were not allowed to cross. One can still see cattle in some towns to-day, and in London herds of sheep cross one of the busiest squares each day to go to graze in the park. Most particularly there were pigs—each household bred enough to provide for its own needs—which strayed along the roads in spite of repeated prohibitions; but this was not an entirely bad thing, for they ate up all the scraps and thus made a contribution towards eliminating one of the sources of refuse in the roads.

In the noisy city, teeming with its unceasingly busy population, the bells marked the hours and their sound also formed part of the 'background noises.' The Angelus, in the morning, at mid-day and in the evening, sounded the hours of work and of rest, playing the role of the modern factory hooter. Bells proclaimed feast days, that is, holidays, called for help in time of emergency, and summoned the people together for general assemblies or the municipal magistrates for special councils. The tocsin gave the fire-alarm, the passing-bell was tolled for funerals, bells pealed on holidays; their chimes marked the life of each day until the evening when they sounded the curfew. Then the lamps were put out in the shops and the bright oven fires extinguished; the awnings were rolled up, carriage-gates were closed, and, if a sudden attack was feared, the city gates were also shut, the drawbridge raised and the portcullis lowered. Sometimes it was considered sufficient to throw chains across the roads and this had the additional advantage in districts of evil repute of obstructing the path of fleeing thieves. Only the dim lights remained which flickered day and night in front of the "montjoys"—the statuettes of the Virgin and the saints which stood in niches at the corners of houses and in front of the Crucifixes at the crossroads—while outside the town, in the harbour, the lighthouses shone, showing the entrances to the roadsteads and the principal reefs.

Late travellers were allowed to go on their way only if they carried a torch: in the seaboard towns the comings and goings of people about to embark were permitted. In times of emergency, or if there was danger from some calamity—fire, serious injury to a ship, or shipwreck, for instance—the authorities had torches placed at the corners of the roads to allow help to be fetched rapidly and to avert accidents.

Then all the members of each household would retire within the protecting walls of their houses—walls they had been careful to build thick and strong as a defence against the cold and the heat and against disturbing noise; for in those days people knew they would find no comfort without solid walls to protect them. According to the resources of the district, these walls were built of bricks or of free-stone if this could be afforded, but a combination of wood and cobwork was most general and has continued in common use right up to the present day. The whole framework of the façade was built of beams, skilfully constructed while flat on the ground. It was then erected all in one by the aid of winches, jacks and pulleys, and the interstices were afterwards filled in with bricks or whatever material was customarily used in the district. The churches which have remained standing are generally indicative of the aspect of the houses: in Languedoc, red brick was predominant and lent its very individual brightness to the churches of Toulouse and of Albi; in Auvergne, stone was used for building, the dark stone from Volvic, of which the Cathedrals of Puy and Clermont-Ferrand present impressive examples. In the clay-soil regions such as Provence in the Midi, houses and monuments were covered with tiles which, in the sunlight, took on that honey colour which is characteristic of villages such as Riez or Jouques; in Burgundy people liked to glaze these tiles, and the roofs shimmered with brilliant colour: the Hospice de Beaune and Saint Bénigne de Dijon are examples of this; in Touraine and Anjou use was made of the slate quarried in those regions. When the churches, instead of being vaulted, were only timbered, as was frequently the case in the North and around the Bassin Parisien, this was because the forests which were more numerous than the quarries made this method of roofing more economical. In these parts, private houses were always thatched, even in the towns, and that inevitably increased the risk of fire. Everywhere the municipal authorities laid down precautionary measures which the inhabitants of the town were to take to avoid disasters—the risk of fire was the only reason for the curfew. In Marseilles, ship-owners were advised—when their men were proceeding with the operation known as the *brusque*, which consisted in heating the hull of the ship so that it was easier to coat with pitch—to make sure that the flame did not exceed a certain height, for, said the city bye-laws, 'it is not always within man's power to control the flames which he himself has lit.' After a fire which, in 1244, destroyed twenty-two houses in Limoges, large reservoirs were built from which the citizens could draw water in an emergency. When a fire broke out it was every man's duty to run with a bucket of water at the summons of the tocsin; and everyone had to place another bucket in front of his own house as a precaution.

The essential part of the medieval house, particularly in the North of France, was the *salle*, the room where all the family gathered at meal-times and which was used for every important occasion: baptisms, marriages and lyke-wakes. It was the living-room, where the family all assembled in the evening beneath the great mantlepiece, to warm themselves and to tell stories before going to bed. This

was true of both peasant dwellings and castles. The rest of
the rooms, the bedrooms and others, were of only secondary
importance; the principal room was the *salle familiale*, which
French Canadians still call the *vivoir*. Where the style of
living demanded it, the kitchen was separate; sometimes,
in the castles, it even occupied a separate building, doubtless
to lessen the risk of fire; the huge kitchens, with their
chimney-cowls, in the Abbey of Fontevrault, and those of
the palace of the Dukes of Burgundy in Dijon, have remained
as they were.

Without mentioning the many store-rooms, banqueting
halls and so on, which a seigniorial mansion could comprise,
the middle-class house included workrooms—if these were
needed—and bedrooms. To enter into more detail, one
also found recesses adjoining these bedrooms which were
called *privés*, *longaignes* or *restraits*, that is, what we are now
accustomed to refer to as W.Cs. Surprising though it may
seem, every house in the Middle Ages possessed this
amenity in which the Palais de Versailles was lacking.
Indeed, fastidiousness was very highly developed on this
point, for it was considered quite indelicate not to have one's
own private W.C.; the general rule was that everyone had
his own and was the only person to use it: manners did not
become coarse in this respect until the sixteenth century,
during which, moreover, all the hygienic practices known in
the Middle Ages were neglected. The Abbey of Cluny in
the eleventh century had no less than forty latrines and—
which appears more incredible, despite its being equally
true—public latrines existed during this period. There is
proof of this in towns such as Rouen, Amiens and Agen,
for their installation and upkeep were the subject of
municipal discussions or mention of them is to be found in
the city accounts. In private houses, the *restraits* were often
situated on the top floor and a pipe running the length of

the staircase led to the sewers or night-soil dumps, or to trenches very similar to those used to-day; a process was even employed resembling that of the most modern septic tanks, for wood ashes were used which have the property of decomposing waste. Thus, one finds mention of purchases of ashes destined for the latrines of the hospital of Nîmes in the fifteenth century. In the Palais d'Avignon, the pipes emptied into a drain which ran into the Sorgue. And it is known that it was by entering through the sewers—the only point which no one had thought to fortify!—that the soldiers of Philippe-Auguste took the fortress of Château-Gaillard, the pride of Richard Coeur-de-Lion.

The rooms were more comfortably furnished than is generally believed: furniture included beds which were 'handsomely adorned and covered with bedspreads and coverlets, with white sheets and fur rugs;'[45] stools, high-backed chairs, chests and sculptured coffers where clothes were kept and of which fine specimens can still be seen, especially in the Hospice de Beaune. The timbers used at this time were very fine: prepared and polished with care, they did not get dusty or attract insect-pests. There were also bread-bins, sideboards and dressers. As for the tables, these were plain boards set up on trestles when meals were served and stacked away afterwards against the walls, to avoid their taking up space unnecessarily. On the other hand, draperies and tapestries were used freely as a protection against the cold and to keep out draughts. Those which are still in existence—for example, the wonderful *Dame à la Licorne* preserved in the Musée de Cluny—show plainly to what advantage they could be put as furnishings and interior decoration. These particular examples were obviously luxuries reserved for the aristocracy and the rich *bourgeoisie;* but the custom of using hanging draperies

---

[45] *Le Ménagier de Paris.*

and arrases was common everywhere. Speaking of the divers duties of the mistress of a house, the *Ménagier de Paris* advises Agnes, the *béguine* who acts as his housekeeper, to instruct 'the chambermaids that the entrance halls of your house, that is, the *salle* and the other places where people come and stay to talk, should be well brushed and cleaned early in the morning, and that the stools, benches and covers lying over the chests there should be dusted and shaken; and that, subsequently, the other rooms should be cleaned and tidied this day and every other day, as befits our style of living . . .'

It is perhaps surprising to find the 'bath-bottom', or bath-tub cloth mentioned in inventories as a part of the furnishings —this was a sort of flannel which covered the bottom of the bath to guard against splinters which were almost inevitable when the bottom was made of wood. Thus, one sees that, contrary to general belief, baths were known and widely used in the Middle Ages; here again, care must be taken not to confuse periods; one must not attribute to the thirteenth century the revolting uncleanliness of the sixteenth and subsequent centuries up to our own time. The Middle Ages was a period of hygiene and cleanliness. A saying in those days shows that cleanliness was considered as one of the pleasures of existence:

Venari, ludere, lavari, bibere,
Hoc est vivere!

In the romances of chivalry one sees that the laws of hospitality required that one should offer one's guests a bath when they arrived after a long journey. It was, moreover, a common habit to wash one's feet and hands when one came in from outside. In the *Ménagier de Paris*, a woman is advised always to have ready for the comfort and well-being of her husband 'a large pan so that his feet can be washed often, and a supply of logs to warm him, a good bed of down, sheets and covers, a night-cap, pillows and clean apparel.' Bathing naturally formed part of the care of infants. Marie de France recalls this in one of her lays:

> *Par les villes où ils erroient*
> *Sept fois le jour reposouoient*
> *L'enfant faisoient allaiter,*
> *Coucher de nouvel, et baigner.*

Even if people did not take a bath every day in the Middle Ages (and could one affirm that this is a general habit in our own time?) at least bathing had a place in their lives; the bath-tub was an item of their furniture; sometimes it was no more than a tub, and its name, *dolium*, which also means a barrel, has perhaps caused confusion. The Roman Abbey of Cluny, dating from the eleventh century, had no fewer than twelve bathrooms, the vaulted cells containing an equal number of wooden baths. In summer, people liked to go and sport in the rivers, and the *Très riches heures du duc de Berry* show the villagers, male and female, washing themselves and swimming on a fine August day, clad in the scantiest attire, for their conception of modesty was quite different from our own and they bathed naked and slept naked between the sheets.

There were public baths or bath-houses which were used by many people. The Musée Borély in Marseilles has preserved a sign in sculptured stone which hung outside the public baths in the thirteenth century. Paris, the Paris of Philippe-Auguste, had twenty-six public baths—more than present-day Paris has in the form of swimming pools. Each morning those in charge of them had it cried through the town:

> *Oyez qu'on crie au point du jour:*
> *Seigneurs, qu'or vous allez baigner*
> *Et étuver sans délayer;*
> *Les bains sont chauds, c'est sans mentir*[46].

[46] Guillaume de Villeneuve, *Crieries de Paris.*

Some of them even carried this to excess: in the *Livre des Métiers* by Etienne Boileau, it is laid down: 'that no one shall cry his baths or have them cried, until after daybreak.' These baths were heated by underground pipes, a process resembling that employed in the. Roman baths. Some private individuals had a similar system installed in their houses, and in the home of Jacques Coeur in Bourges one can still see a bathroom heated by pipes in very much the same way as with modern central heating. But that, obviously, was an instance of exceptional luxury for a private house. This arrangement was also found in the Dijon baths, where the pipes led to three different rooms: the bathroom, properly speaking, a sort of swimming-pool, and the vapour bath. Ordinary baths in the Middle Ages were, in effect, always accompanied by vapour-baths, as is the case nowadays with the Finnish *sauna*. The name '*étuves*', which was given them, indicates that the two belonged together. The Crusaders brought back with them to Europe the custom of adding rooms for depilatory treatment, a habit they had acquired from contact with the Arabs.

The public baths were very well patronised. It may seem surprising to find bishops in the thirteenth century taking the nuns of the Latin towns in the Orient to task for going to the bath-houses, but it does prove that, although the nuns did not have bathrooms installed in their convent they wished nevertheless, to continue in their habits of cleanliness. At Provins, King Louis X built new bath-houses in 1309, the old ones having become inadequate *ob affluentiam populi;* in Marseilles, entrance was controlled and a special day was allotted to Jews and another to prostitutes, to avoid their coming in contact with Christians and respectable women.

The healing powers of springs and the benefits to be derived from thermal treatment were known in the Middle

Ages: in the *Roman de Flamenca*, one reads of a lady feigning sickness so that her doctor shall order her to take the waters at Bourbon-l'Archambaut where she wishes to meet a certain handsome gallant.

All this is obviously far removed from accepted ideas on cleanliness in the Middle Ages and yet documentary proofs exist. The error has arisen from confusion with the periods which followed and also from certain humorous writings which, quite wrongly, have been taken literally. Langlois has made a very just observation in this connection: 'It has,' he writes, 'caused some surprise that certain lessons on the subject of elementary cleanliness and decency are found in the *Chastoiement* of Robert de Blois, which one might have supposed quite unnecessary for ladies whom one imagines to have been not entirely lacking in breeding. For instance, the poet writes: "Do not wipe your eyes or your nose on the table-cloth; do not drink too much." Such counsels make one smile to-day. But the question arises whether they are evidence of the fundamental grossness of the old society of chivalry, or if the author did not write them precisely in order to provoke a smile and if the people of the thirteenth century did not laugh at them as much as we do.'[47] One must not, indeed, take him seriously any more than one could consider as a traditional ceremony of the period this gesture advocated by Villon:

> *C'est bien dîner quand on échappe*
> *Sans débourser pas un denier*
> *Et dire adieu au tavernier*
> *En torchant son nez à la nappe.*

This is roughly the equivalent of saying to-day: 'If you are invited to a reception at the Embassy, avoid spitting on the floor or putting out your cigarette on the tablecloth.' One must make allowances for the humour which was never

[47] *La Vie en France au Moyen Age*, I. p. 161.

absent in the Middle Ages. Refinement of manners was, on the contrary very highly developed: not only were elementary rules, such as that of washing one's hands before meals, observed by all—in the parable of Dives, he grows impatient because his wife, slow in washing her hands, keeps him waiting at meal-times—but people were fond also of certain elegant refinements such as the use of finger-bowls. Thus, the *Ménagier de Paris* gives a recipe 'to prepare water for rincing the hands at table'. 'Boil,' he says, 'some sage; then strain off the water and leave to cool. Add either camomile or marjoram or a little rosemary; boil with some orange peel. Laurel leaves are also to be recommended.' Housewives must have reached a very high standard of refinement in the running of their homes and in their sense of good manners for the need of such recipes to have been felt.

The same work enlightens us concerning the manner in which ordinary members of the household, that is, the the servants, were treated. Their lot could not have been too pitiable, if the writings of the period are any indication: 'At the appropriate hours, have them sit down to table and give them a good meal of one kind of meat, one only, not several, nor over-dainty. And order for them one kind of drink, not one liable to go to the head, whether it be wine or some other beverage; and urge them to eat and drink well and amply; and after the second part of their day's work and on feast days, they should have another meal, and after this, that is in the evening, they should be fed well and generously as before; and, when necessary, they should be given an opportunity to warm themselves and to rest.' In brief, they had three meals a day, plain but solid food, and wine to drink. This is apparent also from the novels about various trades, in which one sees comfortably-off *bourgeois* having their work-people to eat at their own tables and giving them the same foods as they themselves ate, a practice which is common to-day only in country districts. The mistress of the house had to show even wider solicitude: 'If one of your servants should fall ill, put all ordinary things to one side and think kindly and charitably of him; visit him often and remember him solicitously, while assisting his recovery.'

She had also to think of her 'lesser brothers,' the domestic animals, which appear to have been much more numerous then than nowadays; there is no miniature showing indoor scenes or domestic life in which dogs are not depicted running about beside their masters, wandering around the table at the banquets, or stretched out quietly at the feet of their mistress as she spins; and in all the gardens one sees peacocks displaying their brilliant tails in the sunlight. Aviaries were numerous and every man hunted, however modestly, whether with one hound or with a whole pack, falcons, hawks or merlins. Thus, the author of the *Ménagier de Paris* advises his wife that: 'you should firstly think diligently and attentively of the animals which live with you in the house, the little dogs and caged birds; and give thought to the other domestic animals, for they cannot speak and for that reason you must both speak and think for them.'

In the Middle Ages, people appreciated flowers no less than they loved animals. The garden, as well as the house and street, was the ordinary background of men's lives and illuminated manuscripts show us unforgettable pictures of medieval gardens, surrounded by low walls and always with a well or a fountain and a stream running along the edges of the lawns; often we see trellises, wall-trees where fruit is ripening or green groves where, in the romances, knights and ladies kept their trysts. It is remarkable that no distinction was made in this period between what we call a kitchen-garden and what is known as a flower-garden. Flowers and vegetables grew together in the same beds and men doubtless considered a head of cauliflower in bloom, the delicate lace-work leaves of carrots and the abundant foliage of melons or pumpkins as agreeable to the eye as a border of hyacinths or of tulips. The orchard was often chosen as the destination of a walk; it was beneath an old pear-tree that Tristan waited for Iseult the Fair on moon-lit evenings. This does not mean that flowers were not appreciated: French lyrical writings constantly describe shepherdesses and lads occupied in weaving garlands of flowers and leaves; many pictures and tapestries have a background of buds in delicate shades. But the illuminators, besides scattering birds and flowers on the frames of their manuscript pages, also made use of vegetable plants, and the strangely laciniated leaf-artichoke served as a model for generations of sculptors, notably in the flamboyant period.

★

A legend which dies hard has made of the common man in the Middle Ages an everlasting starveling, so that one wondered how a race which was under-nourished for eight centuries and which was, besides, ravaged periodically by wars, famines and epidemics, ever managed to survive and, in addition, to produce passably vigorous descendants. The error arose largely from a misinterpretation of terms then in use. It is true that in France in the Middle Ages men ate '*herbes*' and '*racines*'—(herbs and roots) but that has always been the case, for at that time '*herbe*' meant anything that grew above the soil—cabbage, spinach, lettuce, leeks, beets, etc.—and '*racine*' meant everything that grew below: carrots, turnips, radishes and rapes.[48] People have also been horrified because the thistle was considered a delicacy at this time, but one must read '*cardon*' (cardoon) for

[48] This fact has already been pointed out, notably by Funck-Brentano.

'*chardon*', and then it is no more than a matter of taste. The peasant often collected acorns, but it was not because he liked them himself, but because he fed his pigs on them. It is possible that during certain periods of exceptional distress—for instance at the time of the Anglo-French wars which marked the end of the Middle Ages when the horrors of plague were added to those of war and when mercenaries ravaged a country whose defences were no longer organised—acorn flour may have served as a substitute, as in our own days. But no documents permit one to suppose that this happened frequently.

For it should not be imagined that famine was endemic in the Middle Ages. If one believes Raoul Glaber, a chronicler with a fevered imagination who succumbs easily to writing for stylistic effect, one tends to imagine that hardly a year passed during which men did not have to resort to eating human flesh and the newly-disinterred corpses of children in order to appease their hunger. But the medieval monk, when he relates these monstrous happenings, takes care to avoid accepting responsibility for his assertions and adds prudently: '*it is said.*' It is certain that there were famines in the Middle Ages and that these were numerous—this happens inevitably when the absence or insufficiency of means of transport prevents help from being brought swiftly to threatened regions and hinders the exchange of produce—the personal experiences of our own generation have taught us all we need to know on this subject. During the Early Middle Ages, in particular, when each domain necessarily formed a closed world, when the roads were still not very safe and when, to ensure their upkeep, tolls were exacted which were often very onerous, a year of scanty rainfall was sufficient to cause shortages. But it is certain also that these famines were very localised and did not usually extend beyond the area of a province or a parish. Even during the greatest years of the Middle Ages, the thirteenth century, when feudal self-sufficiency had been replaced by fruitful exchanges and when travel was easy over the whole of France, one sometimes observes very great variations in the prices of produce, especially corn. Each province and each city fixed its prices according to the size of the harvest in that district. The tables drawn up by d'Avenel and de Wailly show fluctuations which meant doubled or even trebled prices—as in Franche-Comté when, in the one year 1272, the price of a hectolitre of corn varied from four to thirteen francs.

One must, moreover, be quite clear as to what one understands by famine. A document quoted by Luchaire, who can hardly be suspected of indulgence towards the Middle Ages, and in a work where he deliberately accumulates texts liable to show the period in the most gloomy light, is calculated to leave present-day readers perplexed. 'This year (1197),' relates the Chronicler of Liège, 'the corn harvest failed. From Epiphany to August we were obliged to spend more than one hundred *marcs* on buying bread. We had neither wine nor beer. A fortnight before the harvest we were eating rye-bread.'[49] If famine consisted for them in having to eat rye-bread, how many people in France in recent years would have envied the lot of their thirteenth century ancestors!

In fact, medieval food was not very different from our own in normal times. Its basis, naturally, was bread, which was made, according to the richness of the district, from wheat, rye, or from a mixed crop of both these; but it is to be noted that even in non-productive districts such as the Midi people ate wheaten bread. In Marseilles, where the land was poor in corn and where exceptional measures had often to be taken for the city to get supplies, there was

[49] *La Société française au temps de Philippe-Auguste*, p. 8.

P

no mention of lower-grade flours in the very detailed regulations governing bread-making. Three sorts of bread were made: white, *méjan*, which was coarser, and wholemeal: the prices were fixed according to a strict tariff which was drawn up by three master-bakers assisted by an expert and responsible man appointed by the *commune*, who took into consideration the waste resulting from grinding, kneading and baking. Many varieties of fancy bread were known in Paris, of which Pain de Chilly and Pain de Gonesse or rolls, were the most highly esteemed. In very poor districts, people ate oatcakes, which are still popular among the Scots, or buckwheat. But no district was completely without bread because the agricultural system of that time, which was based on large estates covering a relatively extensive area, favoured polyculture. In the Middle Ages one never saw one region devoted exclusively to the raising of corn or the growing of vines, and importing the rest of the produce it needed; the system of vast cultivated estates allowed a sufficient variety of crops and, at the same time, a proper proportion of land for each.

Roupnel, in his study of the French countryside,[50] points out that the messuage, the 'local unit', which, according to the richness of the soil, measured from ten to twelve modern hectares, was almost always made up of three parts: arable land, meadows and woods. The two latter represented only a very small fraction—approximately one tenth—of the whole estate; land under cultivation covered an area twice that of the pasture-land. 'This little domain,' he says, 'appears as a whole, a complete picture in miniature of the land itself.' And he adds: 'It is not merely a picture; it has the vitality of the land and its power of endurance.' The illuminated manuscripts, which drew their inspiration from reality, are very revealing on this subject. Everywhere

[50] *Histoire de la campagne française, p.* 366.

one sees a fairly constant proportion of meadows to fields and fields to vineyards.

The vine was cultivated everywhere in France: this fulfilled a religious requirement as well as an economic one, for the faithful, until the middle of the thirteenth century, communicated in both kinds, so that much more wine was drunk at Mass then than to-day. Some present-day wines were highly esteemed at this time: Beaune, Saint-Emilion, Chablis and Epernay; others are no longer as famous now as they used to be: for example, Auxerre or Mantes-sur-Seine. Everywhere local produce had to be protected from imported products, and, in a city such as Marseilles, Draconian measures were taken against the introduction of wines or grapes from other regions. Only counts had the right to import them for their own private consumption—in this case it was probably a matter of fine Spanish or Italian wines. A ship which entered the port with a cargo of wines or grapes risked having it scattered on the ground and the grapes trampled under foot. In the settlements established abroad, also, it was forbidden to offer local wine for sale before the Marseilles merchants had sold their own. The cultivation of the vine was more highly developed in Marseilles then than now and the city bye-laws afforded local produce special protection: hunting in vineyards was forbidden, except to the owner; and the *métayer* was not allowed to pick more than five bunches each day for his personal consumption.

Wine was, in effect, the principal drink in the Middle Ages; beer was drunk, chiefly barley-beer, which the Gauls and Germans had made previously, and also hydromel; but wine was preferred above all and was found on every table from that of the seigneur to that of the servants. It was drunk both for pleasure and as a medicine; all sorts of strengthening properties were ascribed to it and it was included in a host of elixirs and pharmaceutical products, jellies and syrups. People were also very fond of various sweet wines and hippocras, in which aromatic herbs, such as wormwood, hyssop, rosemary and myrtle were macerated, with sugar and honey added. Before going to bed, people generally drank a boiling concoction of wine and curdled milk, which was called a posset in England and Normandy and to which Gallic literature of the period has attributed all sorts of powers, the enumeration of which would bring a blush to the cheek of anyone easily shocked. In any case it ensured the warmth which was lacking in the houses; it is certain that wine, together with violent exercise such as hunting, was what compensated for the inadequacy of means of heating, and yet it does not appear that there was any reason for fearing the evils of alcoholism or the degeneration which goes with it. Doubtless this was because no chemicals and no adulterated by-products were served as drinks; or possibly because general observation of the precepts of the Church allowed its use but checked its abuse.

In addition to bread and wine, there was what was called in the Catalan Midi, the *companatge*, that is, all the other foods. Contrary to widespread opinion, a great deal of meat was eaten and it is obvious from investigations which have been made that the rearing of live-stock in France was on a far greater scale than in our own days. A small place in the Pyrenees which to-day has no more than a dozen head of cattle, had two hundred and fifty previously—and, although proportions are by no means the same everywhere, it is certain that cattle-rearing was practised far more intensively in France until the time when the introduction of live-stock from America at lower prices made it impossible for French cattle-raisers to compete. There was no farm which did not have its own herd of sheep, particularly as this provided the fields with natural manure for which it has since been found convenient to substitute artificial fertilisers, resulting in a considerable reduction in the numbers of sheep in France. Pigs, particularly, were very numerous; in both town and country every family, no matter how poor, reared at least one or two for its own private consumption, and the killing of a pig was a classic scene in the calendars of the months which were often sculptured on church doors or painted on manuscripts. For a pig provided meat and a supply of fat for the year. The methods of salting and smoking which are still used were known in the Middle Ages. Killing a pig was such a common feature of domestic life that the guild of pork-butchers was not formed until very late, and pork-butchers were only sellers of 'cooked dishes' at the beginning before they began to specialise in the making of sausages and the curing of hams. On the other hand, the guild of ordinary butchers was powerful at the beginning of the Middle Ages; the role it played in the popular risings of the fourteenth and fifteenth centuries is well known. According to the *Ménagier de Paris*, the weekly consumption of meat in this city rose to 512 oxen, 3,130 sheep, 528 pigs and 306 calves—without counting consumption in the royal and princely mansions, domestic killing of animals and the various ham fairs and others which were held in the capital or its suburbs. In Marseilles, too, the number of regulations relating to cattle belonging to owners in that city or destined for the consumption of its citizens is striking. In addition to meat, there was poultry: fowls were crammed as they were in earliest Antiquity and goose-livers and conserves formed part of feast-day menus as they do to-day.

Finally, hunting provided plentiful rewards in the forests, which were larger than now and well-stocked with game. There were an infinite number of methods of killing game, ranging from the noose or common snare to specially trained birds of prey, and including various traps, pitfalls, nets and devices such as the bow, the blow-pipe and the crossbow. Partridges were caught in bird-lime and stags and wild boars were hunted. Venison was a common item of diet. Although towards the end of the Middle Ages the *seigneurs* tended to reserve their right to hunt on their own estates, like property-owners and the State itself to-day, their huntsmen, falconers and servants and the peasants who assisted them in the great battues all shared in the spoils. This is commonly to be observed in the novels and pictures of the period.

People also fed on dairy produce, and French butter and cheese were already famous. For instance, there were the rich cheeses of Champagne and Brie and *angelots* from Normandy. In this region butter was practically the only fat employed for cooking and as the use of all animal fats was forbidden during Lent, the inhabitants obtained special dispensations because it was not possible to procure oil in sufficient quantities; the alms which they were required to give for the dispensation sometimes contributed to the building of churches, and the *Tour du Beurre* in Rouen owes its name to this fact. But this is a peculiar case, for the olive tree had become acclimatised nearly everywhere in France and olive-oil was greatly appreciated. Like wine, it was used in the making of several medicinal drinks. Its use alone was authorised on days of abstinence, which were frequent, and the abstinence was very severe since it was extended to include eggs also. The eggs which the hens laid during Lent were hard-boiled in order that they should keep, and it was these eggs which were offered for the priest's benediction during the Good Friday ceremonies, which gave rise to the custom of Easter Eggs.

The same requirements of abstinence led the people of

the Middle Ages to eat a great deal of fish: every castle had its breeding-ground attached, where the breeding of perch, tench, gudgeon and eels became a veritable industry: ponds were also stocked, as still happens in provinces such as Brenne, and after they had been fished they were methodically re-stocked. On the coast, sea-fishing was a busy industry: almost everywhere fishermen's guilds played a great role: on the Mediterranean coast many laws were formulated for their benefit, and to protect their trade against mere middlemen they were assured of a sort of monopoly in fish sales. In Marseilles, for instance, middlemen could offer their wares only after midday; the sale of small fish, or *poissons de bourgin*, fished with a fine-mesh net bearing this name, was left free: sardines, for instance, which were distinguished from larger fish such as mackerel or dolphin, and particularly from the tunny-fish which abounded in the approaches to the port. Men knew how to cure fish as well as meat and each day the 'river merchants' brought full barrels of salted or smoked herrings up the Seine to Paris. A common dish in that period was *craspois*, doubtless a variety of whale.

Finally, there were vegetables which tickled the palate less and were therefore the virtually exclusive diet of monks whose state of life prescribed sobriety and mortification of the flesh. People ate more beans and peas, which took the place of our potatoes. Mahieu de Boulogne can find no better way of voicing his complaints at his unsuccessful marriage and of demonstrating the spitefulness of his wife than by the following verse:

> *Nous sommes comme chien et leu* (wolf)
> *Qui s'entrerechignent ès bois,*
> *Et si je veux avoir des pois*
> *Elle fera de la purée!*

There were several varieties of cabbage: white and garden

cabbages, and cos and round lettuces: the *Ménagier de Paris* speaks of French and Avignon lettuces as being the most popular. Spinach, sorrel, beets, marrows, leeks, turnips and rapes formed part of people's regular diet and to these must be added herbs which were used a great deal to bring out the flavour of meat and vegetables: parsley, marjoram, savory, basil, fennel and mint—without mentioning the spices which were gradually to be brought in larger and larger quantities from the Orient, especially pepper, which was so precious that it was sometimes regarded as a sort of currency and used by some trading communities to pay their dues: for example, the houses belonging to the military Orders.

Fruit was very popular: apples and pears, from which cider and perry were already being made; quinces, which were considered to have medicinal qualities and from which delicious jams were made, especially in Orleans; cherries, dried prunes, raisins and figs, which were used in pastes and preserves, a custom which has persisted up to our own time in certain districts, notably in the North of France. The peach and the apricot, which were introduced by the Arabs, were already popular at the time of the Crusades, but strawberries and raspberries only grew wild for a long time and were scarcely cultivated at all until the sixteenth century. Long before this time chestnuts were sold in the streets of Paris and in the fourteenth century an attempt was made to acclimatise orange trees to the French soil. Almonds, walnuts and hazelnuts were also greatly enjoyed and were used in the making of sweets. And, lastly, there were, as there had been from Antiquity, all that the forests could offer: chestnuts, beechnuts, strawberries and sloes, all of which were very well liked.

General diet varied a great deal according to the district, being more dependent then than now on local resources.

Certainly exchanges of products were frequent and more widespread than might have been expected, since Maltese figs and Armenian raisins were on sale in Paris; Italian and Provençal traders brought exotic produce as far as the great fairs of Champagne and Flanders and, on a smaller scale, the markets attracted traders from almost every region of France. But these exchanges were, naturally, less common than to-day, and in the country, if one disregards the commercial activity generated around the seigniorial castles, people lived on local produce and, as days of fasting and abstinence were very numerous, diet varied from one season to another more than it does nowadays; during the whole of Lent it consisted exclusively of vegetables, fish and wild-fowl prepared in oil; this was also the case on vigils or the eve of feast-days, that is to say, on forty days out of each year. Moreover, it must be noted that religious precepts were in keeping with rules of health: the spring fast and those at the change of the seasons on Ember-days, corresponded to a physical need, while the great festive period, which was reflected inevitably in heavy eating, took place during the coldest months of the winter when people felt the need for rich food.

At all events, from culinary treatises now kept in the libraries and from works such as the invaluable *Ménagier de Paris*, it is evident that food was very well, not to say exquisitely, cooked. Great importance was attached to the serving of the dishes and to the general ordering of the meal. In the seigniorial dwelling those present were seated at long trestle-tables covered with white cloths; often on feast days the ground was strewn with freshly gathered flowers and leaves. The tables were arranged along the square walls and, as the diners did not sit opposite one another, the servants were able to come and go and serve each person with whatever he needed. There were always many guests, for it was the custom for all the barons to keep open house. Robert de Blois is quite indignant at the idea that some *seigneurs* shut the doors of the rooms where they ate instead of leaving them open to all comers; hospitality was a sacred duty then and was extended to humble folk was well as to equals; the *seigneur's mesnie*, moreover, comprised all the squires in his service, the children of his vassals and a large proportion of his kinsmen. Thus, beside the great table where the suzerain sat in the place of honour, a whole host of habitual guests were seated in order of precedence. This custom explains why the Knights of King Arthur, among whom there was perfect equality, sat at a round table—or, rather, one forming a sort of horse-shoe—so that all the places should be equally honourable while it still remained possible for servants to move about freely and serve the diners.

For the greater part of the food was not put on the table: both meat and drink were left on the side-board. Portions of meat were cut for each guest, the carving being the duty of the gentleman carver—generally a young gentleman and, in the romances of chivalry such as *Jean de Dammartin et Blonde d'Oxford*, Beaumanoir's work, it was the lady's attendant squire who performed the task. The pieces of meat were placed either on slices of a special bread known as 'trencher bread', which was of a more solid consistency than ordinary bread—or else straight on to the plates. This custom has persisted in some districts of England where the dishes of meat never appear on the table. It was the same in the case of the drinks: the ewers containing them were set on the sideboard and the wine-butler filled all the glasses and goblets in turn when the diners wished. All pictures of banquet scenes show the squires and servants moving hither and thither during the meal, while the ladies remain seated like the gentlemen of high rank and

the guests of the household, and the slender greyhounds
and small poodles nose about in search of morsels of food
to snap up. Banquets were often interrupted with side-
dishes, during the course of which minstrels recited poems
or performed acrobatic tricks; sometimes a whole mime or
play was performed before the diners.

Great care was taken over the serving of the dishes:
peacocks and pheasants were dressed and recovered with
their feathers, and jellies were moulded in all sorts of shapes.
The courses began with soup, of which there were many
varieties, ranging from elaborate concoctions often containing beaten-up egg, grilled sippets and unexpected
relishes such as verjuice, to frumenties and gruels of oats or
barley, which are still eaten in the country in France and
which formed the basis of peasant diet. The French had a
reputation for being great soup-eaters then, as they have
now. They were also famed for the excellence of their pies
and their tarts: the guild of pastry-cooks in Paris became
justly famous and hot venison and fowl pies were sold in
the streets and also vegetable and jam tarts, seasoned with
aromatic herbs, thyme, laurel and rosemary. At banquets
given by princes on the occasion of some reception,
particularly from the fourteenth century onwards, huge
pies enclosed whole deer, in addition to the capons, pigeons
and rabbits with which they were dressed, larded with pork
fat, dotted with cloves and sprinkled with saffron. Grills
and roasts were greatly liked and so were sauces, among
which each chef had a speciality, and of which the most
highly esteemed—garlic sauce—was sold ready-made for
the use of housewives. Creams and sweetmeats completed
the meal: certain cakes, such as waffles and almond or
marzipan cakes, were among those which are still popular
to-day, and, as nowadays, people liked to give presents of
jams, especially quince jam, which was very popular, and

sugared almonds; these, together with syrups, were the most common sweetmeats.

All this is obviously far removed from 'herbs' and 'roots'. The food and the refinement which could be brought to its preparation naturally varied according to the wealth of the household, but it is certain that canary-bread, pies and exotic produce such as figs from Malta would not have been sold in the streets if there had been no one to buy them, or if they had been beyond the purses of all but the rich, whose catering was dealt with on a different scale and who had their own chefs. In the novels about the various trades one reads of young apprentices buying patties regularly when they went in the morning to draw water from the well for the requirements of the household. This means, therefore, that the price were not prohibitive for them. And, although there was perhaps less variety in the country than in the towns, country-folk could not have lived less well—on the contrary, for the growing of crops and the rearing of cattle allowed them facilities which the town-dweller did not enjoy. When it was desired to create a town it was necessary, in order to attract inhabitants, to promise them franchises and privileges, and this would not have been necessary if peasant conditions had been wretched or if— as in our own time—they had been disadvantageous compared with those of the city-dweller. There is every reason to believe that those sound gastronomical traditions, which have established the reputation of French cookery so firmly the world over, originated during the Middle Ages.

★

Colour is a striking feature of medieval costume; the medieval world was a world of colour and a street scene in those days must have been an enchantment to the eye. Against the background of painted façades with their shining signs hanging outside, moved the figures of men and women all dressed in bright colours which contrasted sharply with the black robes of the clerics, the brown frieze of the mendicant friars and the brilliant whiteness of coifs or hennins. It is hard to imagine such a riot of colour in the modern world, unless it be in processions—still seen in England—on the occasion of the marriage of a prince or the coronation of a king, or in certain religious ceremonies which take place in the Vatican. But in the Middle Ages it was not a matter of ceremonial robes only; simple peasants dressed in bright colours, reds, yellows and blues. The Middle Ages seem to have had a horror of dark shades and everything that has come down to us—frescoes, miniatures, tapestries and stained glass windows—bear witness to this richness of colour which was so characteristic of the period.

One must not, however, exaggerate the picturesqueness or the eccentricity of medieval costume. Certain details of dress which one associates inevitably with the pictures of the time were only worn exceptionally: shoes with long pointed toes, for instance, were fashionable during not more than about fifty years of the fifteenth century—a period of many sartorial exaggerations. Charles d'Orléans mocks the '*gorgias*', the young elegants who wore slashed sleeves—sleeves with slits across them through which brilliant linings showed. Thus, the long pointed hennins which call to mind irresistibly the word '*châtelaine*' were worn far less frequently than the square or round hennins which framed the face and were often attached by bonnet-strings—the general fashion in the fourteenth century.

Generally speaking, the women in the Middle Ages wore clothes which followed the natural line of the body, with a very close-fitting bust and large skirts with graceful curves. The bodice often opened on a *chainse* or linen chemise, and double sleeves were sometimes worn. The outer ones—those of the surcoat or top-garment—reaching to the elbows, and the undersleeves, of a lighter material, reaching to the wrists. The neck was always left uncovered and skirts trailed on the ground; they were held up by a belt, fastened, sometimes, with a jewelled clasp.

Male attire differed scarcely at all from female—at least in the first centuries of the Middle Ages—but was shorter, and the hose and sometimes the breeches showed below the tunic. In the course of the twelfth century, under the influence of the Crusades, long flowing garments were adopted, a fashion which was sharply censured by the Church as being effeminate. The peasants wore a sort of hooded cape and the *bourgeois* covered their heads with felt or fabric hoods. Furs were very popular, ranging from the ermine reserved for kings and princes, marten and miniver, to the simple fox-furs and sheepskins from which the villagers made shoes, bonnets and sometimes coats for themselves. In the fifteenth century, great *seigneurs* such as the Duc de Berry spent fortunes on buying valuable furs and it was also at this time that costume became more elaborate, that breeches were made tight and close-fitting, that tunics were shortened exaggeratedly and drawn in at the waist and that shoulders were padded.

Underlinen existed at the beginning of the Middle Ages and an examination of illuminated manuscripts shows that it was worn by peasants as well as by the *bourgeoisie*. Everywhere in France there were hemp-fields and the hemp fibre was home-spun and woven, giving a fine hard-wearing material. On the other hand, night attire did not exist and the custom was not introduced until very late. Many varieties of materials for garments were to be bought at the great fairs throughout France. All the specialities of the textile industries of Flanders and the North of France were sold in the Mediterranean towns: cloth from Châlons,

strong muslin from Arras, woollens from Douai, Cambrai,
Saint Quentin and Metz, red draperies from Ypres,
'*estanforts*' from England, fine material from Rheims, soft
and hard felts from Provins, not to mention local specialities
like Narbonne *brunette* and grey and green cloth from
Avignon. In another direction, trade in the coast towns,
Genoa, Pisa, Marseilles and Venice, made possible the
importation of exotic produce from North Africa and even
from India and Arabia; some of the records of merchants
attending the fairs of Champagne are as evocative as a
page from the Tales of a Thousand and One Nights: cloth
of gold from Damascus, silks and velvets from Acre,
embroidered veils from India, Armenian cotton goods, furs
from Tartary, leather and cordwain from Tunis and
Bougie, furs from Oran and Tlemcen. Silk and velvet were
for a long time the prerogative of the nobility, the nobles
alone being sufficiently wealthy to be able to procure them.
All these were offered as princely presents: on the occasion
of great rejoicings princes liked to distribute the most
sumptuous clothing among their followers of every rank.
But there was no excessive luxury while the Capets were on
the throne; it was not until the time of the Valois that the
court became magnificent—and then magnificence was
to be found more particularly at the courts of the princes
of apanages, for instance, those of the Dukes of Berry,
Burgundy and Anjou. It is well known, on the other hand,
that men such as Louis le Jeune, Saint Louis and Philippe-
Auguste were conspicuous for the plainness of their dress
which was often more simple than that of their vassals.

As far as military dress was concerned, it would be a
mistake to imagine that the medieval knight wore the
heavy and elaborate armour to be seen in museums to-day;
this did not make its appearance before the end of the
fourteenth century, when firearms necessitated improved

defensive equipment. In the twelfth and thirteenth centuries
armour consisted mainly of a coat of mail reaching to just
above the knees, and a helmet which, originally heavy and
cumbersome, was improved and equipped with visors and
adjustable chin-, forehead- and nose-pieces. A surcoat of
some light material was slipped over the hauberk or coat
of mail to lessen its brilliance; greaves and spurs completed
the soldier's equipment. The fine statue of the Chevalier
de Bamberg gives one an excellent idea of medieval military
dress—a harmonious masterpiece of virile simplicity. But
an extra effort of imagination is needed to reconstruct the
dazzling spectacle which must have been presented by
medieval arms: this multitude of helmets, lances and swords
flashing in the sunlight so that their reflection was often a
cause of defeat for those who happened to be disadvantage-
ously placed.

One can imagine the cries of admiration drawn from the
chroniclers by these shining armies with their pennons and
their standards, their caparisoned horses and the shimmering
silks which opened to reveal tunics of steel. Each *mesnie*
gathered about its *seigneur* and bore his colours. For it was
at this time—at the beginning of the twelfth century—that
coats of arms were first seen. Heraldic terms and most of the
charges were taken from the Arabian Orient, but the
custom rapidly became general in Europe, partly due to the
tournaments, when people relied on the knights' coats of
arms to make it possible to follow their movements on
fields which were often very vast—in the same way that
people in our own days depend on jockeys' colours. Coats of
arms, which are now fashionable again, were an integral
part of medieval life: they gave pictorial expression to the
motto of the *seigneur* or, rather, of the family, and were at
once a war-cry and a call to arms. It is known that each
colour or, rather, each tincture, had a meaning, as did each

charge: azure was the symbol of loyalty, gules of courage, sable of prudence and vert of courtesy. Of the two metals, silver signified purity, and gold, love and ardour. The escutcheon grew more elaborate in the course of the centuries, but even at the time of its first appearance it formed a science and a sort of hermetic language, interpreting in the rich and colourful form beloved of the Middle Ages, all the collection of traditions and ambitions which made up the moral personality of each *mesnie*.

Tools in the Middle Ages were pretty much the same as those which were used until the nineteenth century before the development of machinery and the mechanisation of agriculture. It must be mentioned, however, that the wheelbarrow, whose invention a firmly-rooted tradition attributes to Pascal, was already in existence in the Middle Ages, in a form exactly similar to that used to-day. One can see fifteenth century manuscripts in which the illuminations show workmen carrying stones or bricks in wheelbarrows, one of whose handles they supported by means of a strap slung over the shoulder so that they were able to bear their load more easily; this method is still used by workmen to-day.

We owe many inventions to the Middle Ages and their repercussions on future generations have been too great for us to pass them over in silence: for instance, the pack saddle. The method of harnessing beasts employed until that time had laid all the strain on the animals' breasts, so that a rather heavy load was in danger of choking them; it was in the course of the tenth century that the ingenious idea was conceived of harnessing beasts of burden so that the animal's whole body took the weight, and the strain, entailed.[51] This innovation was to bring about a profound change in men's habits: hitherto, human draught power had been superior to animal draught power, but, by reversing

[51] Cf. Lefebvre des Noettes: *L'attelage a travers les âges*, Paris, 1931.

Q

this state of affairs the suppression of the slave labour which had been an economic necessity in Antiquity was made possible and even easy. The Church had fought for the recognition of the slave as a human being, with the rights of a human being—which in itself constituted a revolution in existing customs. This revolution was decisively completed when horses and donkeys were charged with a part of human labour. In the same way, the invention of the mill— the water-mill and, subsequently, the wind-mill—was to effect a no less important stride forward in humanity's progress, by making obsolete the accepted spectacle of the slave harnessed to the millstone. Less far-reaching in its consequences, but incontestably convenient, was the introduction of the process which enabled vehicles to turn easily on their own axis, thanks to the device which allows the two front wheels to move independently of the two back, and which was to make an equally great contribution to both progress and comfort; one has only to imagine the turning space which must have been needed by heavy waggons loaded with grain and fodder—and the obstructions which must have resulted. It is certain that these inventions had more effect than any others on the well-being of the common people and assisted smoothly and without expense in the effective amelioration of their lot.

To these inventions, which were radically to modify human labour conditions, we must add the compass and the tiller, which have been no less important in the history of the world. Progress in navigation was multiplied tenfold and this explains, in part at least, the immense amount of travelling during the thirteenth century.

The rhythm of the working day in the Middle Ages varied a great deal in accordance with the seasons. It was the parish bell or that of the neighbouring monastery which called the artisan to his workshop and the peasant to his field, and the time of the Angelus varied with the length of the natural day. As a rule, people rose and went to bed at the same time as the sun. In winter, therefore, work began at about eight or nine o'clock and finished at five or six; in summer on the other hand, the day began at five in the morning and did not end until seven or eight at night. This meant that, allowing for two breaks for meals, the working day varied from eight to nine hours in winter and from twelve to thirteen or sometimes fifteen in summer—these are still the regular working hours of peasant families. But it was not thus every day. Firstly, people worked a five-and-a-half day week: each Saturday and on the eve of every feast day, work stopped at one o'clock in some trades and for everyone at the hour of vespers, that is, at four o'clock at the latest. The same rule applied to certain days which were observed without being kept as actual holidays, that is, about thirty days in the year, such as Ash Wednesday, Rogation Days and Childermas, etc. People also rested on the day of the patron saint of their guild and of their parish and there was, of course, a complete holiday on Sundays and on days of obligation. These were very numerous in the Middle Ages—thirty to thirty-three a year, according to the province—for, in addition to the four festivals observed in France to-day, there were, not only All Souls' Day, Epiphany, Easter Monday and Whitmonday, and three days in Christmas week, but also a number of festivals which pass almost unnoticed now, such as the Feast of the Purification, the Invention and Exaltation of the True Cross, the Annunciation, Saint John's Day, Saint Martin's Day, Saint Nicholas' Day, etc. The liturgical calendar thus governed the whole year and introduced great variety into it, especially as more importance was attached to these festivals than nowadays. It was, moreover, from such feast-days, and not from the day of the month, that time was reckoned: one spoke of Saint Andrew's Day, and not of the thirtieth of November, and of three days after Saint Mark's Day rather than of the twenty-eighth of April. People would also waive social obligations, such as those of justice, in their honour: insolvent debtors who were obliged to reside at a fixed abode—a system which calls to mind the debtors' prison, though in a milder form—were allowed to leave their residence and to come and go freely from Thursday in Holy Week until Easter Tuesday, from Whit Saturday to Whit Tuesday and from Christmas Eve until the Festival of the Circumcision of Christ. These are notions which it is hard for us nowadays to grasp.

Altogether there were about eighty days of complete rest with over seventy partial holidays, that is, about three months spread over the year. This ensured infinite variety in the routine of work. During this period people might well have complained, like the cobbler in La Fontaine's fable, of having too many holidays.

The organisation of leisure had a religious basis: every holiday was a festival and every festival began with religious ceremonies. These were often long and always solemn. They were followed by spectacles which, given originally in the church itself, were soon transferred to the parvis. There were scenes from the life of Christ, of which the principal, the Passion, inspired masterpieces which have been rediscovered in our own period. The Virgin and the Saints also inspired dramatic works and everyone knew the *Miracle de Théophile*, which had an extraordinary vogue. These shows were essentially popular—both actors and audience were drawn from the people—and the audience was alert and responsive to the smallest detail of scenes which roused in them sentiments and feelings of a quite different quality from those provoked by present-day drama, since it was not only the intellect and the emotions which were involved but also deep-seated beliefs, strong enough to transport these same people to the shores of Asia Minor in response to an appeal from the Pope. As always, a note of burlesque crept in—a very highly-developed characteristic. Men even went so far as to ascend the pulpit to deliver 'gay sermons', buffooneries seasoned with the most racy vulgarities. The clergy saw no harm in these eccentricities which would have created a scandal in our own time, but participated in them merrily themselves.

Not only purely religious dramas were performed on the stages set up on the public square, but burlesques and satirical farces or plays with romantic or historical themes also. Nearly all the towns had their own theatrical company, and that of the Clerks of the Law Courts in Paris has remained famous. Public rejoicings also had their place alongside religious festivals: there were sometimes magnificent processions which marched through the streets on the occasion of the assemblies and plenary courts which were held by the kings and which recalled the *champs de mars* and the *champs de mai* to which Charlemagne summoned the nobility of the land at Poissy or at Aix-la-Chapelle. On these occasions the French Court, usually so unpretentious, enjoyed displaying a certain ceremonial pomp, and the towns were decorated with all the splendour imaginable, as they were for the entry of kings or great vassals: tapestries were hung along the walls, the houses were decorated with leaves and greenery and the streets strewn with flowers. This was done especially for the coronation of a king: the cities through which he passed after the ceremonies in Rheims were each eager to give him a state reception, but this was in no way a formal or pompous affair: it was accompanied by grotesque processions in which tumblers and professional entertainers, mingling with the public, performed a hundred tricks which would seem to us incompatible with royal majesty: it was not until the entry of Henri II into Paris that it was decided to do away with these merry-makings and 'entertainments of bygone days.' They were the occasion of sometimes unparalleled munificence, particularly in the reign of the Valois: fountains flowing with wine, banquets given to huge crowds and for which travelling kitchens were set up where meat was piled on enormous roasting jacks. It was during the same period that masquerades and fancy-dress balls became popular, and the tragic memory still lingers of one of these—the *Bal des Ardents*—at which the young king, Charles VI, dressed up with four companions as savages, wearing tow covered with pitch and feathers. The group went incautiously close to a lighted torch and caught fire and the king would have been burned to death but for the presence of mind of the Duchesse de Berry who wrapped him in the folds of her gown and smothered the flames. But the danger from which he escaped was not without its effects on the already weak brain of the unfortunate monarch, and on the infirmity which was later to come on him.

All events relating to the royal family or merely to the seigniorial family of the district—births, marriages, and so on, were the occasion for entertainments and festivities. The fairs also brought their share of amusements and it was here that the minstrels displayed their talents. They ranged from those who recited fragments of the *chansons de geste* to the accompaniment of lute and viol, to the simple tumblers who, by their grimaces, their acrobatics and their juggling, attracted a circle of idlers; sometimes they mimed—these ancestors of Tabarin—or showed performing animals or walked the tight rope at dizzy heights.

Next to spectacles of no matter what type, the most popular form of entertainment in the Middle Ages was dancing. There was never a banquet that was not followed by a ball; there was the dancing of the squires in the castles, folk-dancing, round dancing at the maypole; no pastime was better loved, especially by the young people; novels and poems often refer to it. Singing and dancing were sometimes combined and some refrains served as a pretext for dancing in the same way that the bonfires on Midsummer's Day were an excuse for jumping and round-dancing. Athletic competitions also had their devotees: wrestling, running, high-jump, long-jump and archery were practised in village competitions between the parishes and also among the pages and squires who formed part of the *seigneur's mesnie*. Hunting was often followed by banquets and re-joicings and remained the favourite sport; and, of course, jousts and tournaments were the principal attraction on feast-days or at great receptions. The children, as in every society, imitated their elders in their games, or played endlessly at *cligne-musette* or hide-and-seek, and at quoits.

Indoor amusements were not lacking: firstly there was chess: during the Crusades this was played with enthusiasm both by the crusading army and the Saracens and there are many manuscript treatises on the game in our libraries to-day. It is known that the Old Man of the Mountains, the terrible chief of the Assassins, made a present to Saint Louis of a magnificent chessboard in ivory and gold. There were also enthusiasts of the games with board and counters which needed less skill, such as draughts and backgammon. But, most especially, dice-throwing was the craze. It was the ruin of vagabonds and minstrels. Rutebeuf had bitter experience of it more than once and relates pathetically the constantly disappointed hopes and the anguished awakenings of the unfortunate ruined players. People played even in the royal household. As one easily slides into the habit of cursing at such games, the authorities took measures against blasphemers; in Marseilles, people who had acquired this bad habit were dipped three times into a muddy ditch near the Vieux-Port. And there were also punishments for those who used loaded dice or cheated in any way. As for the children, they played at knucklebones. Various more refined intellectual pastimes were preferred in polite society: riddles, anagrams and *bouts rimés*. Christine de Pisan has left some *jeux à vendre*, little impromptu verses in the style of '*Je vous vends mon corbillon*'—full of charm and delicate poetry.

CERTAIN features stand out clearly from the rather perplexing composition which the medieval period presents, and one must not lose sight of these when studying this era which differs greatly from those which preceded it and those which have followed. These characteristics permeate it so thoroughly that the examination of even a single detail can be completely falsified if they are not kept in mind. It is all the more important to have some understanding of the medieval mentality when attempting to assess the period, because each part is so closely related to the whole; the family nucleus is a microcosm which reproduces the macrocosm, that is, the seigniorial *mesnie*, and, indeed, the State as a whole. This is also the case in other respects, so that to consider one institution without taking into account the general atmosphere of the period would be to run the risk of falling into grave errors. This is true more especially of this age than of any other in history.

One of the most outstanding traits is practical common sense. The men of the Middle Ages seem to have had no other criterion than utility. In architecture, in art and in the background of everyday life, they allotted no place to ornamentation, they had no conception of art for art's sake. If a waterspout was transformed for them into a gargoyle, this was because their vivid imaginations were ceaselessly alert and reacted to everything of which their senses made them aware; but they would not have had the idea of sculpturing gargoyles which did not perform the function of waterspouts, any more than they would have thought of laying out gardens merely to please the eye. Their aesthetic sense enabled them to create beauty everywhere, but for them beauty could not exist without utility. It is, moreover, astonishing to see with what facility they were able to combine these two conceptions —beauty and utility, and how, by an exact adaptation to its purpose and a quite natural grace, a simple household utensil, such as a ewer, a goblet or a pitcher, could acquire real beauty. It would seem that they were never in the dilemma of having to sacrifice one to the other or of having to add one to gain acceptance for the other—a common notion in the last century. All that remains of medieval life, from the history of the formation of the royal domain to the evolution of the architecture, demonstrates this practical, realistic spirit, which has sometimes led to the people of the Middle Ages being regarded as prosaic —a view which is perhaps exaggerated, but nearer to the truth than the romantic tendency to see them as fanciful eccentrics.

Their love of poetry will be raised as an objection to this view. But the fact is that unlike our modern age, which has seen in poetry a whimsical thing, an 'escape', and in the poet a sort of Bohemian, a being apart, a degenerate, the people of the Middle Ages considered poetry as a natural form of expression: it was for them an essential part of life, like material necessities or, more exactly, like man's faculties properly speaking, such as thought and language. For them, the poet was not an abnormal being; on the contrary, he was a complete man, more complete than one who was not capable of artistic or poetic creation; they would not have thought, like Plato, of banishing him from the Republic, because poetry played a part in their republic, as did oratory in Ancient Greece.

Their practical common sense was expressed among other ways by a very cautious approach to life. Men made use of everything, but with moderation. They felt a sort of instinctive wariness in face of their own powers—a wariness which co-existed curiously with the vigour and audacity of the great enterprises witnessed during the period. One of the adages which helps to elucidate the history of the age is that of Roger Bacon: *Natura non vincitur, nisi parendo* (One can subdue Nature only by obeying her laws). There was great respect for tradition, for the existing order of things and for customs which were no more than the corroboration of this existing order. All that was time-honoured became unimpugnable and discoveries in art, in architecture and in everyday life, compelled recognition only in so far as they were founded on experience. There was no attempt to make innovations, but rather to strengthen and improve whatever had been handed down from the past. The Middle Ages was a period of empiricism: although life was not based on predetermined rules of behaviour, nevertheless the guiding principles of existence developed out of the conditions to which existence had to adapt itself.

This aspect of the medieval mentality is significantly illustrated by an expression used in French legal terminology: *crime de nouvelleté*. By this was meant anything which broke violently and brutally with the natural course of things or with their established order; it covered misdemeanours ranging from trespass to any interference with a man's quiet enjoyment of his rights. The unforeseeable consequences of this disruptive element, this act of breaking with a past which had already proved itself, were feared; there was here a sort of humility before Creation. It was realised that man can become enslaved by forces which he himself has set in motion, and, for this reason, the men of the Middle Ages were wary of all that had not been hallowed by tradition. Thus, the most usual methods of investigation or of proof consisted in an appeal to the memory of the oldest witnesses; when it was proved that a right which was being contested had existed from time immemorial, the contestants bowed to that argument. It was by virtue of this same attitude that a farmer who settled on a piece of land and cultivated it undisturbed during a prescribed period, was subsequently considered to be the rightful owner. It was thought that those who had reason to appeal against this should have perceived it during the course of the legal period of a year and a day, when the *nouvelleté* was transformed into an established fact.

Still more significant was the medieval conception of individual liberty. This was not regarded as a natural heritage or as an absolute right, but more as an outcome. A man whose security was assured, who owned sufficient land to stand up to the tax-collectors and who could protect his estate himself, was called free because he had, in fact, the possibility of doing what he pleased. The rest of the population aimed at security above all else and appears not to have suffered overmuch from the restrictions which were necessarily imposed on its freedom of movement, nor was this freedom claimed as an indisputable right. This was true, of course, only where individual liberty was concerned, *'atomic'* liberty, as Jacques Chevalier says;

for people were most particular about the rights of the group to which they belonged which were regarded as indispensable for its existence: the rights of the family, of the guild and of the *commune* were always claimed and disputed with great passion, and were defended by force of arms if necessary.

This practical common sense, this innate horror of abstractions and theorising, was combined with a very highly-developed sense of humour. Medieval man was amused by everything: drawing easily became transformed for him into caricature and emotion bordered on irony. This is a characteristic to be remembered when one studies the period, for more than once writings have been distorted and rendered prosaic by a tendency to take them too seriously. People have imagined them to be examples of the famous medieval 'naïveté', or seen lurking schemes of revenge harboured by the weak against the strong, where in fact the author sought only to amuse and nothing more. When canons in ridiculous postures with grotesque heads were carved on cathedral stalls, where a certain chronicler, describing the effects of Greek Fire, exclaims about this 'water' which spreads flames that 'it is very expensive, like good wine,' when in the *fabliaux* the curé is beaten with a stick—one must not read into such passages anything more than a sense of the ridiculous, a desire to laugh and to make others laugh. Nothing escaped this tendency, not even those matters which were held in the greatest respect. The tavern scenes and coarse jests which are included in the *Mystères* have sometimes been considered shocking and it would be utterly impossible in our own days to reconstruct some of the religious or official ceremonies without scandalising a public accustomed to more gravity.

It is particularly in reading the manuscripts of the time that one becomes aware of this faculty for combining laughter with the most earnest matters, that sort of natural mischievousness which made the men of the Middle Ages incapable of remaining serious to the end. For instance, following one grave treatise on the different weights and measures in current use and their equivalents, one finds this unexpected conclusion added on his own responsibility by a copyist who was obviously jibbing at his task: 'and weights are measures and personally I hate measures.' Another, at the end of a certain philosophical work, serenely formulates the following shameless wish: '*Scriptori por pena sua detur pulchra puella,*' (May the copyist for his trouble be granted a beautiful girl). All this is without transition, in the same hand-writing as the rest of the work and in manuscripts intended for very august personages. If one passes on to the drawings and miniatures decorating some of the pages, one finds countless examples of malicious wit or irony scattered here and there with a verve that bursts out constantly and finds opportunities for expression even in the most erudite philosophical treatises.

This medieval humour is, moreover, curiously linked with the religious faith which animated the period and which must be borne in mind when one considers even the smallest incidents of history or of everyday life. Religious faith in fact taught the people of the Middle Ages the unique powers of the Divine Being to whom nothing was impossible and who could, consequently, turn situations upside down as He pleased. The *Credo quia absurdum,* attributed to Saint Augustine, is a part of the very essence of the medieval mentality: divine meditation thus added a quite unbounded field of realisable impossibilities to all the actual probabilities of this earthly life. The little scenes in which the sculptors and image-makers of the period liked to depict, for example, a cock carrying off a fox or a hare slaying a hunter, only express this state of mind in which the humorous note is closely linked with belief in an omnipotent God made man.

If one attempts to summarise the occupations of these people one realises that they are epitomised in two words, two opposite but not contradictory poles: manor and pilgrimage. Every existence was concentrated upon the home, the family, the parish, the domain and the group to which it belonged. There was no custom, no feature of men's habits which did not tend to strengthen this attachment or to enforce respect for it. A city would defend its liberties as jealously as a *seigneur* his castellany, the guilds proved to be as intransigent where their privileges were concerned as the father of a family regarding his fief, however tiny it might be. The manor, the place where one remained, was considered as a sanctuary; that is evident from all that it is possible for us to know of medieval history: individual rights, family and municipal institutions—even the formation of the royal domain, the result of patient tenacity and of the skilful combination of inheritances and marriages, was only one proof among many of the practical and realistic spirit shown by the men of the Middle Ages when it was a question of strengthening and safeguarding their patrimony.

And yet, these people who were inseparable from the soil, bound to their ancestors and to their descendants, were perpetually on the move. The Middle Ages was a period of building and also of travelling—two activities which may appear irreconcilable, but which did nevertheless co-exist without bother or catastrophe. There were enormous displacements of people and more active travelling than has been known in any other period in the history of the world excepting our own. What were the colonial ventures of, for instance the Greeks, or those of the last century, compared with the exoduses of population at the time of the Crusades? And these were fruitful exoduses, having nothing in common with the lamentable herds which represent for us a mass of people on the move. As soon as they arrived on enemy shores which they had conquered in fierce battle, these handfuls of barons transplanted from their provinces of Flanders or Languedoc, proved their worth as builders, jurists and administrators, with an astonishing genius for adapting themselves to countries whose language, customs and climate had been unknown to them a few months previously. Two centuries sufficed to witness the birth, growth and decline of a civilisation forged piece by piece, and one whose relics still astonish us to-day.

We can guess at the work represented by a fortress such as Château-Gaillard or a cathedral such as that of Albi, but it is more difficult to realise that these were built by people whose lives where a ceaseless coming and going—from the merchant who left his shop for the fairs of Champagne or Flanders or to trade in the settlements of Africa or Asia Minor, to the abbot who went off to inspect his monasteries; from the students travelling from one university to another to the barons visiting their estates or the bishops touring their dioceses, from the kings who set out on Crusades to the humble people who made their way to Rome or Santiago—all shared more or less in this fever to travel which made of the medieval world a world on the march. When Guillaume de Rubruquis visited the court of the Khan of the Mongols at the request of Saint Louis, he was not surprised at all to find a Parisian goldsmith there, one Guillaume Boucher, whose brother kept a shop on the Pont au Change and who, having settled in the *Horde d'Or*, was making a 'magic tree' for his Asiatic patrons from which golden serpents, twined about the trunk, poured forth milk, wine and hydromel. The architect, Villard de Honnecourt, ventured as far afield as Hungary, broadcasting the *opus francigenum* at random, so to speak, and it was a Frenchman, Etienne de Bonneuil, who built the cathedral of Upsala in Sweden.

This casual attitude towards journeys was deeply rooted in tradition. As soon as he was capable of acting for himself, that is, at the age of fourteen or fifteen, each individual had, according to family tradition, the right and the possibility of leaving home, of founding a family and of working on his own account and he could be deprived of no part of what was due to him from the paternal heritage. However extraordinary it may seem, the very ties which bound him to the soil ensured his liberty. The father of a family could set out on a Crusade, leaving his land, his wife and his children; his property belonged to the family more than to himself and others could take his place in the capacity of manager. The vagabond in him was in no way prejudicial to the administrator, and nothing prevented him from assuming each of these two roles in turn. This taste for adventure was such that even the serf attached to an estate had permission to leave it to go on a pilgrimage. Custom bound men to the place where destiny had set them, but, equally, the spirit of the age produced an understanding of that need for escape which counteracts and compensates for a sense of stability. Certain customs even authorised the traveller to take with him on his journey whatever was necessary for his own sustenance and for that of his mount, and everywhere the obligations of hospitality were regarded as the most sacred there were; to refuse shelter to travellers was considered a grave sin, entailing a sort of malediction.

That the Middle Ages witnessed abuses of this order of things is evident from, for instance, the measures which the Church had to take against vagabond scholars. And the peasants' tendency to leave home resulted in great movements of shepherd folk who sometimes gave themselves over to the most unruly disturbances. But it is none the less

R

true that this delight in travelling was without equal either as a sign of life or as a source of vitality. Thus it was that exchanges multiplied in mediæval Christendom, as they did between Europe and the East. The Middle Ages was the era of great discoveries: it was then that strange and splendid fruits were acclimatised to France, oranges, lemons, pomegranates, peaches and apricots; thanks to the Crusaders, Europe came to know rice, cotton and sugar-cane, and to learn the use of the compass and how to make paper and also, alas, gun-powder; at the same time, French industries were introduced into Syria: glassmaking, weaving and dyeing. French merchants explored the African continent, a European architect built the great mosque in Timbuctoo and the Ethiopians sent for French artist-craftsmen, painters, engravers and carpenters. In the Middle Ages a peaceable citizen of Toulouse, Anselme Ysalguier, brought back to his town a black princess whom he had married in Gao—and, at the same time, a doctor from the banks of the Niger, whom the Dauphin, the future Charles VII, consulted. Manor and pilgrimage, realism and fantasy these were the two poles of medieval life, between which mankind evolved without the slightest trouble, combining one with the other and passing from one to the other with an ease which has not since been recaptured.

From this whole there emerges a confidence in life and a joy in living which have no equal in any other civilisation. That sense of fatality which weighed on the Ancient World, that fear of Destiny, the implacable god to whom even the gods were subject, was wholly unknown in the Middle Ages. The lines of the Latin poet are applicable to this period:

> . . . *metus omnes et inexorabile Fatum*
> *Subjecit pedibus* . . .

In the philosophy of the medieval period, in its architecture and its way of life, everywhere a joy in existing bursts through, and a positive power, which call to mind the laughing reply made by Louis VII when he was taxed with the absence of pomp at his court: 'At the Court of France we have only bread, wine and gaiety.' A magnificent comment, which summarises the Middle Ages, a period when men knew better than at any other time how to appreciate simple, wholesome, joyous things: bread, wine and gaiety.

AINESSE, DROIT DE. (Right of Primogeniture.) This was the system which was found most effective in the Middle Ages in preventing the parcelling out of land which resulted in the abandonment of the rural areas, and also in arousing a spirit of initiative among the younger sons of the family. The fact that Britain now has the greatest Empire in the world can probably be attributed to Right of Primogeniture.

AMERICA, DISCOVERY OF. Dates back to round about the year 1000; is attributable to the Vikings who took six to seven days to travel from Norway to Greenland, where a See was established. The Greenlanders, in response to an appeal for support of the Crusade launched by Pope John XXII in 1327, sent a cargo of walrus-teeth and sealskins to Rome as a contribution towards the expenses of the undertaking.

AN MIL, TERREURS DE L'. (Terrors of the Year One Thousand.) The historians of the end of the sixteenth century, who are responsible for the invention of these terrors, surely merit at least as great a reputation for their feeling for the romantic as Michelet who drew his inspiration from them.

ASILE, DROIT DE. (Right of Sanctuary.) This right rested on quite different bases in the Middle Ages than today. The difference is chiefly apparent in the fact that then it allowed even a criminal his chance, whereas in France in our own days, on the other hand, an accused man is regarded *a priori* as guilty. Whence detention on suspicion, of which an innocent man, in theory at least, runs as much risk as a guilty one.

BONDSERVICE. The difference between bondservice and slavery enables one to grasp precisely the contrast between the society of Antiquity and that of the Middle Ages, since, unlike the slave who was treated as an object, the serf was a man, with a family, a home and property; he was independent of his *seigneur* when he had paid his rent, in exchange for which he was protected from unemployment, military service and tax-collectors.

Bondservice aroused vigorous protests—those of the serfs when it was attempted to give them all their freedom. As a result of their opposition to this measure, they went down in history as the '*serfs récalcitrants.*'

BON PLAISIR, CAR TEL EST NOTRE. (For such is our good pleasure.) The first sovereign to employ this formula was none other than Napoleon.

BOURGEOISIE. Came into being towards the end of the eleventh century at the time of the expansion of the towns; did not begin to take an effective part of the central power until the end of the thirteenth century—this coincides with the decline of the Middle Ages.

CHIMERAS OF NOTRE-DAME. Added by Viollet-le-Duc at the time of the restoration of the buildings in the nineteenth century.

COMPASS. First known in the West in the twelfth century; described in 1269 by Pérégrin de Maricourt; perfected in the fourteenth century.

CORPORATIONS. The word dates from the eighteenth century; the thing, save for a few exceptions, from the end of the fifteenth century, at least in its narrow and exclusive sense, for the *bourgeoisie*, who always evinced a stronger caste feeling than the nobility, without shouldering the same responsibilities, soon reserved the monopoly of the mastership for themselves.

COUR DES MIRACLES. Jacob, the bibliophile, represents the typical historian, for whom the Middle Ages existed between the Cour des Miracles and the Charnier des Innocents. It is to be regretted that he did not live long enough to know the flowers of civilisation which now blossom on the outskirts of Paris and in certain of the suburbs of the great French towns; he would have found there a more genuine theme for his powers of evocation.

CRUSADES. These were not limited to eight expeditions, as one might be led to believe. We must imagine a Society of Nations, founded on a common faith instead of on a temporary identity of interests, and organising expeditions overseas.

CUISSAGE, DROIT DE. When one is confronted with certain interpretations, based on a play of words (cf. BON PLAISIR, EMMUREMENT, FEODALITE), of which '*Droit de Cuissage*' is a striking example, one wonders if the Middle Ages have not fallen victim to a regular conspiracy of 'historians'.

EMMUREMENT. (Lit. Walling in.) The '*emmurés*' of Carcassonne have provided one of France's most popular academic painters with a theme for a work which is moving for its admirable intentions. In the Middle Ages '*emmurement*' signified imprisonment.

EPIDEMICS. If it were possible to draw up a list of their victims in the Middle Ages and compare those with the victims of alcoholism and tuberculosis in the last century, it is not at all certain that the balance would be in favour of the latter. (As both these attacked *the people*, just as the plague in the sixteenth century, do they not merit the name epidemic?)

FAMINES. These were numerous, particularly in the eleventh century, but it is difficult to form an exact idea of them because those of modern times cover vast areas, while in the Middle Ages they were always very localised, the equivalent of one or two counties, at the most, suffering from a bad harvest.

FEUDAL SYSTEM. The only society in the world in which men's relationships with each other have been based on mutual loyalty and the protection owed by the lord to the humble people on his estate. It is hard to explain why the expression has been employed in connection with the trusts of our own day, for it is impossible to find in any document the slightest hint of a conspiracy among the *seigneurs* to exploit the people.

FROGS. 'The serf . . . spent his nights thrashing the water to silence the frogs which disturbed his master's sleep.' The writer, who has spent two hours at night thrashing the water of a pond in an attempt to silence the frogs, offers a large reward to whoever can demonstrate the possible truth of M. Devinat's assertion. (*Manuel d'Histoire, Cours Moyen*, p. 11.)

GOTHIC ART. The word 'Gothic' applied to medieval art remains the only 'obscure' aspect of the period, since it owes nothing to the Goths or to the other barbarians, and saw the light of day in the Ile-de-France towards the middle of the twelfth century.

GRACE DE DIEU, ROI PAR LA (King by the Grace of God.) The two meanings which this formula has acquired are, by their very antithesis, significant of the evolution of the monarchy. For Saint Louis, the expression '*Roi par la grâce de Dieu*' was a humble formula which recognised the hand of the Creator in the various tasks assigned to his creatures; as Louis XIV understood it, the same formula became the proclamation of the privilege of a predestinate.

HYGIENE. 'To be received by the king seated on his close-stool was a privilege conferred by special licence, the *'brevet d'affaires.'* (Lavisse, *Histoire de France*); the Palace of Versailles had no lavatories and Louis XIV took only one bath during the whole of his life. These few reminders of the customs of the seventeenth century demonstrate the magnitude of the evolution in men's habits which had taken place at the Renaissance Courts. One has only to recollect that the Paris of Philippe-Auguste had twenty-six public bath-houses.

INNOCENTS, CHARNIER DES. Cf. *COUR DES MIRACLES.*

INQUISITION. Burning at the stake was a penalty inflicted on heretics for the first time by the Emperor Frederick II, the 'enlightened' sceptic monarch who was several times excommunicated and considered by all historians to have been a precursor of the Renaissance. It was in the course of this same Renaissance that the Inquisition took on, especially in Spain and the Low Countries, the character it has retained in history and in tradition.

MONKS. One must bear in mind that the greatest scholars, the greatest artists and the greatest philosophers of the Middle Ages were monks. (Cf. St. Thomas Aquinas, Roger Bacon, Fra Angelico, etc.)

NAÏVETÉ. 'M. Bédier has divested my mind of prejudice regarding the ingenuousness and lack of intelligence of the authors of the *chansons de geste*. Why, indeed, should one suppose that they did not intend and understand what they were doing?' (G. Lanson, *Histoire illustrée de la littérature française*, second edition.)

NOTRE-DAME DE PARIS. The mutilations inflicted by the revolutionaries must not make us forget that we owe to the French Revolution the fact that the façade of Notre Dame has been preserved, if not in every detail at least as a whole. It had actually been planned during the latter years of the eighteenth century to pull it down and rebuild it in the style of that of the Panthéon.

ORLEANS CATHEDRAL. Cited as the model of the Gothic style by the Romantics; dates from the eighteenth century.

OUBLIETTES. No hint of an explanation is to be found in authentic documents of the strange mistake which has led fiction writers to confuse the prison, which was in fact a part of every feudal castle, with the underground store-rooms.

PATRIOTISM. It may be indisputable that French nationalism dates from the Revolution, but patriotism existed long before Joan of Arc, as Charlemagne's knights bear witness, who died with their faces turned towards 'sweet France'.

PONDS. Cf. FROGS.

PRUD'HOMME. Represents the Ideal Man of the Middle Ages, as the *honnête homme* was the ideal of the seventeenth century. According to Ménage, the latter had to possess 'a balanced mind and a temperate heart; one is a mental virtue which combats error, and the other a virtue of the heart which prevents extremes of passions, whether good or evil.' In the Middle Ages, the requisite qualities of the *prud'homme* are summarised in the following lines:

> *Tant est prud'homme, si com semble*
> *Qui a ces deux choses ensemble:*
> *Valeur de corps et bonté d'âme.*
> (He is a 'prud'homme', it seems to me,
> Who possesses these two things:
> A fine body and a noble soul.)

RENART, ROMAN DE. An example of popular artistic creation and one which had such a vogue that the surname 'Renart' came to be used as a substitute for '*goupil*' (fox). Goethe, moreover, did not scorn to make an adaptation of the work himself. It remains an example of that liking for practical jokes and of that sense of humour which it is no exaggeration to consider as the key to the Middle Ages— humour for its own sake since, unlike the fables of Antiquity, it veiled no moral.

WHEELBARROW. In common use during the Middle Ages. It was possibly a practical joker who ascribed its invention—which added nothing to his fame—to Pascal.

WITCHCRAFT, SORCERERS. The abuse of trials for witchcraft was denounced in a work by P. von Spee, S. J., the *Cautio Criminalis*, which appeared in 1631. This date may seem surprising, but the fact is that such trials, though they began to occur during the decline of the Middle Ages at the end of the fifteenth century, did not become really numerous until the beginning of the '*Grand Siècle*'.

*T*HIS book is set in 12-pt. Monotype Garamond on 14-pt. body, a type-face originally cut by Jean Jannon at Sedan in 1621, and recut for the Monotype in 1926. This design was later ascribed to Claude Garamond whose name it took when the Imprimerie Royale took over the punches in the XVII century.

Garamond is a light and elegant face, a feature particularly evident in its italic version. The italic capital letters differ in slope from the lower case letters (minuscules), a characteristic of Garamond. The Monotype version differs from other revivals, the strokes are thinner, the capital A ends in a sharp upper point which lies slightly above other capital letters. As in many other type-faces of the time, the capitals are slightly lower than the ascenders of b, d, h, l, and other letters.

The ornament used on the title-page has been redrawn from an old illustration.